MUSE, ODALISQUE, HANDMAIDEN:
A Girl's Life In The Incredible String Band

Muse Odalisque Handmaiden

A Girl's Life In The Incredible String Band

Rose Simpson

MUSE, ODALISQUE, HANDMAIDEN: *A Girl's Life In The Incredible String Band*
by Rose Simpson

First published by Strange Attractor Press 2020.
Text © Rose Simpson 2020.

ISBN: 9781907222672

Cover Design by Tihana Šare.
Book Design / Layout by Maïa Gaffney-Hyde.
Set in Bembo and **Tremolo.**

STRANGE ATTRACTOR PRESS
BM SAP, London,
WC1N 3XX, UK
www.strangeattractor.co.uk

Distributed by The MIT Press, Cambridge, Massachusetts.
And London, England.

Printed and bound in the USA by McNaughton & Gunn.

Acknowledgement

Without Adrian Whittaker's ongoing encouragement, patient advice and encyclopaedic knowledge of all things ISB I couldn't have written this memoir. Dropping in on the ISB world for his showing of the re-edited *U* film in 2018 persuaded me it was worthwhile to try.

As I began to look again at that time it was Wolfgang Rostek's diligent archival work and his vast collection of ISB ephemera and concert reviews that coloured and dated memories of performances.

Thanks to both and to all those whose enthusiasm for the music of Mike Heron and Robin Williamson is undiminished despite the years that have passed since we walked out on stages together.

Contents

Preface

In general I believe that people already talk and write too much, dissipating useful and hard-earned energy. My Yorkshire legacy seems taciturn but sensible: "Do something rather than talk about it." So I never wanted to write a book. But when my story is being narrated and sold, in the process becoming a public commodity embedded in a monolithic history, I'm not content any more to let it be entirely out of my hands.

The story could be that of any of the girls on the psychedelic album covers and posters of 1968, these deluded or exploited air-heads, as they're now often seen. We seemed so wilfully to be ignoring the enlightenment of the more political feminists and so can be dismissed from the public gaze.

We hear plenty from the men whose names appear on the same records, sitting on the platforms of literary festivals and TV studios, hoping we don't notice their thinning hair and the stooped frailty of the age they conceal.

Political women and academic ladies, radical female artists and thrusting businesswomen have all demanded their voices be heard – but most of us just "*stroll along the path that time is taking*," doing the ordinary things of ordinary lives. But we too were claiming equalities, on the terms that mattered to us – more erratic and physical perhaps than ideological – and that story also needs telling.

A woman's story is often less strident than the narratives of the men surrounding her, more visceral, sometimes more homely and aware of its own vulnerability. My Incredible String Band years are rooted in domestic detail, but such detail runs behind all exciting lives – it's how we recognise that the poets and prophets we looked up to are human too. I can only tell here how it seemed to me, as an intimate observer of the lives lived so close to mine. It has been important to me not to retell others' stories. Over the years I have avoided reading, watching or listening to anything at all about ISB, mostly because it hurt to be reminded of what was for me, in many ways, Paradise Lost. So while any resemblance to other accounts simply confirms mine, divergence paints my own picture of how it was.

Memory makes individual meshes of significance, overriding frameworks of time and place. I am choosing to follow mine down its own meandering paths. The resulting picture is, I believe, truer than if I forced reminiscences into a straitjacket of dates and facts. The timeline at the beginning of each chapter strings the beads of events according to an outsider's vision of how it all happened. I didn't live according to that chronology. Some days were a fog of yesterdays, others a bright view of the days ahead and the memories are shaped by that internal ordering. We never thought that there was only one Truth amongst the 5000 layers of our onion lives, as they carried all of us forward into the shared future.

My cave was bright with sulky gems
That paled the stars like diadems
Silver lost and buried gold
Such was my home in days of old.

Robin Williamson, *The Iron Stone*

Strange Meetings

July 1967

5000 Spirits or The Layers of the Onion is released, establishing the Incredible String Band as the UK's answer to Flower Power in the US. In October, ISB consisting of Robin Williamson and Mike Heron, plays the Royal Festival Hall, on a bill with Shirley and Dolly Collins. In Temple Cottage outside Edinburgh Licorice mostly lives with Robin. She also contributes to the recording of *The Hangman's Beautiful Daughter*, trilling and whispering on some of its songs. I am a twenty-year-old English student at York University, though I prefer mountains to lecture theatres. Temple Cottage is also a haven for mountaineers, and I find my way there.

Winter 1967

My introduction to The Incredible String Band was entirely by chance and extremely unlikely. I had never read a music magazine or been to a pop concert. I had heard of Bob Dylan, the Beatles and the Rolling Stones but had no idea of the two Scottish musicians later said to have influenced them.

With its iconic psychedelic cover, their second LP, *5000 Spirits or the Layers of the Onion*, had just come out – and my personal metamorphosis began. Within months I changed from an unmusical working-class student into a member of a band of international reputation, complete with photoshoots for American *Vogue* and ultimately an appearance at the Woodstock Festival. I was at the centre of the back-cover photograph of the next album. The transformation was startling, and a new creature emerged to stagger, uneasily at first, into the bright lights of 1968.

While Mike and Robin were taking LSD in hip London clubs, developing a psychedelic British answer to Haight Ashbury, I was reading English at York University. Yorkshire's bleak moors and harsh industrial valleys were my playground, its austere faces and dour ways teaching me how life was going to be. The university environment bore little relationship to any "real life" I could imagine. An academic formalism I couldn't understand was spoiling literature for me. Afraid to question it,

Rose, far right, on The Hangman's Beautiful Daughter album cover, 1967

I lost interest. The freedoms offered by the Mountaineering Club were comprehensible and, more by accident than design, I became its President.

The Rock and Ice Club was the home of Britain's "hard men" of mountaineering. Tougher than the students and better climbers, they made no concessions to politeness, and made derogatory comments if they resented a girl's presence out on the fell. But this was no discouragement to me – I'd been brought up on "Put up and shut up" to silence childish complaints. "I'll give you a jam butty if you send her across later," one old joker called over to my climbing-companion as we sat around the primus stove after a hard day in the Lakes. I was fair game or I wouldn't be there, he thought.

The next day, on a slippery cliff and feeling precarious, the same codger asked me to drop him a rope from the top of the crag. Now he trusted to a woman's protective instincts. I aimed the coiled rope at his head and watched with satisfaction as anxiety overtook arrogance. He was safe enough, and by asking for help he was also humiliated, the laugh of the day.

It was in 1967, after a freezing day on a Scottish mountain, that I first headed for Temple Cottage. My anorak, climbing breeches and thick woolly socks were soaked through. I wanted to be warm and dry again, I didn't care much where. Mary Stewart's name was legendary then among the Yorkshire climbing fraternity. Strong as an ox, she had carried one climber with a broken leg miles across the moors. Walking up the muddy track to her house I had no idea what to expect.

The front door was open, the porch full of wellies, old climbing boots and muddy shoes. Children were racing through the stone-flagged hallway, chasing a tiny boy stumbling over his grown-up's shirt. The little girl waved a fairy-wand, made out of a paper star on a stick. Used to random visitors, she took no notice of another one, and Mary was just as unfussy.

Sturdy old farmhouse furniture coped with innumerable children and pets. The big armchairs and settees had deep, thick cushions and worn upholstery that you could throw yourself down into as a nest against the cold. Nobody was bothered about damp muddy trousers and dirty hands.

Closing doors was obviously not a household rule and the warmth from the Aga escaped through the front door as the children ran in and out. The house was chilly and draughty, but no one seemed to notice. If the children stopped long enough to care, they just put on another old jumper.

Tink, the eldest girl, was perhaps 12 then but competent to take care of everything when the phone went and Mary was called out to any

Rose, another wet day in the mountains, 1967

animal or mountaineering emergency. She was quiet and thoughtful, aware of her responsibilities as eldest daughter and I soon found I could rely on her for advice on everything, from the whereabouts of the nearest bus stop to how the clothes drier worked. Little Robby was a rosy-faced cherub, curious and persistent, eager to get involved but quickly distracted. Preoccupied with their own lives, the others tried to ignore him. They found their own odd socks for school and threw their own clothes into the big washing machine after muddy games of football. They were encouraged to be self-reliant.

No one had much time for housework. Like the stairs and all untouched surfaces, the sills were dusty and a bit gritty in the corners, one of them strewn with small bleached bird-skulls, dried-out flowers and toys the children had collected. The landscape had crept in along with the souvenirs and stayed. Newspapers lay dropped in corners for days, until needed to get the fire going. Then they were like gold-dust because dry sticks or kindling weren't always available, and the old chimneys needed coaxing before the fire would take.

In the daytime the kitchen was the warmest place, with the faint iron-and-coke smell that was part of the old Aga's charm, with socks always on its rail. The Handy Betty drying rack hung over the range on its pulley, lowered and hauled up again to dry out everyone's clothes. After a big wash, the smell of clean wet wool seemed natural and homely, like the sheep outside on the rainy hillsides.

It was only a small narrow kitchen, and when the house was full, you had to squeeze past the others to reach the sink or ladle food onto a plate. Cooking, like housework, was a necessary chore, though not one that needed much finesse. Fried rice and vegetables emerged from vast cast-iron pans, with soy sauce from a catering-size bottle. We mostly ate with chopsticks, which took up less space and needed less washing up than knives and forks, a proficiency we later rejoiced in at the superior oriental restaurants which ISB visited.

The Temple Cottage bedrooms were Spartan, old eiderdowns, candlewick bedspreads and little furniture, but their windows looked out over the valley. The children's rooms spilled their clutter out onto the landing, but other doors were shut so it was difficult to know who else was staying. Acceptance from the house's inhabitants had been immediate and unquestioning, my climbing breeches and rucksack establishing my identity. But it wasn't just climbers that stayed there and befriended Mary.

When night closed in, the house felt warmer and looked more cheerful, lights were turned on with their coloured shades. The faded patterns of cushions and mats which were dingy in the morning light of a snowy winter, were lent a glow by firelight. Someone called from the kitchen for hands to peel and chop vegetables, and life came in from the outdoor cold as everyone started to congregate for supper.

The general move towards the kitchen brought out some of the upstairs residents too.

Will o' the wisps

Someone told me they were folk singers, but the people that came down the stairs one by one didn't look like that to me. Folk singers wore corduroys and Icelandic sweaters. Folk singers toured all corners of the UK hawking traditional songs to a rowdy audience. They were part of the mountaineering scene and we scree-ran off the hill to get to the pub, with its folk-club in the back room. These odd-looking strangers looked too soft and frail to even manage the travel.

With her long hair framing a pale face, the girl looked folksy and very quaint in that utilitarian household, with her long skirts and embroidered jacket. The children called her Licorice, but I thought that was just their joke. The two men were even more outlandish, in curious clothes like drawings of medieval minstrels or wandering players. The taller blond was Robin, the dark-haired one Mike.

I looked at them with some detachment, as if they had just walked out of a picture book. Slightly stooped, Robin Williamson roamed in loosely and erratically, as if by chance, with his long hair falling over his face as he poked around the pots and pans. As ever, his clothes flapped about him as he moved, held together with tags and strings and laces. A threadbare jacket with missing buttons hung over cotton jeans of an indefinite pastel colour and a zip that gave up occasionally. No one was bothered, despite the lack of underwear.

Almost on a level with my own, Mike Heron's wide dark eyes gazed out of a face that looked to me like the prince in some story of the Faery Folk. Films and my mother's magazines had wanted me to admire "tall, dark and handsome", and this never interested me much. But this face of wonder entranced me, all compact energy and a voice which spoke music veiled in smiles.

I was the peasant girl who'd strayed by accident into the prince's chamber, yet his soft Scottish accent spoke sense and kindness. His bright-green wool flares struck me as warm and practical. Made from an old frilled Victorian nightdress dyed crimson, the shirt was unusual, bizarre even on a man, but he wore it with unassailable composure. He transformed clothes in the wearing. As he sat playing his guitar in the corner the next day, looking out at the frosty landscape, perfectly ordinary trousers and polo-neck jumper looked like fancy dress.

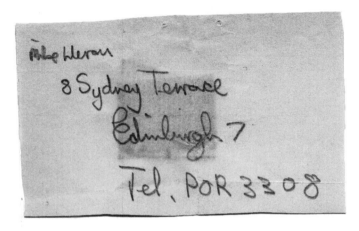

Mike's address, scrawled in pencil on a scrap of paper, 1967

Perhaps the name Temple Cottage should have told me this would be no normal climbing interlude, to be forgotten on the next rock-face. Back in York and student life, the romance of Mike and Robin hung on in my mind, like some visitation from a dream. They arrived in Harrogate one day to play at a local folk club, but I didn't go to see them play. They were staying in an empty house belonging to a friend of Mary's in the climbing world. We called in after a Sunday afternoon on Almscliff Crag, and all sat on the floor eating fish and chips. There was no furniture, just a couple of sleeping bags and a foam mattress.

In Scotland, Mike had given me his Edinburgh address, scrawled in pencil on a scrap of paper. But I never got in touch. What relevance could this musician whose life I knew nothing of have for me? He didn't write quick notes or send letters, music was his instant way of talking.

Despite the austerity of their surroundings, they still looked rare and strange, blond and dark together as they huddled in Afghan coats, leaning on saddle-bags from India and talking with the phrasing and intonation I now slightly recognised. A friend from the Art School, with hip aspirations, had bought *Layers of the Onion*, and I had been curious. In university we talked about poets and utopian idealists, fantasy islands where we could start again and make a better world. I was picking up ideas that undermined the old dominance of classical music and great writers of the past. In odd moments, I wondered if these two poetic players were leading us into a new future. I couldn't get the singers or their song out of my mind.

Castles in the air

A couple of months later, I set off back to Scotland on the train, and back to Temple Cottage. This time I left my ice-axe at home. I'd made myself a long, dark blue wool skirt, the most exotic garment I could imagine myself wearing. I hoped I would fit in better and look less of a hearty outdoor girl for those gentle creatures who lived upstairs. I rolled the skirt up in my rucksack.

But I took my climbing boots too, to keep options open and not betray the real reason for my visit. I even set off across the moor one day, but the attraction lay back at Mary's. I wanted to join the soft loungers on cushions rather than head for the hills.

Real life is the chaotic homeliness of the ground floor of the house, where people work and children play. But slipping quietly upstairs I drift into another land. Robin's and Licorice's door opens onto an ethereal dimension of fable and mystery. I'm cautious, maybe even apprehensive, as I knock very quietly, knowing that Mike is there with them and hoping for a welcome. I'm eager to enter the dreamland.

The downstairs walls were whitewashed long ago and are now greyish. But this room is radiant with colour, the rough corners and angles softened by strewn possessions: hand-painted mandalas and draped beads fill the spaces between the technicolour holiness of Krishna posters. Sometimes Robin or Licorice pick up a brush or a crayon, drawing another whirling circle to trap the conscious mind.

The room always smells of the incense cones burning on ashtrays and of the wax from perfumed candles, which gradually drips in trails over nearby cushions, and on my skirt if I sit too close. Clothes are left lying around everywhere, heaped contents spill out of open drawers onto the floor: filmy scarves, embroidered bags, braided waistcoats, strange pantaloons. Even books aren't lined up sensibly, but fall over to show their pages. Pictures have been torn out and lie strewn over the bed and the mats, along with music magazines and letters from friends.

The astrological diagrams and sepia photographs of Eastern mystics mean nothing to me. They call all that claptrap where I come from. But Robin and Lic talk to them and call the images their friends. I've never seen musical instruments like those on the wall, these peculiar and strange ornaments contributing their own small echoes, clicks and buzzes to the room's melodies.

Robin is often playing and singing when I go in, not to entertain or to practise, but because it is his way of speaking to the world and it makes them both happy. He and Licorice lie wrapped warm in everything from old flannelette sheets to silky oriental bedspreads. Licorice can look unearthly while swaddled in the many-coloured layers. The old patchwork cushion makes a soft pillow and she slips off into reveries, then sleepy dreams. But the stitching leaves trails on her cheek when she rests her face for long. When it lifts up from the velvet it carries patchwork imprints.

More an inhabitant than a visitor, Mike is clearly used to the room. At first he sits alert and upright on the old leather pouffe in the corner, then he leans against the wall as they talk and smoke until finally he ends up slumped on a cushion on the floor. His face is as beautiful in the stillness of sleep as when lit up by his dark eyes. I know I am being swept along by the romance of it all, mixing fact and fantasy, but after several hours I can't distinguish dreams from reality.

Our conversations and routines included drugs, not as a frantic escapism or search for mad fun, but as a quieter pursuit of deeper, more serious visions, unreachable via thought or consciousness. We smoked marijuana and felt we were drifting into an unconscious world of nature and cosmic being. In those reveries, the eternal truths of the universe would be revealed. We believed this.

Actually after a few experiments, I suspended this expectation. But at first I did see it as the way of enlightenment and intensified awareness. I had read the books and fallen under the spells of the opium dreams of poets. Perhaps musicians and creative beings might experience the glories I couldn't find in the chemical haze. This seemed right.

When everyone was out and Licorice had other amusements for the day, Robin sometimes got restless, a naughty child trying to outrage the elders: "Pass us that spliff man, if you've got nothing better." This meant he was bored and wanted someone to play with. He couldn't be serious and spiritual all the time. Drugs suspended the day's times and rhythms, dissolving the present into rainbows. We all shared the little world of that room. But it was no griping absence when no one had been to Edinburgh to score, and we were forced back into our books and music.

Days glided by with hash-hazy evenings, as happy breaks from Mike and Robin's gigs and recording. Away for a few days, the two would return with tales from the city: gone out with Joe Boyd, been to a Yoko Ono Happening, met the Beatles. Something about molten polythene dripping from the ceiling, Mike wasn't clear. Licorice and I listened, knowing well that the days hadn't ended with a good night's sleep. They were a novelty in London, for their looks as well as their talent – but living in the moment was the watchword so we never asked.

Lord of the Dance

Climbers still came and went at Temple Cottage, but I didn't go out on the hill any more. I visibly lost muscle-tone and weight, no longer the small Amazon who had first walked through the door. The house Mary kept was like some medieval hostel on the route across the mountains to a holy shrine. She offered a refuge for all strivers after truth, whether at the remote mountain-top or at its spiritual equivalent. Mike and Robin were genuine pilgrims, looking to achieve the insights Mike hoped to realise through his writing and music, and to enhance the visions Robin already believed were his.

The children have gone to bed and the house is all locked up: it is the enchantment of one of those evenings, in an oasis surrounded by night, that floats me off again into the past time. The big, low-ceilinged, sitting room glows faintly from the log fire, but the corners of the room are dark, lit only by the few candles still guttering on their saucers. Mike and Robin have been playing lazily, but now they fall back into the cushions of the big old settee. Conversation is just occasional murmured comments now, but we are all unwilling to leave the warmth for the cold upstairs.

A knock at the door surprises us all, at this hour of the night and far from anywhere. Even in that house of surprises it seems to me a wild and fantastic arrival when a Buddhist monk in his robes walks in. I am wondering what was in the tea, but Robin makes the introductions – he knows Trungpa Rinpoche from the Samye Ling monastery in Eskdalemuir.

As more tea is chivvied from the kettle on the Aga, Mike whispers the background story to me. For those not following the well-worn trails of Enlightenment in India, the Eskdalemuir monastery was an alternative venue, and Trungpa was already a legendary figure for Buddhists, across generations. The spiritual pathways between the monastery and Temple Cottage were just more of the mysterious cosmic conjunctions Mike saw as directing our little lives.

Rinpoche's dark rusty-red robes are pulled around his waist with a knotted cord. With his bare legs and sandaled feet he looks as active and athletic as any of the climbers here. But his ascetic, good-natured, smiling face is smooth and tranquil, unlike their battered, weather-worn and often bearded ones.

He settles round the fire with his cold hands around a bowl of tea, but it is late, and we are all too tired to talk much, even with this welcome new arrival. Someone puts another record on Mary's old Dansette record-player. Mike and Robin's tastes are always eclectic, and the music has been changing all evening, from West Coast rock to evening ragas and back again.

Whatever is now playing, Rinpoche suddenly jumps out of his chair and starts to dance to it. This may be meditation for him – whirling Dervish via Tai Chi – but the sudden surging energy snaps me out of drowsiness into clear waking. Rinpoche looks like pure embodied joy, his impassive face above the whirling limbs expressing absolute loss of self in the movement and the moment.

No one seems disturbed by this eruption of activity into the sleepy room. We sit around and watch. Once I collect my thoughts, I am curious, puzzled by what is happening in front of me. I am entranced by the dance, and the others gaze with rapt, absent stares, caught up in the sudden drama. Rinpoche is tall and slim, and his robes whip round as he spins and sways and leaps. It is a storm of a dance which seems to have no cause or reason, just to be.

I don't believe there's a single way to Enlightenment, but if anything could have persuaded me otherwise, that dance was it. It stops as suddenly as it started, Rinpoche fades away into one of the rooms in the black house and we all go to bed as if nothing had happened. I once heard temple gongs on a radio programme and their echoing, reverberating sound haunted my imagination. The living presence of a monk dancing his beliefs in his robes in a Scottish farmhouse was proof this was an other-worldly place. By morning he was gone and I never saw him again.

Family portrait

Another visitor from Samye Ling found himself on the cover of *The Hangman's Beautiful Daughter* album, looking more Renaissance than Buddhist. He was quiet and unassuming, cheerfully amusing the children as we walked through the wood for the photo.

The *Hangman* photo-shoot was just a weekend diversion for the children and for us, or so it now seems. If it was Christmas Day, as is often claimed, then we had a very quiet celebration – odd in a house full of children with grown-ups always willing to play games. Dressing-up boxes and drawers were turned out. Little Robbie was wrapped up in someone's summer kimono over a warm jumper, wound in a scarf and topped off with a sun hat. The smaller girl of the family grabbed an elf-hat. The elder, more aware of style, wore a fashionable wide brim and smiled at the camera properly. This was a hat Robin sometimes wore, and the two were always close, talking seriously about all the grown-up things that others were too young or too old to be interested in. Not having anything even vaguely decorative of my own I borrowed a jacket from Licorice – who insisted on the dog, always at her feet whenever possible anyway. Everyone else chose outfits from what they could find and whatever took their fancy.

I dislike being photographed and was glad to hide behind my hair as I made sure that Robbie wouldn't fall out of the tree where Mike had perched him, much to his delight. Up on a branch, he could get a good view of everything. The elder brother behind him was having too much fun pretending to ride his hunter to worry about the little one.

The abandoned mask Mike had picked up was made by one of the children, probably for some school project. Robin found the toy lying around somewhere, or perhaps it was a gift. Only when the contact-sheets came round did I notice how mask and toy dominate the image, both presented to the camera's gaze. Whether or not they planned to give them a symbolic significance, their serious expressions as they held them invited the interpretation.

The possibilities of the meanings were infinite, and the eager fans we heard from later examined the sleeve, asking each other what message they conveyed. Did the mask have mystic significance? Was the spinning toy a prayer wheel carrying messages to the cosmos? Mike and Robin never said – but the presence of those objects singled the two of them out from the rest of us, as we draped ourselves around the trees.

There was much laughing and fooling about, the dog chasing the children and refusing to sit still. Then someone fell over, hurt their knee and had to be consoled. The two visitors in the back row, who had taken most advantage of the costume-opportunity, arranged their poses. Despite all the hilarity, the photographer caught a moment of seriousness, our expressions all very true to how we were at the time. No wonder I look tired. Nights and days were all muddled up and I was two people in two different lives.

The distances between us four are clear. My central position next to Robin I still think of as accidental, but it had unforeseen consequences. I had no doubts who I felt closer to and preferred on aesthetic grounds. Robin was with Licorice, as far as I was concerned, while Mike had been on his own on the occasions we had met. Mike's cheerfulness lightened the day and he laughed easily at small pleasures. I knew already that he was quite serious about his pursuit of a better, more spiritual life. But he never weighed me down with mystic utterances, his philosophical observations never made me feel I stood outside some circle of initiates.

Free flight

Back in York, a Final Year student, I lived in Hall the odd weeks I was there, when not on a mountain or at Temple Cottage. When Robin appeared at my door one afternoon – Indian shirt, beads and the inevitable thonged flares – I didn't ask how he had found me, or why. As day passed into evening, with instant coffee and catch-up chat between friends whose lives followed different ways, he mentioned that he was planning to stay the night. Not unusual after the fluidity of Temple Cottage hospitality, but inconvenient.

York University retained some rules, despite its liberal reputation. Miscellaneous hippies sharing rooms was a step too far down the path to freedom. The cleaners would be horrified if they arrived in the morning to find Robin on the premises. The refectory staff had already collapsed into giggles at the sight of him, his bead necklaces clicking against milk jugs and the heavy silver rings on his fingers catching his hair as he pushed it back.

Unwilling to disturb the free flow of the Cottage ethos, I hoped some solution would present itself. Perhaps someone who had seen him play would take him off my hands. Unfortunately, no one claimed acquaintance in time. He told me he planned to head off to London in a couple of days to meet Mike. He willingly agreed tomorrow morning would be better. Our presence at breakfast in the refectory wouldn't go unnoticed, but that was just unfortunate, he had to stay. The narrow settee-bed of a student study room conveniently dictated sleeping arrangements. I was used to sleeping on damp mountains, so a warm floor was no suffering.

My tutor was also escaping for an indiscreet weekend on the train the next afternoon, so blank stares in both directions sealed the deal. In a kaftan made from an Indian bedspread found in a jumble sale in Harrogate, with wooden beads and my aunt's silver nurse's belt, I could match Robin's style. We arrived at the flat where Joe Boyd was staying, and there was Mike.

The flat was one of Joe's many homes and hideaways in London, near Kensington Gardens, on the ground floor of a porticoed terrace, very grand from the outside but not unlike Temple Cottage inside. It was untidy, cluttered with paperwork and the peripatetic possessions of a frantically busy life. Joe and his friends seemed to live in public, to be always on display. Home was both the office and an exhibition area for a lifestyle. The bedrooms were arenas for the business combats of these new gladiators: cushioned zenanas, full of Eastern promise, rather than private personal spaces.

Even to my naïve eyes, it was clear Joe was different. He seemed to know everything about anything and, without being good-looking in film star terms, was somehow glamorous. He was also boyish in his unconcern with all the things that mothers nag about, like tidy bedrooms and regular habits. This charm ensured the constant background presence of a girlfriend, always "the best and most beautiful," as Nick Drake once said. Work finished, supper eaten at a nearby restaurant and plans for the next day made, we all ended up back at his flat.

But now I had a problem. Robin had turned up in York without encouragement from me, confident that I would be delighted to see him and follow in his wake. There had been no subtle hints to suggest Mike found my arrival with Robin odd. He seemed unperturbed and gave me no chance to talk about it.

Indeed everyone had followed Robin's lead, acting as if he and I were together. I was disconcerted, unsure how to react as the weight of group expectation carried me along. I didn't know anything about this world or these people. Outside the enchanted space of Temple Cottage, even the hippie language was strange.

It was only when I was alone with Robin that I could gather my wits, as he fell asleep in the semi-dark of a city room lit by the streetlights outside. I didn't want to be there and was not going to hang around. There were no words to explain. Instinct carried me along as I crept out into the unlit hallway. All was quiet in the flat, and I relied on primitive, blind intuition to draw me to where Mike might be. It worked. He was surprised, but glad to see me. I was sure that this was the right place to be and I stayed, happy and content in a warm nest.

I didn't care what others thought. If those men in their trendy clothes could flit from pretty face to pretty face, as they had been saying all evening, then so could I. Not one word was ever spoken to me about this, by anyone who was there. Whatever tensions there were between Mike and Robin in the following days were not shared. Joe was clearly puzzled the next morning. Concert bookings even had to be cancelled, to Joe's great dissatisfaction. But this was not my problem.

Krishna Colours on the Wall: Roman Camps

March 1968

The Hangman's Beautiful Daughter is released, bringing widespread press attention with it. Mike and Robin undertake the first big UK tour, often with dancers Mimi and Mouse. The unique influence of ISB is being noticed and other music-makers want to meet them. Film-maker Peter Neal begins making a documentary to capture the bright fun and hopefulness, starting with the trippy performances at the Festival Hall concert at the end of March. I give up on rock-faces, dissertations and Finals. Mike buys a tiny cottage and we play at making a home. Left behind for the first US tour, I discover the drawbacks of this new life.

✦

As Mike and I greeted the morning together, after a night of choices and meandering, many questions were left unasked. Not willing to spoil the day with disagreements, we wandered off into London to find another temporary lodging. We had a new life to think of. If ISB was the background to it, it was not at the forefront of our minds. The next weeks would bring their own solutions as the personalities, times and places of Mike's musical life moved into mine and ISB changed from a duo to a quartet.

We didn't think about it much, just seized the day and lived in the moment.

Initially we stayed with a couple of lecturers from Hornsey College of Art, friends of Mike though more from my world, of college gossip and university terms. Back in York, talking about my new Scottish friends, I had described ISB as the personification of a wider cultural movement – in that context I could hardly celebrate the hazy evenings and ecstatic mornings. But in London, with Mike beside me, the words didn't matter any more, I didn't care about the theories, or about whether I sat my Finals or not. There were more important, more attractive things to get on with.

Disagreements flared up between Mike and Robin over the next few days, far more than tiffs over a girl. Given the success of ISB's records and

Joe's interest, they really did now have a prospect of fame and fortune. Record contracts signed, bigger venues booked, they could no longer ignore the changes this would force upon them. Their partnership was vital if they wanted to pursue these opportunities, they could see that. From the start, Joe had advised they record their own songs rather than a traditional folk repertoire. He continued to encourage them to exploit the originality of their talents. But like their looks, their personalities, were very different. Keeping this difference complementary rather than oppositional would be a problem.

Despite shared spiritual beliefs as a common ground to meet on, their musical aspirations diverged widely. Both brought the Scottish landscape into the concert hall, but Robin's song swept over the glens like a wind. Mike showed us how the ferns grew, the small woodland flowers and the quiet morning lake.

On-stage, Robin would sing meditations on Maya one minute, then change tack for 'Big Ted' and chat about the Welsh pig's sexual prowess, before seizing his gimbri to fly us all off again into a mystic dimension of colour and sound. Mike brought us back to the beauty of homely things and childlike images, so joyful that we didn't need to leave the earth any more. So their most individual songs appealed to different ends of their audience spectrum, particularly in the earlier LPs. The more esoteric and intellectual chased Robin's references, pondering his deep thoughts, while the more physical and sybaritic identified the same intensity in Mike's funny, whimsical lyrics.

As with their techniques and their instrumentation, how they chose to write their songs had little in common. Robin favoured inspiration, dreaming entire lyrics, creating accompaniments spontaneously in ever-varying forms. Repetition of fixed versions was not his preferred style. Mike went away alone with his guitar and spun the songs from his conversation with the strings. He had enjoyed his time with the Edinburgh beat group The Abstracts, their rock aspirations clear from their newspaper advertisements: "Lock up your daughters, The Abstracts are in town." Looking eagerly forward to all that success with ISB might offer, he was willing to work for it, and to make the necessary compromises.

Robin's dedication was less certain. The moment he had the advance for their first LP, he headed off to Morocco, without thought for Mike, the partnership, or making commitments for the future. It was only when the money started to run out that he returned to revive the project. From the start, he clearly accepted only reluctantly any disciplined approach to creative or spiritual quests. He tolerated restrictions imposed by management or record companies, but also resented them.

The Abstracts announcement, 31 December 1964

A whole new world

When I first joined Mike in London, Licorice had vanished somewhere in Scotland, but she re-emerged shortly afterwards, to stay with Robin once more.

Meeting occasionally at Joe's flat or in restaurants, we were an uneasy foursome. The advent of another girlfriend intent on being an active part of Mike's life merely aggravated matters further, in Joe's eyes, especially if it meant cancelling dates in a tour already booked.

One visually memorable date survived this wreck. The support band were Tyrannosaurus Rex. Robin, Mike and Marc Bolan looked like Elizabethan jesters in their motley of colours, flares, ribbons, beads and curls, against the ancient setting of an Oxford college chamber.

Away from Temple Cottage, I was realising how different Mike and Robin's lives were from anything I knew or could understand. However much they resisted its claims, they belonged to the music industry. These were not just the intriguing and lovable men I had been sharing happy times with. When Mike and Robin returned to full schedules of playing, rehearsing, recording and performing, the hours of my days changed. Dawn departures, uncertain and uncontrollable destinations, midnight meals and unknown faces invaded my life.

I found myself wondering when and what the next meal might be. Perhaps I should always try to eat a lot, then I'd be sure to get through whatever the day brought. Getting up each morning I had little idea where I would be that evening. I learned to go with the flow and wonder at the strange shores I had drifted onto, the thrills and spills of cutting loose from a lifetime's habits.

I had seen contemporary psychedelia in newspaper colour sections and advertisements, but now its swirling electric colours and startling imagery decorated my life. The Dutch art collective Simon and Marijke had painted the album cover of *5000 Spirits or the Layers of the Onion* for Mike and Robin. Nigel Waymouth of the Granny Takes A Trip boutique designed their concert posters. He dressed London trend-setters but to us he was a friendly face we occasionally met at Joe's. I didn't have much time for his shop's over-self-conscious staff and customers. The clothes were too expensive and seemed to us like a uniform of fake rebellion, a rejection of the personal spontaneity we cherished for ourselves.

Dancers Mimi and Mouse, embodiments of the West Coast flower children, adorned Mike and Robin's stage appearances – but they also seemed to belong to this world of dressed-up people pretending to be free-spirited. They performed meditative Tai Chi before each appearance. I was puzzled by the slow rituals of their movement, but never admitted my ignorance when Robin sat beside me and remarked on the technique.

A great advantage of our habitual disinclination for small talk in those early days was that I was saved many a faux pas exposing my bewilderment. It also allowed the equivocations and mysteries of our inter-relationships to spin out longer. As Robin's hair brushed my shoulder, I wondered how it had been with those other girls below us on the stage. Their mask-like smiles and heavily contrived gestures felt so artificial, so unlike the clear truth that Mike and Robin seemed to radiate, that I decided it didn't matter anyway. I was never going to be a painted doll and I was already beginning to make my own rules for this new game.

Mimi and Mouse's appearances with ISB ceased after the cancelled tour, and soon Licorice and I replaced them on stage, much to Joe Boyd's disappointment. With our intrusive presence we may have lessened Mike and Robin's hypnotic intensity as a duo. We certainly modified the Boyd influence, not always for the better. But perhaps we also made them more accessible for a wider audience, prolonging the time they could live and work together with a degree of mutual pleasure.

Crossing roads

Perhaps my suddenly being at the heart of this band seems hard to reconcile with how things had been before, but the incongruity is not as great as it seems. Common features united all our lives, with family pasts that ran parallel and shared experiences of a less personal kind. Despite obvious differences of style, language, habits and interests, I could still fit in here.

I don't know what similarities or differences existed between our family lives before the four of us were brought together in Mary's house. Just as our parents didn't discuss their pasts with us, we never talked about it. We met each other as if there were no time before. I never wondered how old they were or even thought to ask their proper names. It is only now that I find that Mike was the eldest, nearly twenty five, Robin a year younger than him and Licorice just twenty two. The numbers were irrelevant. I arrived on the scene to find the three of them already living the life of their album covers, being the figures others recognised from the photos.

Before that they had done other things, lived with other people in other places. Mike made jokey references to his past. He talked about Michelle, his previous girlfriend. There was vague gossip about Licorice and Robin. But I had no idea where they came from or what else had happened to them, who their families were. This silence encourages me to generalise from the history I know at first hand, and from the need to establish some origins on which to base the coming three years.

The four of us now together so unexpectedly and randomly were all from the Baby Boom Generation, generated in the frenzy of returning soldiers seeking escape, oblivion, security and affection. War causes all sorts of collisions, mostly painful, occasionally creative. Our fathers and mothers had been active in the war effort, had seen and felt the horrors, griefs and fears of total war at home as well as abroad. Whether they admitted to trauma or not, their trauma shaped our early lives, and we failed to recognise its manifestations. And there were so many of us that these minor derangements of everyday life – now called post-traumatic stress – were our normality.

The World Wars had also forced people together to share the common experiences of battle in the field, and on the Home Front, generating the songs, stories and images we all grew up with. Tales of old soldiers were told at family meetings, 'Goodbye Tipperary' sung along with the housework. Williamson's song 'Darling Belle' tells of 1914-18. Memories of that distanced past were current gossip rather than the fresher traumas of World War Two.

War had been a temporary leveller for people of very different backgrounds, generating conformities in daily life across differences of class and income. Everyone was subject to rationing and its evasions; all schools took on returned soldiers and a few popular magazines instructed housewives and mothers how to raise their children. My family was not like those of the other three, but still our childhoods overlapped in the national saga.

The war had dominated my childish vision. The fabled buoyancy of the 1950s, the ballroom dancing under glitter-balls, rested on a sombre bedrock. My parents' marriage had been an unhappy accident. My father wore his battledress as weekend gardening clothes, although the "Dig for Victory" ethos didn't survive carrot-fly eating the crop and the potatoes wilting. His back-injury, acquired in battle along with a medal for gallantry, added pain to the daily burdens of marital misery and financial stress.

All four of us in ISB had known family loss and a post-war deprivation – though I only understood the latter as the absence of fruit and sweets. A certain hardship had made itself felt in scratchy jumpers, knitted from the unravelled wool of worn-out adult sweaters. Shoes had to last, so metal segs were hammered into toes and heels to save the soles. Footsteps clicked in rhythmic accompaniment as we ran along. New clothes were rare, limited by the availability of clothing coupons as well as poverty. We had no say in the choice of fabric, style or colour.

At school, girls learned to sew and knit, while boys did woodwork and handicrafts. Licorice, Mike and Robin seemed to lack these useful skills, though by choice not incompetence. A clever girl who got to Grammar School might have a secure and comfortable future as the wife of a professional man. We learned plain cooking, economical household management and the basics of thorough cleaning – including how to make soap from the fat left over from the Sunday roast.

All this came in very useful when hippiedom took over and the simple life became an ideological banner. I had articles saved still from wartime magazines about making a "fashionable jacket from grandmother's fur coat" – debates about the fur trade did not yet cloud our consciences. So I could sew Mike a warm red velvet winter coat to brave a Canadian winter in, with an old fur to line it. It stood up to the elements much better than the yellow embroidered Afghan jacket he had bought on some earlier tour. That now looked like a dirty tabby cat and didn't smell much better.

Home thoughts

My parents were an ill-assorted pair who made each other miserable every waking hour. When they left the home, always separately, they switched to the characters they wanted to be. Play-acting as daily life was the way I grew up. My mother's chosen play was respectability, avoiding the neighbours' gossip being more important to her than happiness. The forbearance and reticence I learned from her were convenient habits in the early band days, when Mike was away and I was alone in Scotland. They came in useful later too, in bleak dressing rooms, before the band's status enabled clauses in our contracts requesting water and salad bowls, or whatever the whims of the moment were.

My father's involvement in amateur dramatics and his endless round of productions and drama festivals allowed him to present himself to strangers as a pastiche of the famous actors of the day. With a clipped Noël Coward accent, he sometimes had the thin, haunted face of Gielgud playing tragedy. Expensive blazers and slacks from the town's second-hand shops completed the transformation. Setting off to work every morning on his bike in a threadbare old gabardine over cheap grey trousers gathered up in cycling clips, he was invisible to everyone he met in his evenings at the Dramatic Society and the Opera House.

I learnt my part in his personal play. As soon as I could read, I spent boring hours as all the other characters in his scripts, as he learnt his lines for the latest show. As a teenager in the theatre-club bar, I smiled politely as the Thespian community of a regional town pretended to take me for his sister. And I absorbed the language and the manners of backstage – because impoverished repertory theatres were only too glad to get voluntary help from the amateur community, as long as no jobs were threatened and the hierarchy preserved. Thus performance as life-style was second nature to me, and I was happy and comfortable in the labyrinthine corridors, dressing rooms and black dustiness of behind the scenes. The transition from student life to the new fantastic home of international stages was easy.

Like many other working-class girls at the time, my notions of the future oscillated between the imagined adoration we felt was our due, according to films and fictions, and the drudgery that was a daily reality for the women we saw around us. An independent life with a career of my own never occurred to me as a serious possibility. In quiet moments schoolboy boyfriends gave us sweet and respectful affection. They too had seen the films and knew a girl expected some romantic gesture in return for a grope in the back seat of a borrowed car.

We listened to our mothers complain about children and chores, straying husbands and insufficient housekeeping money. In their experience the short-lived delights of love and marriage were inevitably followed by misery, and they expected the same for us. If education got us a good job as a nurse or a teacher it might go better but this was unlikely as far as they could see.

And I blew this faint possibility of salvation by running off with a "psychedelic folk group" in my final year at university. For a while I lived the images the band sang about: flower-child, down-home lover. I also painted the ceiling in a blaze of cocaine and made jars of macrobiotic ice-cream from wholemeal flour and coconut, putting it outside in the winter snow to freeze. We had no fridge, keeping the mechanical world as far away as possible. I shared the hopeful ideals of ISB's earlier years –

but also walked the muddy miles to the village for the shopping, in the "real world" of rural Scotland.

Wanderings

In the newly peripatetic life Mike and I now found for ourselves, we met each other anywhere his music took him and a room was free. There was a fortified country house in the Scottish borders, which centuries ago had sheltered its family as marauding rievers tried to steal their cattle. Its Tudor ceiling mouldings were a renewed delight every morning, as we opened our eyes and looked upwards. We hung mirrors from the ceiling of a backstreet room in Cambridge, and watched them turning in the sunlight, seeing rainbows and our reflected laughing faces. We hardly knew the hosts of these houses, or the address, but we were happy as we came and went, and everyone round us seemed to reflect our pleasure.

When the invitations ran out, we returned to York, staying for a while in a flat more subterranean than basement, all that was available so late in the term. In the song 'Douglas Traherne Harding', Mike later sang about enlightenment as embodied in the man in the basement with no head. Douglas Harding was a mystic philosopher, author of *On Having No Head*, but Mike was referring to his own hours of contemplation, I think, as he sat in the semi-dark while I was on some errand in town. Later, we met Douglas Harding, in another basement, at the Baghdad Restaurant on the Fulham Road. There, all was warmth, colour and well-being as kebabs and sweet tea were stuffed into the hungry mouths of very visible Heads.

The low light crept in from the one front window in York, showing up the black mould in all the corners. Moquette armchairs had soaked up the pervasive wetness into wilted cushions of indistinct colours. If we dried them out in the sun they acted as damp-barriers – if we didn't sit still too long. The grease on every kitchen surface was deep-ingrained. The condition of the mattress was indescribable. We bought cheap sheets and covered it up, hoping that the nastiness was only skin-deep.

The nearby park and the university campus felt like countryside. Water-fowl nested on the island in the lake and their chicks tottered over the lawns. Peacocks screamed, displaying iridescent feathery tails against the topiary. It was Yorkshire so it must have rained, but I don't remember. I never made it to lectures. Why choose to waste the time snatched from Mike's musical life when it always seemed too short?

In my present state of contentment, I felt I'd already spent too many weeks on mountains. I had never enjoyed the drunken university parties, or the pretentious intellectualism of Hampstead maidens talking loudly in corridors about counter-tenors and medieval consorts. Once or twice

The Roman Camps terraced cottages with nearby slag-heaps, as seen from the fields beyond

Mike and I walked hand in hand around the campus at night and I showed him what my life had been before he came along.

When he had to go away I went too, as often as possible. Eventually I saw universities from a band's viewpoint – Ents students hoping for careers in the media were always the same in their officious vanity and insecurity. Later on, as an established member of the band, I sometimes travelled with the roadies for fun, helping them unload and set up. The Entertainment Committee saw me as the roadie's moll and talked down to me. Their shocked embarrassment when they realised their mistake amused me.

I now had a reflected glory. The band's reputation was spreading. Even in Yorkshire, boutiques and discotheques were diffusing London taste to the provinces. Our multi-coloured raiment continued to attract attention and we were invited to stay in Wilfred Mellers' home, a blessed release from the damp basement. He was Professor of Music, and his kind support saw us through for a while. Instead of water biscuits spread with apricot jam for breakfast, we had proper meals.

This temporary and disjointed existence couldn't last. Spending a couple of dutiful days with my parents, I was evading discussions about missed weeks at York and imminent Finals. Unfortunately the *Harrogate Advertiser* had spotted and photographed me as "Hippy on Parliament Street" and my mother was devastated by the public shame.

Mike phoned to tell me he had bought a house and we could now have a home together. I got the earliest train back to Edinburgh.

Nesting

Mike met me at the station and we drove out to the little house at Roman Camps. The name predisposed me to like it, historic, international and totally incongruous for a huddle of industrial buildings near the main road between Edinburgh and Glasgow. Mike had bought the place for £500, most of the money in his bank account, left to him by an aunt. We inherited some of her possessions too – she evidently had a taste for the unconventional, so must have been pleased by her unusual nephew.

Dilapidated, the house was a palace compared to the York basement, a two-roomed single storey, ex-miner's cottage, one of maybe 50 built in terraces of four around a large grassy square worn bare by children's games in summer and muddy in winter. It was surrounded by a spoiled countryside of ditches and streams, fields and slag-heaps. No one bothered to plant anything in the small gardens, which were full of dock and nettles.

Everyone dried their weekly laundry on the rows of lines on the green, one line per cottage. On Mondays the other women turned out with their washing baskets, rain or fine, to hang out at least the sheets. We had no choice, there was no room inside. We didn't visit or have visitors, and the green was my one link with the daily life of the families around. Although we lived there for some time, we were never really part of the community.

Our washing was different too, strange foreign garments in brilliant colours. And the Monday Wash ritual required possession of a washing machine. My mother never had one and I had rarely used the college launderette. I was used to hand-washing – but fingertips already sore from playing metal bass strings didn't cope well with scrubbing stains off linen. Long immersion in hot suds made my skin raw and, pain aside, this didn't look good in photographs.

I was aware I was an object of local derision, from the looks I got when I took my few things out of the washing-up bowl that was my laundry basket. They had rows of matching bed linen and white underwear – some using a second line, to demonstrate their prosperity and cleanliness. But at least when the greyish tinge of wear crept in I could dye my sheets another startling colour. Soon they were all tie-dyed fuchsia pink and purple, which leached out into the paler textiles.

As soon as we took possession, I painted the kitchen orange. Accessories were a fashionable brown. The washing-up bowl with matching brush and waste basket seemed cool and sophisticated to me, though Mike's visitors from Edinburgh didn't seem impressed.

From left, transitions – hearty sweater, Indian skirt; paint myself hippy – Roman Camps, 1968

But the colours were important. Pastels represented a repressed aesthetic, whose day had passed. We wanted intense, strident colours, clashing and shouting, breaking all matching conventions. We wanted the impermanence of posters and postcards, to announce our tastes and ever-changing allegiances to gods or gurus, so unlike the mock oil-paintings from Boots the Chemist which were a fixed presence in the parental front room.

I sewed yellow gingham curtains for the kitchen and towelling ones for the bathroom, and Mike hung them up with cheerful enthusiasm. He borrowed a car to bring over the aunt's Benares brass coffee table, some African baskets, and a Victorian sewing box. A mattress on the floor was fine, with an Indian bedspread and lots of cushions and the red double sleeping bag Mike bought from the camping shop – too hot in summer and a bit cold in winter but we didn't mind.

We jointly painted the bedroom walls sunset colours and the living room sunny yellow. Mike drew an intricate mandala on the wall with felt-tip pens and we hung the guitars up for decoration. We stripped and sanded the wood floor with a hired machine, covering the house with dust, then varnished over it and went to Edinburgh overnight leaving it to dry. Our amateur efforts left small globules of polyurethane varnish all over the roughly finished boards, which collected dirt as time went by and ripped up the foam on my squeezy mops.

Warm rooms and hot water depended on the open fire in the living room, and keeping it going was a constant chore. Mike needed warm hands to play, and his days were largely sedentary. The coal man from the village delivered to the bunker by the back door. We foraged the countryside for sticks and kept every newspaper we could lay hands on. We rarely read them, more concerned with "the pure life within us" than the world outside.

We decided a joint bank account was the only way, an astonishing gesture of commitment on Mike's part. The bank manager in Edinburgh gave us a lecture on financial responsibility and warned Mike that he had taken me from my home and had a duty towards me. We just laughed and never referred to it again, once we had signed all the papers and escaped from the quiet office. I appreciated the paternal concern and Mike's quiet acceptance of the message, but I did not plan to rely on either if I could help it. When a man from the Inland Revenue called at the cottage one day to ask about my income I told him I was a Kept Woman and laughed at his astonishment. Respectable people made up excuses but I saw no reason to do that.

When Mike brought an acetate print of Art Nouveau girls in a garden back from San Francisco, with "Flower Children" printed across it in wavy purple script, I had no sense of making a statement about our lives. Newspaper reports of the strange goings-on in Haight Ashbury or LA depicted others, not us, as far as I was concerned. We stuck the image on the window and lit it from behind with candles at night so passers-by could see it. Our life – from its domestic routines to the working world of music – had already become normality for me, and I was surprised when people thought it strange. It was only later that I looked at the dates on an ISB concert poster and realised that the exotic, sinuous, semi-naked girls might be taken for me and Licorice.

In the few weeks we had together at Roman Camps in between life with the band, we played at home-making. I never had a pet, though one day I rescued a tiny Indian whistling toad from the school bus. Some boys were poking it, and this cruelty to a helpless creature aroused the Valkyrie in me. Fierceness must have radiated from the weird witch – there was no argument as they gave it to me. We put it in a box full of damp moss, with a Pyrex pool. Mike caught flies for it, and we gave it the freedom of the cottage. But it soon disappeared. We looked everywhere and never found anything. I hope it went out into the world and prospered.

Sharing with Sister: her room was a haven when Mike was touring the US, 1968

Lives of poets

When Mike and Robin next toured America, I was left at home. Lic went with them, but I never knew this or I might have made more of a fuss. Besides, I still had to do my Finals, at York. I wrote a dissertation on French Symbolism. My sources were Mike's books on mystic signs, references to the lyrics on *Layers of the Onion* and the small, cheap, poetry paperbacks I could find in Edinburgh bookshops. This saved me doing one of the exams, and I turned up for two more, with enough background knowledge to write through one. The next was Middle English. The first question was on the 14th century dream vision poem *Pearl*. I had never read it and gave up. I sat for a while, then walked out. The following days I was officially ill but in no mental state to see a doctor, staying in Harrogate feeling lost and astray. Then I fled back to Roman Camps.

Mike's Victorian nightdress-shirt became my cover-all and security garment, a comforter when I felt lonely and a talisman towards his return. There were very occasional postcards, but I only learned about the trip afterwards, unpacking the new shirts made for him in LA by some part-time groupie and friend of the stars. We had not yet seen these things in the UK: the brilliant, gauzy clothes, the thonged leather bag with fringes. and a psychedelic tinplate toy with a wheel which spun into rainbows and sparks.

He played me his new song about puppies, written one early morning in the sun in a homestead-garden watching the little animals greet the new day. The music brought the novelty and the golden light of California into the greyness of Scotland. There was no point envying the days I hadn't shared, or the girls who maybe had. All that was the prejudice of the old world, and we were making a new one.

Lives of the Poets tells an imaginative girl what not to do. The wives and mistresses of genius patiently endured all impositions, until relegated to the footnotes. But I had no feel for martyrdom. When Mike's diversions bothered me, I found my own. It looked so simple to me, and I had little sympathy for those who chose to suffer and whine rather than do something about it.

Domestic bliss and country walks

Besides, Mike was now home and all was going well. Broxburn was the nearest small town, dark stone and hard corners, all local shops except the bank. We bought cheese from the grocer, cut by wire from a wheel of Cheddar which was always mouldy and odd-tasting. I asked about its age but was sternly advised that mould was the nature of such cheese. Muddy root vegetables, tinned food and basic household essentials were all the shop offered, with oranges an extravagant import.

Joe's Witchseason Productions paid Mike and Robin a basic wage to keep us alive, with more after big concerts. When money came in and we felt rich, we went into Edinburgh, the big city with its fancy shops. Mike had already acquired a taste for delicatessen his mother would never have bought, and we sought out new ingredients for my forays into cookery. There were cheeses with fancy names and weird tastes, bought after deep discussions with the owner, in a quiet shadowy grocery with marble counters and gleaming brasswork on its wooden dressers. Abernethy biscuits were on every shopping list.

Meals were haphazard, fitted in around the passions of the day. If we had been up all night on acid then milkless porridge was our saviour. The milkman who delivered to the neighbours had soon got fed up of bottles of sour milk on the doorstep and the late-paid bills when we went away. On a sociable day, Fanny Craddock was the height of sophistication and I tried out her recipes in the little orange kitchen. Crème Brulée was a favourite,

Slipping and sliding: Mike and Sister climb the heaps, Summer 1968

and we bought a Bain Marie. I enjoyed making puddings and Mike usually liked eating them. All this was before diet became part of our spiritual crusades, when ideology, rather than taste or pleasure, dictated food choices.

Walking to the shop and the bus took a fair part of each day, across the fields beside the beck, then over the bridge where it flowed under the main street. The red ashy slag-heaps from past mining operations looked like a Martian landscape in a science-fiction film, piled one after another. As the sun went down behind them, they blazed crimson and black.

Roman Camps was a very coloured countryside. We never stopped to ask what they had been mining. Grass had grown in places, but the ground slipped and slithered as we walked up the heaps and jumped

Brother and Sister

down, sliding with the shale and dust. One day Mike's sister came to play with us in this giant sand-pit on our doorstep. She looked like an Angela Brazil hockey-playing schoolgirl in her nice tidy coat, with short dark hair cut pudding-bowl style. After a day on the heaps, picnicking by the beck and catching tiddlers, she went home dusted with red despite our best efforts to brush her down.

Sister of mercy

We called her Sister, and she was a great help to me when Mike was away. She was a teacher at a school for children with multiple and severe physical problems. The motherly love and kindness she extended to them, uncritical care and protection, she also poured out on me, as her beloved brother's girlfriend. She had taught Mike to sing harmonies when he was a boy, sitting together in the back seat of their parents' car when they went on outings, and his songs and his success were clearly the delight of her life. Not that she would ever say anything so sentimental.

She shared her bedsit in Malvern with me for a week while Mike was in the US, cooking dinner after work and making sure I was healthy and happy. She hoped for a family of her own, picturing it in the little oil paintings which decorated her room. She went to art classes to learn technique but continued to paint happy families with three children lined up beside their parents in front of a house. Mike had the family looks, but his sister's goodness shone out of her.

When the Maharishi became the latest fashion for Enlightenment, and we were initiated into his meditation system, Mike and Robin enjoyed celebrity introductions with the guru himself, while Licorice and I were welcomed by his acolytes. But Sister found her own quiet way through the hierarchy, exercising all the self-discipline in which we failed: the hours of silently repeating mantras, sitting quietly and breathing in the universe. We kept this up for weeks before getting bored, but she maintained it for years. I did make the time for stillness, seeing it as a useful habit, stripped of its spiritual significance.

Sister was killed in a road accident on a later trip to an ashram in India. We were on tour in the US when we heard. In the confusion of uncertain news, it felt to me more like a half-believed-in disappearance than a real, permanent loss to mourn. Happening in a world outside the group bubble, it seemed irrelevant and unreal, like all family matters. I didn't even make a note of the day or the year and Mike didn't talk about it.

Deck the halls

Our first Christmas at Roman Camps, in 1968, was a celebration of the band as a family and Robin and Licorice came to stay. Licorice arrived beaming over a bunch of arum lilies, like a pre-Raphaelite Madonna. We put the white, perfect blooms in a brass vase on the floor. We only had one of Auntie's oriental chairs to clutter up the small space, so most things happened on the floor, eating and sleeping, talking and playing. When the world rocked on its axis and the room spun slowly, whatever the reason, the floor was the safest place

In stories, people always dug trees up in the forest for Christmas, and Mike and I had already dug ours up in the forestry plantation up the road, late one afternoon when there was no one around. We carried it home in triumph through the dusk. It had to be a live tree for our first Christmas, to be taken outside after Twelfth Night and replanted in the garden opposite. I looked in every hedgerow for decorative holly with berries on, but in the end had to buy it at the grocer's.

Over several weeks I had been collecting glass balls and Lametta, and on tour I bought a turquoise bird with a peacock-feather tail. I made a wobbly tinsel star for the top of the tree, and we had proper wax candles, bought from the Norwegian shop on Princes Street, with candleholders rescued from my childhood. The ritual of bringing in the greenery to ward off winter seemed right for us, as we made a living from the folk music that celebrated country ways. On gloomy days the fairy tale sparkling reminded us of the turning seasons and the promise of Spring to come.

On Christmas Day we exchanged presents and I cooked some approximation of a traditional dinner, while Mike, Robin and Licorice played and sang together cheerfully. I had made the Christmas puddings in August, according to best housewifely traditions, and put them away carefully, wrapped in greaseproof paper – but now there was a difficulty. September and October we were mostly on tour and hungry mice had got in to nibble them around the edges. I washed them in brandy to disinfect them, cut off the worst bits, stuck one or two together and put them away again, this time in tins. On the day, no one noticed the mis-shapes amidst the flaming spirit, as I brought them while everyone sang "*We all want some figgy pudding.*"

We sat around, smoked hash, fell asleep watching children going past the window on their new bikes, got bored and read books, ate mince pies and talked. A proper family Christmas at home. Huw Price, the Witchseason tour manager, would later show me how to re-glaze a window cracked when throwing a misdirected present across the room, but that was in summer.

One day Claude Picasso turned up at Roman Camps, with baguettes and camembert and a bottle of wine we drank at lunchtime, not recognising whether it was from a superior French vineyard or the Co-op down the road. Joe must have arranged this, and very Montmartre we felt, part of the Left Bank in Paris and rather superior.

Claude and Mike sat on the floor chatting as the morning passed. Mike played a little, but the conversation flagged, so I took Claude walking past the slag-heaps, along the damp field-edges to the main road, the familiar way to the nearest bus-stop. I showed him the little flowers that grew in wet corners, looked for newts in pools and talked about everything. Even Scottish peasants knew the name Picasso, and we dropped it into the chat when we called in the shop after he'd gone. We were getting the bus into Edinburgh and Mike wanted cigarettes, not to smoke but to dismember for the tobacco – "Those'll do," he said, when the requested brand wasn't forthcoming. "That French chap smoked all of mine, Claude Picasso he was, you know, the artist's son." *You may think we look like vagabonds and doubt if the music is any good*, we were hinting, *but we have visitors with serious art credentials and they believe in us.*

The new jacket. A novel creation in orange Binca with vivid embroideries. Roman Camps, Summer 1968. The trousers were bright green.

Some months later I met Claude again, this time on his ground in New York. Lasers were the new wonder. He was shining the intense green beam up into the New York sky at night, through the maze of buildings. He told me where to look and explained the nature of its intense light. We went to an exhibition of laser art in Philadelphia, with very early holograms. I didn't quite understand how the three-dimensional images worked, hovering uncertainly in these spaces – but I was willing to be impressed by the people who could conceive of it. We worshipped nature and the mystic past, so it was diametrically opposed to what we were doing, but there was the same sorcery in the process, the same will to redefine and upturn.

After a couple of weeks in the quiet of Roman Camps we always set off back into the other world, of cities and crowds pulling us in all directions. But in those days Mike and I also always returned, to the peace of our little house in Scotland. It felt a bit chilly as we walked through the door, but everything was where we had left it and we picked up the threads of our life together again.

'Scattered Brightness' in Edinburgh

April-July 1968

Mike and Robin record tracks for *Wee Tam and The Big Huge*, tour the US coast-to-coast and embark on a summer of festivals and clubs in the UK and Europe. Home is still Scotland. At first the front cover of *The Hangman's Beautiful Daughter* features just them, but on later pressings back and front are reversed, with Licorice and I now central to the group photo. Publicity photos and radio and TV appearances treat all four of us as the group and Licorice and I are now both there in the studio. She sings sometimes and I join in for choruses when needed. She already plays guitar. I have a beginner's grasp of violin and recorder and start to learn bass when Mike brings one home.

◆

Another entertainment in my new life was frequent journeys by road, rail and air from Edinburgh to London. ISB was on its rapid rise to fame, but home was still important to us all, and each of us dragged the past behind us into the unfamiliar territory of celebrity. After penny-pinching years forced to travel cheaply, Mike and Robin enjoyed the luxuries of a first-class train ticket and lunch in the restaurant car. Guards and waiters often looked uncomfortable, unsure how to deal with these strange young people in fancy dress in their tidy carriages, though some enjoyed the oddity as much as we did.

Edinburgh had a place in my imagination before I ever got there. My childhood had been fuelled by stories of how the wild Scots under Wallace had sacked York long ago, presented as a reason to distrust both Scots and Catholics. I was warned that York Minster would revert to the Pope if the renovation works were ever finished. But Edinburgh was the acceptable, anglicised, intellectual and artistic face of Scotland.

Living in a musical bubble with Mike, distanced from the concerns and ordinary conversations of those around us, it was the folk legends and imaginary lives of Scotland that still peopled my head. I fretted over the mourning fidelity of Greyfriars Bobby, visited Holyrood castle with the tourists to see the bloodstains of the murdered David Rizzio on the floor of the Queen's room and sympathised with her penchant for her young lute-playing secretary.

Mike knew the scenes too well to be much interested. As if to place our curious life in a more normal context, he explained to me that Edinburgh had always been notorious for strange carryings-on. Stevenson's fictional characters came from its drawing rooms, while grave-robbers Burke and Hare had supplied cadavers to the students at its schools of anatomy. Rowdy bands of students roamed the drinking dens of its wynds, as the narrow alleyways of the old town were called. After a day dissecting cadavers, alcohol was a necessary antidote. But with his folk-club days behind him, Mike had no wish now to show me round the bars.

Robin and Licorice too had a past in Edinburgh and knew its quiet back alleys as well as the displays on Princes Street. They could always find a friendly welcome and a floor to sleep on, so family or childhood friends were only a phone call away. But now people were coming up from London for the Festival and to visit Mike and Robin in their native environment.

Our trips into Edinburgh for shopping or work usually became social events, bringing me into Mike's world of acquaintances, old and new. Someone would recognise him and spread the word. He enjoyed the attention, meeting admiring strangers with the same ease as old pals. But as the new girlfriend I faced curious stares.

Sometimes we visited people who had contacted us through the office, knowing that this was work as well as pleasure. I wasn't paying much attention and often failed to find out who the people were, or to recognise them. I greeted the face in front of me not the name attached, and never remembered half of them. We visited a concert pianist one night, Aldo Ciccolini I heard later, in an elegant drawing-room in Edinburgh. Long velvet curtains ran behind his grand piano, so the room had the impression of a stage. He played Satie Nocturnes and Mike chatted briefly with him. We bought the LPs of Nocturnes and Gymnopédies and played them a lot. I waited to hear their influence on Mike's music but never identified them directly.

Comedy hours

I could see why Robin and Licorice often steered clear of the town, and I only knew their Edinburgh lives by hearsay. On one occasion we spent an evening in town together in the old haunts, a room full of pint-drinking folkies. What made the evening notable was the vivid presence of Billy Connolly in the small room of some city folk club, then playing with a group called The Humblebums. With his wild hair and wilder wit, he couldn't be missed. After their set he and Mike found each other and the fun began.

Mike didn't even try to keep up with the boisterous Connolly, but he could stop him in mid flow with his own quiet humour. Mike was always willing to sit back, appreciate and be entertained. They laughed at each other, Connolly's admiration for Mike clear. But Robin couldn't resist the challenge of another teller of comic stories. This was his performance too. Verbal sparring continued, with no great good will on either side, apparently, until Robin turned away, looking arrogant and disdainful. This was his fail-safe expression when defeated and angry.

A night out in Glasgow was different. That city's reputation was as brutal and harsh as its accent. The day we were there, a vicious storm the night before left dead birds on pavements, backs broken by the wind so I was told. I bought another workbox for my sewing things, an old souvenir from India, and filled a compartment with sandalwood, mothproofing it as well as making it smell good. Mike wasn't one for sightseeing but we had a purpose for the visit.

In Glasgow, they still put on Music Hall, supporting this relic of Victorian theatre with full houses of rowdy audiences. There were old velvet seats with shiny stains, sweet wrappers stuffed down the sides, cigarette stubs brushed underneath them on the dirty lino floor. Working-class audiences flocked to the shows they had known since childhood. Mike revelled in the vigorous caricatures and clichés and took me along. Even the performers fulfilled the stereotypes, the wavery soprano past her best, the ingenue who hadn't yet reached hers, a few dancers in tired chorus-girl outfits.

The comedian the show revolved around was raucous and obscene, but luckily I couldn't understand most of the jokes, the delivery as unlike English as any foreign language. As we went in, Mike's Scottish accent too became stronger, and by the end of the evening he too was cheering along in Glaswegian. His ability to find pleasure in the most unlikely places was both a challenge and a delight to my sterner temperament. In Otley, "laughing like a fool" was to be avoided at all costs – as my mother once admonished me and someone was taken off to "the madhouse" when seen in the park with no stockings.

This music-hall comedian played unashamedly to all the worst prejudices of an audience who seemed to take pride in a reputation for heavy drinking, domestic violence and racism. But I could see that for Mike it was an escape from ISB's rarefied atmosphere, with its enforced gentleness and fey pretensions. This was real folk-culture, not the politely cleaned-up Cecil Sharp House version.

Hippie shopping

Back in Edinburgh and looking for Scottishness, I bought a Shetland shawl you could thread through a wedding ring, and a tam o'shanter from the tartan shop. We carried an enormous log-basket from Workshops for the Blind between us to the car, with all our shopping in it. At home, bags of coal and sticks for the fire made sooty dust which leaked out onto the floor and our bare feet. Then we trod it into cushions, sheets and clothes, making more washing and impossible stains.

Soon swirling light shows and psychedelic daisies were decorating the shop windows of Princes Street. Our hip tastes had gone mainstream. Without wanting or intending to, we were now at the forefront of an alternative cultural movement. To maintain the distances between us and straight people, ever-more obscure manifestations of our cultural difference were needed.

Edinburgh's little back-street antique shops became our hunting grounds. Mike stretched his city knowledge to its limits as we searched out ever more recherché adornments. There were narrow passages in the Old Town with places tourists would never find, genuine Old Curiosity Shops with proprietors out of Dickens. Souvenirs of Empire had arrived in Scottish ports, to be stored in Edinburgh castle, along with all the opium kept there for medical supplies.

This was a past world of high tenements, with bath-houses still advertising on the street for those without facilities. Old grocery shops hung on in corners until their elderly keepers and customers died off. In one we could buy hemp seed, officially for canaries, loose by the pound. We did intend to grow it, hoping it would be narcotic and smokable, but the project was eventually abandoned. Coming and going as we did, plants couldn't survive for long. My geraniums never flowered cheerfully on the windowsill.

It was in one of the old Edinburgh tenements that I saw my first drug-dealer. I'd read about opium dens down the alleyways of Old Shanghai and was appropriately fearful. My father had once casually mentioned one of his boyhood errand-rounds in London's East India Docks. He took packages for the "Lascar sailors" that frequented the worst corners of Poplar, smoking opium in dark rooms between voyages.

My copy of *Edwin Drood* had a Doré illustration of such a place. As we entered the high building it felt as if we were heading into the book. The long, steep staircases with their dirty walls and rusty banisters led to landings with rows of doors hiding unknown horrors. I clung onto the filthy stair-rail as we climbed, aware of the drop beneath and envisaging the melodrama that might emerge any minute.

Mike knocked quietly on one. His "Hi man, anyone in?" was normal and unthreatening, though the room was full of dark shadows, as in the illustration. In the corner was a homely Baby Belling stove, and a kettle simmering away, offering tea to customers. The unremarkable person Mike was conducting his business with didn't come from Dickens either, he was just a hippie like us, talking in a perfectly ordinary way about the relative advantages of Lebanese versus Black Moroccan. After a mug of tea we left, both a bit tense and watchful until we were back home. When night fell, we dug a hole and buried the cannabis resin in the little garden opposite our cottage, telling each other to form a clear mental picture of exactly which stone marked the spot. By that time of night neither of us was too clear about anything and certainly too lazy to dig deep.

Visiting the parents

Visiting Mike's parents showed me the more conventional life of the town. His father was the archetypal public-school English master, scholarly and sensitive. We didn't have long conversations, but I enjoyed his quiet wit and felt welcome. Even Mike's very proper, well corseted, church-going mother seemed ready to accept the new girlfriend and be willing to ignore the outrage of "living in sin".

Like teenagers, we sat on his narrow bed in the little bedroom while Mother got the tea ready downstairs and suburban Edinburgh carried on its routine lives outside the window. Unless an undercurrent of wildness hid behind all those other windows too. As we drove up a nearby street Mike pointed out a garden below which a well had been dug, and a previous owner's corpse lowered into it in chains. The body was said still to be suspended there, the well once more covered by lawn. I never discovered what faith in what afterlife would lead to such laborious preparations, or how neighbours past and present felt about the void beneath that lawn.

I began to form ideas about Mike's earlier life. We took a bus from the town centre to Pittenweem, and on the top deck he told me about family days on the beach, digging sandcastles and making moats for the sea to fill. Old school friends lived in the terraces of fine old houses that we passed, some the sons of Edinburgh gentry. Robin could mimic their accents very effectively and often did, both at home and in concerts, mocking the bourgeois philistinism we had left behind.

Visiting the past

One day we visited Michelle, Mike's ex-girlfriend. He had left stuff at her place and now wanted it back, taking me along as moral support, or maybe a defence against his own precarious inclinations. She and Mike had the familiarity that comes from living together, when so much is understood and there is no need, or any inclination, to charm and impress.

Her small flat was like Robin's room at Mary's, draped in hangings and oriental fabrics, cushions everywhere and colourful cotton rag-mats over the old carpets. Dusty incense holders still held the collected ash of burnt incense sticks. Empty wine bottles, with wax dripped down the green glass, had grubby candle-stubs in them.

Curtains hung where doors should have been, softer and prettier but not so good at shutting out the world. A long-gone husband with DIY skills had taken the doors down and they still sat in the back yard. The bed took up an entire alcove-room, the atmosphere exotic and seductive. I didn't feel too welcome and the inclination to curtail rather than extend the acquaintance was mutual. Mike grabbed a few possessions and we left. Maybe he went back some other day. I never asked.

Was this where Mike was on the days he left Temple Cottage? It had never occurred to me – nor that our freedom to love as we pleased left casualties in its wake. But the enforced fidelity of marriage was a misery that I knew, and anything was better than that. When first Mike played 'Hedgehog Song' to me, I had been amused by the whimsy of this *Wind in the Willows* story, in which the funny little hedgehog told him home truths. Years later I discovered it had wandered into Mike's imagination off one of Michelle's wine-labels, and I suddenly saw him as a part of Michelle's life, lying hazily around those rooms, guitar in hand.

After that difficult encounter we couldn't just go home so we ended up in town for the day, in Rose Street, more notorious for pubs than elegance – but Jenny Richardson's second-hand clothes shop and Bruce's Records were there. First Mike looked through the new LPs at Bruce's, then we poked about among Jenny's boxes, and racks of outfits that had graced the refined gatherings of 50 years before. When we met Mike's old friends, contrived remarks covered the awkward moments while they worked out his new living arrangements – "This must be the street for Rose to shop." Like Michelle, Jenny was a part of Mike's past that I couldn't know, as her polite acknowledgement made clear.

I told myself it wasn't worth worrying about. I could make my own way, albeit a different one. In their snakeskin shoes and chiffons these women couldn't survive a night camping on the hill in a storm, waking up soaking wet to climb all the next day. They apparently couldn't mend the broken zips or the torn ribbons in their own old clothes either, never mind making whole outfits for beautiful men. If I envied their apparent confidence and the easy way they hinted at past intimacy, I was not going to be put down or – even more ridiculous in my eyes – get jealous. The French rock-boots were always waiting in the cupboard somewhere, for another outing.

Without her knowing, it was Licorice who helped me to come to terms with the women who floated around Mike and Robin. Some were old lovers, others wanted to be new ones, all enjoyed being seen in their company. Licorice had the same style, language and shared experiences as these women who were strangers to me. She knew what she was dealing with. And because she seemed largely indifferent to their presence, it was easier for me to be the same. She always seemed so sure of her position, never tried to attract or demand Robin's attention, or to wheedle and coax and play games, apart from occasionally in parody. She kept her distance and retained her freedoms. She knew, and I learned, that this was the best way.

Both Mike and Robin placed their own thoughts and their music above everything else. However much they enjoyed the admiration and availability of the women who draped themselves on the periphery of their days, they also demanded absolute autonomy. Not that either ever needed to demand independence from Licorice or me, because it was always freely offered. I put no constraints on what Mike did, at home or abroad. I rarely asked how he passed the time when I was not there – which was wise as I have since found out. In return I expected the same and got it.

Joining in

Then Mike gave me a Syrian drum, to play as he and Robin did a quick run-through before some gig. The drum was a great delight to me, as much for itself as for the implicit suggestion that I could make music too. Its shiny silver mushroom-shape, the curly engravings on its stem and the grains of its stretched skin made it a pleasure to look at, to carry around and to play. It stood around in corners wherever we were, a portable love-token and a musical part of our home.

Everything's fine right now

June 1968

Mike and Robin return from the US, their aspirations seemingly at odds. Licorice and I both float around the stage at the Royal Albert Hall concert. Two wildly creative musicians have become two couples, a touring band of four with ever-longer schedules, in search of a way of working to suit. From late July Mike and I reluctantly follow Robin and Lic to their communal home, Penwern in Wales, to live alongside the dance troupe Stone Monkey. Here Peter Neal films the *Pirate and the Crystal Ball* story. Later, as part of his plan for ISB's new direction, Robin works on the performance of *Creation* with Stone Monkey. In August, Lic and I take part in the session for 'The Iron Stone' at Olympic studios.

◆

"I'd like to introduce us. I'm Robin Williamson and this is Mike Heron. We're singers and players. We're prophets from the North and Seers Extraordinary, by appointment to the Wonders of the Universe." That was how Robin introduced one concert when he and Mike were still just a duo. Joining them at those mystical heights was never my ambition, and Mike had doubts about his own status as a prophet.

By the time they played the Albert Hall in June, after the release of *The Hangman's Beautiful Daughter*, their most successful LP, we were a generally amicable group of four people, sharing lives. A fluctuating hierarchy had been established, with Robin demanding his own way, generally supported by Licorice, and Mike more conciliatory, concerned with longer term group cohesion and success above momentary whims. When Licorice decided she wanted to be a stage performer as well as a disembodied voice, my presence redressed the balance.

There were no discussions or arguments, decisions or arrangements made between the four of us – none that I know of, anyway, or that Joe Boyd remembers. There were no rehearsals, either, beyond the usual casual playing together in the latest rented flats Joe had found us. Of late, when stages were set up, Lic and I had usually been there, gentler than roadies for frazzled nerves, quieter and more affectionate. The little Syrian drum was usually on stage and I now knew 'Hedgehog Song' well. It had not lost its charm, and nor had Mike's face as he sang it.

It seemed natural and inevitable to join them all in the song, and it made little difference to me that it would be this important occasion at the Royal Albert Hall. The *Hangman* LP had made waves, big names in the music world were now paying attention and wanting to know more.

No special attention was paid before the gig to appearance. No hairdressers, no make-up. We brushed our hair and hunted out clothes from the coloured bags that went everywhere with us. The dresses Licorice and I changed into were ones we wore anytime. Mike and Robin were searching for strings, cutting a broken fingernail, finding a plectrum. Lack of artifice and spontaneity were the most important factors, to truly be the people we were rather than pretending to style or perfection.

As I sat on-stage, all that mattered to me was that we were happy and having a good time together. The colours and lights were exciting, and everyone out front was there to share the fun. They looked friendly. Never having been in front of an audience before – except in one school play – I had no fears of criticism or rejection. Someone whispered backstage that the Beatles were in the audience but we never saw them. Neither Mike nor Robin showed any interest in their presence.

There were songs from previous albums, but it was *Hangman* they wanted to play and everyone to hear. For us on stage, the music was an outpouring of our lives. Mike and Robin's childhoods, the loves of earlier years and our shared present were all there, laid open truthfully for everyone to see. The "*earth, water, fire and air*" chorus of 'Koeeoaddi There' seemed to assert our unity, four of us fused by the harmony of our astrological birth-signs. Tagged onto other songs it often reappeared on-stage, as if to renew the bonds.

I knew that the wealth of Robin's musical and literary references, the fantastic instrumentation, the vocal play-acting in 'Minotaur's Song' were not affectation, but just how he'd been back at Mary's. The trippy meanderings and final joyful chant of 'Very Cellular Song' were Mike. To me this was more a shared celebration than the performance of a new LP. This was how we all went through each day, and the audience knew it too. In *Melody Maker*, Karl Dallas picked this up, and the counter-cultural notion of "anti-showmanship" which lay behind it. He called it a "private party into which several thousand people have somehow strayed."

The crowd in the dressing-room was bigger at the Royal Albert Hall, and the wait to escape longer, but otherwise it was just another concert. There were always lots of people on the edges of our stages, friends or people we'd met somewhere. Robin liked audience participation, inviting them to roar with 'The Minotaur's Song', drawing them into his own emotions as look and voice took on the character of a lyric. Like a village pantomime he called people up on-stage, arranged them in a line, to grunt alongside the song about Big Ted. One time a young and carefree Salman Rushdie was on-stage, making sounds of wind or water, whistling, hooting and laughing along with us at Robin's jokes.

Venues were still expecting a duo, but after the Albert Hall, we girls were part of the group, and the roadies had to set up two more mics. And chairs too, though we mostly sat on the floor, close together at the side with our tambourines and finger cymbals, Swanee whistles, ocarina, and a collection of small drums or rattles. We would stand up to clap or to tap a drum, walk around to hand something to, or find something for, the players, never feeling that it was a performance, then settle back wherever convenient when there was nothing else to do. We rarely left the stage once on it, feeling part of the music even when we didn't play.

Licorice already had a place in the music but made little of her skills in those first performances. Both of us played the percussion instruments nearby when a general atmospheric accompaniment was needed. Hand-clapping and smiles were involuntary rather than rehearsed. But she took her contribution more seriously than I did mine. She had spent longer with musicians and could play guitar, although she rarely did when I was around. One day she announced she had written a song and wanted to play the accompaniment, and I was surprised by her competence. Perhaps, in the shadow of Robin's easy virtuosity, she had lacked the confidence to play earlier, or the encouragement.

We both knew that musical ability was not why we were on-stage. It was part of our understanding with the audience that we should make mistakes, giggle helplessly behind the amplifiers sometimes or snivel in a dark corner on a bad day. Nigel Planer's parody single 'Hurdy Gurdy Mushroom Man' very accurately caught the sense of arcane lyrics tumbling into technical ineptitude.

Although Joe Boyd didn't welcome the two of us as part of the band, our presence probably helped the relationship between Robin and Mike survive the initial turmoils fame was about to bring. Each now had someone at his side, with support and sympathy. Before the audience arrived, when theatres and halls were just cavernous empty black spaces, Licorice and I were there. When Mike or Robin wanted to flee from the world outside, we were part of their flight.

Most of the many instruments we took around with us found their way on-stage in case we needed them, so the stage layout invited disaster. I lived in fear of stepping on something fragile or getting tangled in a mic lead and unplugging it at a vital moment. Cables were a constant hazard, becoming tripwires when caught on stands or under a cushion. A discarded coat or shoe could flip into the air when we moved something. Gaffer tape was our only solution, and slick production techniques were not a priority. We wanted the casual and extempore on-stage and off.

When we eventually got guitar stands, like a proper rock group, that peril was diminished, but if a stand got knocked over in a careless dash for a forgotten plectrum the domino effect would be a chaos of falling instruments. Then we all giggled, although Mike wasn't very amused. The audiences picked up their reactions from us and laughed along.

Earthly pleasures

I knew from meetings with fans that some already viewed Mike and Robin as godlike figures, transforming lives through their music. As all the Hindu deities we hung on our walls had handmaidens, Licorice and I fitted the image. This never weighed heavily on either of us. In those early days, our mutual willingness to serve the divine manifestation of music flowing through Mike and Robin was tempered by the strong wills of two very real-life girls with a strong resistance to personal sacrifice.

Despite the worship, I never saw Mike or Robin as anything other than beautiful men with an earnest intent to tell truths through music, and the original talent to achieve that aim. Even during a performance they were earthbound. Robin would amble on-stage as if he just happened to be going in that direction and might as well play to this audience he'd found. Mike was always more concerned beforehand with technicalities of stage, amplification or mixing board, especially his guitars and their tuning, and he cared lovingly for the vagaries and sensitivities of the sitar. He walked on-stage briskly, usually smiling and acknowledging the onlookers. Once there he was at home enough to take easy minutes out, delving in bags and pockets and laying out around him what he needed to feel comfortable. His peaceful confidence and willingness to share the music rather than show off, won allegiance from audiences.

He never seemed abashed when small difficulties arose. If one of us broke a string or came untuned it was he or Robin that put it right. If a mic was in the wrong place, he called out across the audience to the roadies or those on the mixing board as he adjusted it. His cheerful companionship on-stage flowed across the footlights. The audience felt that he would be their friend. He entertained them as companions and confidantes, sharing his life for a little while.

Usually there was a set-list, pencilled hurriedly on a scrap of paper by Mike and Robin at the last minute, or found in a guitar case from the previous concert. But it was a secondary consideration. As they came together for the first song and looked out at the auditorium, any differences of approach and opinion were lost in the pleasure of performance. I rarely saw a time when the creative friction of their personalities was not soothed by the admiring presence of an audience.

Lic and I were another source of affirmation and appreciation and the two of them melded more easily when we were present, until habit and emotional distance reduced the tranquilising effect. In those early days and for most of the time I was with them, we were a mutually supportive group of four, often very happy in each other's company and welcoming the audiences of strangers who became our temporary friends. Reviewers with little sympathy for our ideas, ourselves or the music found it easier to write of clashes and feuds and cat fights. We thought them Philistines and "straight people" not worth worrying about.

Joe made it easy for Mike and Robin to be part of the wider world of London's counter-culture. With his friend John 'Hoppy' Hopkins, he had initiated much of it. Hoppy was still in Wormwood Scrubs for cannabis possession when I landed at the flat in Westbourne Grove where Joe was living. There were vague rumours about a rift with Joe, but he turned up again to film ISB's *U* show at the Roundhouse so the disagreement can't have been serious. The scandal of the jailing had garnered powerful support and the notoriety of the UFO club had become national news. Everyone had been intrigued to see Boyd's new protégés. Mike and Robin were only too willing to join in the curious and exciting world he opened to them, and Lic and I went along for the ride.

Wandering minstrels

Theatrical dressing-rooms were our temporary shelter from both inner and outer worlds. I usually brought my sewing bag to concerts. A roadie could replace a lost plectrum or broken string, but couldn't sew Mike back in when the zip broke. I made clothes for him, and most of my own, ever more wild and fantastic, with the knitting, crochet, embroidery and drawn-thread work taught to me by my aunt. I made caftans from old damask curtains before anyone else thought of it, and choir-boy tops in bright silks and satins, from a paper-pattern. Velvet trousers also came from curtains, but as we got busier we bought girls' flares from Granny Takes A Trip in Chelsea's World's End, in shiny crepe. We were the same size, each trying to claim the orange pair. I pulled in the waists for myself with embroidered belts. We were strange apparitions, the images ever-changing, our only style the inclination of the moment.

Licorice was a magpie, always able to find treasure, or that one special junk shop with antique embroidery and small exquisite textiles. I went for the more obvious Chelsea or Kensington second-hand clothes shops, and clear-out sales from theatrical costumiers. One great day I found that Anello and Davide sold off dance shoes when a West End show closed. In their warehouse I found shoes for all fantasies, including soft leather boots for ballet-dancers, clogs for character peasants, all in glorious colours, and the buttoned shoes the hip girls wore with their 1920s flapper dresses. Even when the search for my size was fruitless, I enjoyed the footwear dreamscapes.

Robin's decorative talents he applied more to his rooms and instruments than his clothes. He gradually covered his guitar in swirling drawings, adding another winding colour in the bored moments before a gig. Mike was more concerned with sound than look. He was not content until he owned a Gibson Les Paul bought in the USA, along with a flat-back mandolin of mine, sold long after to Robert Plant when poverty struck.

But usually it was Robin who brought the instruments from remote corners of the globe, which most of us had never heard of before. He could coax a tune from all of them, his virtuoso musicianship amazing us as much as his audiences. Faced with Robin's versatility, Mike could nevertheless redress the balance in the enterprise, with flawless harmonies and original guitar-playing, while learning to play the sitar added a new dimension to the band's sound and look.

At first we dragged our households of instruments and clothes to theatres and clubs in a caravanserai of bags, cloths, boxes and suitcases. My needlework, Mike's books, Robin's latest hobby, and now and then Licorice's dog. On one occasion there was even a basket of puppies. The roadies picked up what got left behind, and that was then all dropped in dark dusty corners, to be unearthed when needed next. Later a road crew travelled separately with baggage and instruments, so we should have been able to stroll into a dressing room and out onto stage all set up and ready. But this rarely happened.

Sometimes a trip ran to a strict schedule but delays were not unusual, and we'd arrive to a litter of cases and instruments, lost stands or microphones, and angry voices at the sound and lighting boards, as our crew clashed with the residents. Mike and Robin would appear still fretting and harassed by the journey, calling for missing boxes and lost objects that now they couldn't perform without. Knowing the owners' habits, Lic and I could often find things that the roadies couldn't. In the shared hours of travel and performing there was little personal privacy. We had neither the time nor the energy to be restrained and polite. While mental space was private, physical space was tight. So we kept our own ways and our own secrets in the hours we spent apart.

At some point in the shifting confusion of amps and instruments, we'd be summoned from our peaceful corners for a sound-check. With the auditorium in darkness we walked out onto the barely lit stage. Joe and the others were gathered at some primitive sound board, and someone, usually Joe, would call, "Do a quick verse of 'Log Cabin' and then something with sitar."

We talked very little. We'd ask was it a full house and what was happening after, while mics and amps were adjusted. But Robin and Lic usually wanted to snatch a rest in the dressing room or shoot out on some errand, while Mike was keen to organise his thoughts or his music. I preferred a few moments of quiet on-stage, feeling the silence and the peace of the empty theatre, hearing its own life and anticipating the presence of an audience transforming it. I liked watching the lights come up and dim, as if the work behind the show was real life and we were somehow imaginary.

If one of us was unwell or having a bad day we didn't get to indulge in feeling ill. Our appearance on stage in a more or less functional state was a contractual necessity, with minimal regard for long-term consequences or immediate suffering. The next show was the deadline for recovery, and we never missed one for simple health reasons.

The adrenalin of being on stage cured most minor ills. If Robin felt queasy, or less than vigorous, he swallowed a couple of raw eggs, and that always worked. A couple of roll-ups, contents unknown, spun between his fine fingers and often smoked with Oscar Wilde gestures, cheered him up. He always had little baccy tins in jacket pockets or guitar cases and we didn't enquire what was in them. He was remarkably tranquil about being sick ten minutes before the gig started, and it was so common that we hardly noticed it.

Mike was the most resilient of us all, self-contained and calm about unease and disease when the rest of us were fussing and moaning. He never seemed to get ill, and his sturdy health set the standard. We survived and performed on whatever remedy a roadie could fetch from the nearest drug store. But the names of "patch-you-up-in-half-an-hour" clinics were an essential part of any good road manager's address book, and we saw several.

Medical staff were never startled by the multicoloured caravan that walked through the door as we outraged medical conventions of tidiness. Perfumed oils, trailing garments, scarves, bags and odd possessions spread all over their clean and sterile surfaces. The staff were usually only too willing to tell us which band had been in before, to divert us from our own problems.

There were lurking fears and rumours of incurable diseases, mostly sexually transmitted, with mysterious origins, perhaps soldiers returning from Vietnam, or foreigners with strange strains of virus. We ignored advice when we roamed, hoping for the best, and got away with it.

Routine days

In those days Edinburgh airport was a large shed with a drinks machine. Often arriving before dawn, we would park ourselves and our instruments on hard benches in the bare hallway area. A small café sold bacon butties to liven us up on cold dark mornings as we dragged ourselves across the tarmac to whatever small plane was flying to London.

When in London for a while, usually for recording, we were picked up at Heathrow and driven to hired serviced flats, with a tactful distance between each couple. We needed the space between us but sometimes chose to ignore it, all piling in together until the inevitable frictions arose and each pair went its separate ways. But when the four of us were sharing all our time, ideas and hopes, and many of our possessions, it created a skin-to-skin intimacy that never quite disappeared.

We spent some months on and off in a typical London terrace near Queensway, with stone steps up to a front door and net-curtained bay windows on each side. It felt as if our every arrival and departure was observed, and we played up to the watchers. Robin and Licorice made faces, we threw ourselves into dramatic poses over the balustrade, Mike serenaded the curtains.

For Mike's birthday, I bought him a cake with his name iced on it. He was 26, but I didn't know that and didn't care. We lit its candles and sang 'Happy Birthday' – then it was abandoned on the cooker for weeks until rock hard. We never cooked when away. The habits of life in public left no time for domesticity.

The first black and white four-piece group photos were taken in this flat, all of us leaning against one other, seated on a single bed against the blank beige wall. We look cheerful, young and ordinary, with Licorice's missing front tooth adding to the careless spontaneity. Despite the elaborate curling text beneath there was none of the mystique of previous band photographs.

To make more fascinating pictures, we were taken off to the mock-rural setting of Hampstead Heath, to pose around its steps and fountains. The photographs were not good. We felt uncomfortable, aware of our failure to project magic or glamour. Joe's disappointment was clear as he tried one background after another, and none of them improved our mood. We only felt more awkward than ever in that initial, forced and public display of group identity.

None of us ever welcomed photo-sessions, an infliction that couldn't be avoided. The contact sheets sent round in envelopes for our inspection were a necessary evil, and we chose the least unsatisfactory.

First group photo session, Queensway Flats, Spring 1968

Places to go,
people to meet, things to do

There are patterns to touring with a band, even one as unique as ISB, that make each day and each concert like beads on a necklace, all sharing common features but each one slightly different. Regardless of continent or audience the routines go on, the same faces, crates, equipment and wires. Hotel rooms aren't very different. Days and crises stand out in memory, but when exactly they occurred is gone. What lasts is people and the impressions they made.

Away from Roman Camps, Joe's Witchseason office at 83 Charlotte Street, W1, became our official mailing address as well as the anchor for our wanderings and the hub of our contacts with the wider world of friends and other musicians. Sandy Denny, then of Fairport Convention, was not relaxed with any of us when our paths crossed. We were told she found touring difficult and refused to fly. Hence her unease at Witchseason, we thought, however well it was going with UK gigs and in the studio. With Fairport people there she was more cheerful but we never spent time together at the bar after a gig. Fairport musicians were called in for ISB recordings sometimes. The working atmosphere was "all in it together", and nobody claimed superiority or preferential treatment, but no close friendships developed, despite our admiration for their work.

Another shadow gliding through Witchseason was Nick Drake, looking quiet and withdrawn. Perhaps he shyly saw Mike and Robin as big names. We said hello once or twice but that was it. The girls in the office told me he was Joe's latest enthusiasm but they thought he was too introverted to cope with life on the road. Joe could see a successful future for him, and the two seemed to have a mutual admiration society. By then, Mike and Robin were more critical of Joe's passing fancies.

Once Joe started working for Warner Bros, we never saw Nick again. Directly or indirectly, those left behind at Witchseason ran our lives for us. When I wanted to meet someone whose address or phone number I had mislaid, I phoned the office for them to arrange and usually this worked. If we needed money, Joe's office was the bank. There was a fast-changing array of pretty secretaries and other beauties, occasionally attracted by the chance to meet Joe or his bands rather than the work.

Pop musicians were the new aristocracy of London society. I rarely knew the girls' names and identified them mainly by clothes.

There was the chirpy little cockney hot-pants girl, the droopy hippie-skirt one who didn't last long, the smart American whose stay was even shorter. Iris the efficient book-keeper was later found murdered, a casualty of the times, and we hardly remarked on it. The most permanent face, Anthea, was the exception, with a music-management background of her own and the confidence and contacts to go with it. Her office was towards the back, near Tod Lloyd's and Danny Halperin's lair. What they did there was never clear to me. Tod was something to do with the money, Danny did art things, and this accounted for all the other strange characters who called on them. I never got through their door.

Anthea's wry expression and edgy, caustic way of talking deterred casual chat. But when we did ask her something, as she walked through with a letter to type or a note for Joe, she was never dismissive. There was kindness and understanding beneath the shell. We were confident she would find someone to sort out the difficulty, whether it was the leaky bathroom back home or a crack in the fat body of an old mandolin.

The Witchseason office wasn't far from the music shop where the photos for the first album cover were taken; Robin, Mike and Clive in jeans, hair short, holding instruments and gazing hesitantly at the camera. We often called in as we passed. Mike liked to handle the guitars hung round the walls. If other musicians came in, they were sometimes taken down, tuned and played.

Acting cool

For all the hazy memories, there are also very clear ones. I knew this was not likely to be a permanent way of life for me, and I wanted to tie the memories down. I took more happy snaps than the others, aware that publicity photos were archived while the incidental faces of daily life might be lost. I wanted the realities of life with the band kept, through all the dissensions and boredoms of coffee shops, streets and home. The brilliance that sang itself into strangers' memories was only enhanced for me by its constant collision with the everyday.

Once I had found my feet in all the language and habits of the new world, I could work out my own compromises. Looking like a "hippie chick" was a game I enjoyed. There were no rules, just self-expression. Like our home, our clothes showed what we held dear, rejecting conventions of style and fashion.

If the colour magazines showed us as silly girls with no sense of propriety or responsibility, I knew different. We showed our flaws to the world because our mothers had hidden theirs in respectability, and then been miserable. We didn't want to compete with our male companions. We wanted our own lives not theirs. They didn't intend working for life at a job they hated, so why should we? Equal wages or opportunities didn't define the futures we saw for ourselves. We weren't even sure that there would be a future, with nuclear weapons and another world war due along any minute, if the first half of the century was the pattern.

For us girls, contraceptive pills had solved the main problem of unwanted pregnancies and sexual freedom was a new right we could claim, so we did. Woe betide any man who suggested that monogamy and fidelity was natural for women and not for men. We were not going to protect them from their own sexuality by smothering ourselves in petticoats and corsets. If naked flesh upset the poor dears that was their problem. Our clothes were about liberation, not a come-on. The vociferous Women's Libbers taught us we could comment on and giggle at men's bodies just as much as they had always done at women's, but we wanted to be kinder. We didn't want to take on male faults along with the freedoms.

So we wore what we liked and our companions did the same. I travelled with Mike on the train to Edinburgh looking like a Victorian lady in deep mourning. My long black skirt, jet-beaded bodice and bonnet with trailing ribbons attracted attention in the Dining Car but felt very proper and fitting to me.

I swept over stages and garden lawns in a blue damask, gold-braided Scarlett O'Hara gown, with wide full skirts which swayed as I walked. Beads dropped from 1920s flapper dresses, and the fine chiffon threatened to disintegrate when shopping bags got caught in the frills. The original owners of our dresses had worn them when the Oxford Street department stores first opened, and they also had claimed liberation.

Over a flesh-coloured body-stocking and wrapped in embroidered shawls, the white lace dress I wore for Woodstock was not too transparent for an evening out. No white wedding dress was planned in my future, so I was making the most of the present. Peasant shirts, which perhaps once held treasured memories of an exile's homeland, were a useful standby, wearable with anything. And the longer ones Mike could share, as he did the lacy blouses I picked up on market stalls and in old-clothes shops.

Here come the girls

The Royal Albert Hall concert was a game-changer. It was almost immediately acknowledged publicly that Mike and Robin were now permanently accompanied by their girlfriends. Where dancers Mimi and Mouse had defined roles, Licorice and I were neither dancers nor musicians, nor in any sense a backing group. At first we were just there, singing parts then joining in alongside on percussion or sound effects. Sometimes Licorice would do a little dance and I might join in, or we simply sat and watched as they played. Then Mike realised I had learned violin a bit, so I collected my old fiddle from Harrogate and played my part on 'Log Cabin Home' while Lic also widened her scope.

No one else was doing this. Women in bands were usually singers, adding shiny glamour to the men around them. Lic and I never tried to look alluring and rarely did. Flirting was not our way. If we wanted something, or someone, we asked straight.

One day Mike came home to Roman Camps with a Paul McCartney-style bass guitar. Fifty years later, Fairport Convention's Dave Pegg suddenly remembered that Mike had borrowed it from him, and now wondered when it might be returned. It had a very heavy leather strap, oddly adorned with horse brasses. "If you can play a fiddle, you can play bass," said Mike, "and there'll be less problems with hitting the right note. That's why frets are there, you just have to remember the tune." He pointed out it was even fiddle-shaped, so I should feel at home with it. It looked a bit old-fashioned when everyone was playing Gibsons and Fenders, but I was ecstatic. I liked the idea of playing bass. I knew from the school orchestra that this was what grounded a tune and gave it depth.

We agreed that Mike would work out the bass line for his songs, and I would play it. That suited me fine, his version would be far better than anything I could put together. After a trying week of very sore fingers, I was already on-stage with it. A year later, I could admit in interview: "He's a hard task master, at least he was at first… But now Lic and I are becoming much more independent members of the group. Much more out on our own". Mike's version was this: "I probably just shoehorned her in a bit more. There was a danger of it getting to be this airy-fairy kind of thing, which was an area where Robin was quite happy, so getting Rose on bass put a bit of balls underneath it all and stopped it floating away on this musical cloud".

He recognised that the duo couldn't move on without adapting its performing style. Encouraged by Joe they'd left folk music behind, though we often played it together for fun. Robin saw the band's increasing resources as an opportunity to develop all the dramatic storytelling and performing that he had to squeeze in as eccentric interludes before.

In the early days of the 'Noah and the Dove' dialogue, Mike's comments punctuated the verse as Robin declaimed his tale. Mike's head was encased in a tube of dishcloth cotton with a cardboard beak sewn to it, which he pulled aside when he needed to breathe. Robin had roughly painted a large head on a sheet of cardboard packing case to illustrate the poem. This was propped up on a mic stand or waved about as necessary. Mike seemed to enjoy the brief diversion and to appreciate the intention, but this wasn't his mode of expression. As Robin began to dramatise the mysteries, Mike wanted to influence the direction of change, and Lic and I were part of his answer.

Licorice's guitar playing now came in handy and she seemed better acquainted with keyboards than I was. I could now attempt electric bass and very basic fiddle. Recorder lessons from school were remembered and even a few guitar chords learned, although I never got the hang of key signatures. A simple keyboard part, I was told, shouldn't be beyond rote learning without any technical knowledge. As song after song was written, our repertoire of instruments extended.

On recordings for radio and TV as well as concerts, we played our part, though the hosts often seemed reluctant to acknowledge us. While audiences were happy to embrace the counter-cultural freedoms of our amateur performances, music professionals were uneasy and showed it. Even the doyen of cutting-edge music John Peel, who fulsomely welcomed Mike and Robin as he escorted them into the studio, merely gave us a perfunctory nod and left us to trail behind. We played two sessions of *Nightride* and two of *Top Gear* without him affording Lic and I more than a casual glance. But he was championing the music and was not known for charm, so we didn't mind.

He obviously noticed us though. As we left the studio once he was heard to say, "Harness those voices properly and you could cut steel with them," a tribute more to Licorice's clear, sparkling and entirely accurate top notes than my more tentative ones.

Julie Felix, England's imitation Joan Baez, had clearly picked up some of her model's arrogance. When we turned up to record the *Julie Felix Show* she too ignored Licorice and me. Our own crew had to ensure we had microphones and were seated on stage with Mike and Robin. This was not welcoming. Laughing ruefully together afterwards, we came to the flattering conclusion that she felt her shiny image threatened by our more genuine, rougher-hewn folksiness. After all, the folk scene traded on its position as the authentic historical voice of the countryside, music of and for the people. Our lack of training and artifice was just that. But for a wider, less discriminating audience, hers was the predictably well-groomed, pretty face between Mike and Robin's.

Licorice and I now had our own technical concerns with strings, seats, microphones and speakers, and our own instrument cases to find, pack and watch as well as Mike and Robin's. I was not conscious of any shift in our relationships, but there must have been some difference of emphasis. No longer decorative handmaidens, we improved as musicians and contributed to the musical work. My amplifiers became bigger and more powerful as the band's amplification increased. Mike and Robin would sometimes play my bass, but it was still mine and I took it home.

We played on bills in Britain, Europe and the USA, with every type of group, from folk singers to rock bands, accepting incongruities as part of the serendipity of touring. Acquaintanceships were usually transitory, even non-existent. Shepherded by road crew or organisers, it was easy enough to ignore the other band, and get away quickly and gladly from the venue at the end. We didn't want to think about their performances or hear their thoughts about ours, and it wasn't the time for gossip. Mike and Robin's friendships with other musicians weren't generally shared, and were as changeable as the rest of our lives.

Old friends of mine from school or college came to gigs sometimes and it felt awkward. They couldn't understand how my life went and were bemused by my being in a band appearing on world stages. Their current talk of family and careers meant nothing to me, like voices from a long time past, so we went our separate ways and lost contact.

If family turned up, as happened only a couple of times, it was even more difficult. In York I spent an uncomfortable half-hour trying to hide behind my bass guitar, to divert paternal attention from a near-transparent peasant blouse. My former best friend, now working for the Inland Revenue, appeared at the stage door in Leeds, in "psychedelic" patterned mini-dress and high back-combed hair. Escorted in by a grinning roadie, she looked entirely incongruous and obviously felt unwelcome. I struggled to say something to thank her for her interest while avoiding an invitation for an after-show meal. I was unsure at what point her legal sensibilities would flare and her connections become a threat to our peace of mind.

Fans and fantasies

Every major city we toured had its own group of ISB fans, who gave new and bizarre colour to the décor of provincial theatres and halls. Some found their way backstage, friendly or devious enough to sidestep locked doors and bored roadies, becoming familiar faces tour by tour. They thought themselves our friends and might be around the stage door when we were dropped off, but we preferred to be alone until the gig was over. The routines of arrival, preparation and performance were understood by us separately and together, so outsiders were a nuisance.

There were many fans, most of them really, who wanted to give not take. They sent us letters and photos of what they were doing without asking for replies or meetings. Fate and Ferret, two schoolboys from

c/o 83, Charlotte Street,
London.

Dear George and Andy

Thank you very much for the great box-full of good things. It was a beautiful 'Welcome Present' because we got them just when we arrived back from America. We were all quite knocked-out by your paintings and poems. They're incredibly beautiful. Michael used to spend all his holidays at Pittenweem when he was little, and his aunt lives very close to you, so he was delighted by the big picture. We have both of them on our walls now. It's such a joy to see them, and read the poems.

We spent three weeks in America and enjoyed it a lot. Even the big city was good to see. New York seems like the crystallization of everything a city is supposed to be, and it's very exciting. Especially with all the lights and Christmas things. The central happiness and ecstasy of Christmas gives the commercial decorations an ecstatic sparkle. 'Beauty' and 'ecstasy' and 'joy' seem to have been repeated a bit in

my letter, but I'm very happy now, and these fall soonest to my mind. It's as if good things are accumulating every day towards a completely radiant Christmas. We all wish that yours is good too, and that Next Year follows on from that.

Love from us all

Rose. (who usually gets to write the letters)

Rose's reply to fan-letter from Fate and Ferret, Winter 1968

Scotland, sent us notes and drawings, of us as well as themselves. They made up conversations between us and wrote stories around them. I was always pleased when a Fate and Ferret bundle found its way to us via Joe's office. I wrote a letter or two back, to tell them what it was really like, and they kept them:

> "We spent three weeks in America and enjoyed it a lot. Even the big city was good to see. New York seems like the crystallisation of everything a city is supposed to be and it's very exciting, especially with the lights and Christmas things. The central happiness and ecstasy of Christmas gives the commercial decorations an ecstatic sparkle. 'Beauty' and 'ecstasy' and 'joy' seem to have been repeated a bit in my letter, but I'm very happy now and these fall soonest to my mind. It's as if good things are accumulating every day toward a completely radiant Christmas."

71

It was a mystery to me why we turned up at some of the houses we visited after gigs. We had to eat, and if it was at someone's home, I assumed it was one of Robin's unpredictable fancies. Mike and I went along with them and tried to avoid conflict. Joe encouraged this, never quite confident of group unity or understanding that we could get on together and even like each other, despite the frequent distances between us.

The vicar's house in Bristol was one of those imposed visits. Luckily, we were not exhausted at this point or the outcome might have been different. Kind people had clearly made a great effort, and we usually tried to respond – but that evening Joe was not pleased at having to be polite to strangers, while Mike and I wanted to get back to the hotel. He had a song to work on and I didn't want to meet anyone else that night.

But Robin and Licorice insisted, and were willing to answer the questions we had been asked a million times: "Do you all live together?", "When did you meet?", "Did you learn to play sitar in India?" As Mike and I were about to make excuses and go, copious wine saved the evening, smoothing ruffled feathers and relaxing strained nerves. As the bottles drained, they all became lovely people, Licorice was adorable, Robin an inspiration, Mike a delight and Joe our guardian angel. We ended up singing in harmony for our supper, but this was a rare conclusion to such an evening mid-tour.

Day after day we would arrive at buildings with monumental facades and strict rules enforced by bored staff. Municipal theatres on busy streets, with wide staircases, plush seats out front and dark alleyways behind, and down-at-heel dressing rooms in shades of dirty cream paint and brown varnish. Barren spaces that smelled stale, the rubbish bins full of cans and fag ends from previous visitors. They were like school cloakrooms, with benches and coat pegs, chipped washbasins, ancient toilets and bars on the windows in case we tried to escape. We were relegated to the back entrance and attention to our comfort was grudging and resentful.

Once on-stage that was forgotten as the music carried us along. Despite the increasing organisation as the financial stakes got higher, we still operated on an emotional level. Tour schedules were presented to us, but Mike and Robin were largely unconcerned by when and where. They relied on the office to make the best compromise between financial and personal demands.

Once a tour started, we were swallowed up in its routines, but we never became indifferent to a performance. And after their years in smaller venues, Mike and Robin felt the energy of enthusiastic audiences in large halls. We were as high as kites and tired out after many a show, needing to be shepherded and sheltered, but with little inclination to come down to earth. Joe knew how to find restaurants where we could unwind. Others often turned up, mostly invited by Joe as far as I could tell. Sometimes an evening encounter prolonged itself, and a new face met us over breakfast. But often we just wanted to get away and be quiet, to unwind in a private space.

Once Mike had bought his Gibson Les Paul guitar, the one he'd been looking at for some time, I too wanted something better than an old McCartney-style violin bass. We bought the Gibson bass in the US, leaving the old one behind somewhere.

I now knew the tuning of a mandolin was the same as a fiddle, so I bought a fine old Gibson flat-back in the States, only to be stopped and searched at Heathrow flying back. It had never occurred to me that I needed to declare it as a purchase, but technically I was smuggling it. My innocence, at least on this score, must have been fairly obvious, and there was nothing else illegal to be found. But I had no proof of purchase or a receipt, or even a clear memory where it came from. I was rescued first by a roadie then by Joe, who produced sufficient documentation to allow the necessary duty to be paid. I never asked him whether all the other instruments we casually imported were ever declared. I was too glad to rejoin the others in town, as a free person.

Failed in translation

We played Europe too, with its ever-growing band of hippies, but our lyrics were complicated for non-English-speakers, and differing definitions of what made a counter-culture hindered appreciation. They seemed more serious and political than us. Saving the world through art and frivolity had lost its appeal for a continent traipsed over by warring armies fairly recently. Traditions of training, thoroughness and order were at odds with our deliberate chaotic amateurism. Mostly it seemed that, while they identified with Mike and Robin's sheer musicianship, they couldn't think what Lic and I were doing there.

We played the Concertgebouw in Amsterdam a few times, my main recollection being good hotels, with bowls of Advocaat topped with cream for breakfast, and perfect tomato soup for lunch. An early-morning outing to the flea-market was a chance to buy Oriental mats and a pair of stone medieval statuettes. They were heavy enough on the short trip back to the hotel in a taxi but a nightmare for the roadies, who had to carry them around the rest of the venues. They graced my fireplace at the Glen Row house once they finally made it back to Scotland.

Much later, in October 1969 Joe saved Mike's life in Amsterdam. A radio-station had left some live wires on the rigging, and when Mike's

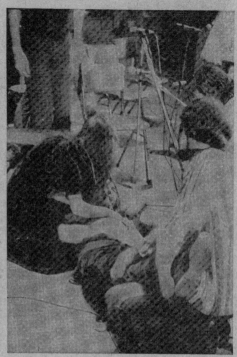

Britse gitarist Mike Heron stond onder spanning

GEVLOERD DOOR VOLTTREFFER

Van onze verslaggever

AMSTERDAM, 20 okt. — Het optreden van de *Incredible Stringband* zaterdagnacht in het concertgebouw in Amsterdam, ontaardde in een letterlijk en figuurlijk schokkende gebeurtenis toen één van de leden, Mike Heron, onder stroom kwam te staan tijdens het verzetten van een microfoon. Hij had ook een gitaar in zijn hand en tussen deze attributen bleek 220 Volt te staan. Na enige ogenblikken van verwarring wist één van de zangeressen, Rose, hem de gitaar uit zijn hand te slaan en werd ook de aansluiting van de microfoon verbroken.

Volgens de technische assistenten van de groep was hun hele circuit een afgesloten en geaard systeem. Zij weten het incident aan de opnamemicrofoons van de VPRO, die eveneens op het podium stonden, voor radio-opnamen van de daarna optredende *Fairport Convention*. De opnameploeg verzekerde echter, dat ook hun apparatuur geaard was, hetgeen ook bleek bij het door de politie ingestelde onderzoek. Omdat na het gebeurde beide installaties direct afgesloten werden, was het verder zeer moeilijk om alsnog de ware oorzaak van het met een sisser afgelopen ongeluk op te sporen.

Mike Heron van de Incredible Stringband ligt getroffen door 220 Volt op het podium van het Concertgebouw. Zangeres Rose buigt zich zorgzaam over hem heen.

„INCREDIBLE STRINGBAND"

Dutch newspaper article, Rose cradling Mike, Amsterdam 1968, courtesy of the National Library of the Netherlands, The Hague.

guitar came into contact, the electric shock threw him into the air and across the stage. He landed, slumped down and rigid, fingers clamped round the guitar neck, unable to let go. Joe flashed across the stage and tore him free. I rushed to his side, self-consciously aware of the visual cliché of dying heads cradled on loving knees. The photos of his blank face, as press huddled round wondering whether he would die or not, are very beautiful, the perfect features and wide eyes like a death mask in their frozen stillness.

In others my long hair fell over his pale, semi-conscious face and I gazed agonised. This was an appropriate scene for a musician's girlfriend, and the Dutch press discovered a rationale for my presence, my role now vindicated.

Less dramatic but more convenient, he recovered quickly. We had a short break in the dressing-room to pull ourselves together, and check Mike was essentially unharmed and able to sing and play. We then returned to the stage, continuing the set and taking no more notice of the incident.

London blues

On a touring calendar's blank days, or at the end, we often landed back in London. Instruments and equipment were unpacked, and what we didn't immediately need around was stored for the next round of gigs. We had a couple of days to take stock, emotionally and financially, before going home again for a while. These were awkward days of readjustment, changing tempo and getting back to ordinary routines.

We all found our own ways of dealing with the strains. Mike often disappeared, either on errands unknown or into the exclusive retreat of his own thoughts, leaving me wondering how to pass the time until we could go home. When reading was too static and shopping too boring, I would go to the British Museum, conveniently near the Witchseason office. I sat in the vast cool spaces of infinite time in the Egyptian galleries, with the turmoil outside gone quiet. I imagined, in a faraway future, when I finally gave up on life, that I'd like to be in one of those magnificent mummy cases.

One day I sat in the museum's great hallway, surrounded by Abyssinian colossi, thinking about how things were going with the band. It was changing, as Licorice and I became more involved in its creative life. She was writing more as we travelled, and at home she often had a guitar to hand. I knew that she worked out songs for herself, but maybe she had a more definite aim.

When Mike was at home, I had noticed how he picked up fragments of tune or phrases from the books and music of our everyday. Later I heard them blended into his own work. I had no idea how to go about writing a song, but a poem might work as a lyric, and maybe Mike would make me a melody. Buying myself a notebook in the museum shop, I found I could stick some words together in the form of a poem with some rhyme and metre, but I didn't have anything that I wanted to say to the world, so I gave up.

Later I got as far as a whole song, lyric and melody. I knew it was probably not a good idea, but with Licorice demanding more equality in the creative work, it was more from duty than inclination. A tune I found vaguely pleasing was adapted on my tenor recorder from some other woodwind piece. The words were nondescript and insincere. When it came to performance, as usual after minimal group rehearsal, I was overwhelmed by terror, unhappy and unable to get out of it.

It was the first and last time I tried anything of the kind. I think my plight was so obvious to the audience that I got sympathy rather than criticism, and once I had got it over with, I told them straight what was going on and apologised for wasting their time. After this, no one suggested I try again, and I erased all traces of the song itself from my memory.

Golden lads and girls

A favourite London haunt for all four of us was the Baghdad Restaurant on the Fulham Road. We would sit in the basement on cushions, drink rosewater and honey from silvery tin cups in curtained alcoves and eat Turkish Delight, listening to music played on ouds. We met a host of young aristocratic hippies there, the types photographed for *Tatler*'s Deb of the Month, taking a walk on the wild side instead, sometimes with younger brothers on jolly holidays from their public schools. Thrilled to be able to go back and tell their pals about the London Scene.

Their looks, manners, connections and money got them to the centre of everything, and they became the girlfriends and boyfriends of the stars, way beyond the safety of their homes. They appeared in magazines, films and advertisements. Alice Ormsby-Gore looked dreamily beautiful, walking through wheat fields with Eric Clapton to advertise diamonds for De Beers. But like several of the Golden Boys and Girls we met on the cushions of the Baghdad, one drug led to another, and she ended her days unhappily.

In their good days, they came to our gigs and we met them in clubs and restaurants. They took for granted their shiny hair and perfect teeth. They threw away clothes we could only dream of, and given half a chance would gladly have picked up. However much they tried to tone them down, their accents gave away their class and education. But now they wanted to be part of a world much more exciting than their own, rebelling against distraught parents. The same parents, or so I heard, tried both bribery and threats of drug-busts to separate them from undesirable companions like us, who could only harm their career and marriage prospects in the world they were born to.

We regarded them as privileged and protected and never thought of any responsibility towards them. Some became victims of addictions, or of callous men. When their dependence became inconvenient rather than charming, the harsh worlds they moved into soon abandoned them.

Better to remember the good times than contemplate the wreck of promising lives. To the best of my knowledge, ISB never exploited or abused such admirers. They never went to the "fuck a 14-year-old" parties that we heard were not uncommon. We sat quietly with each other in the basement of the Baghdad, and with us the boys and girls were safe.

At the end of a tour, we sometimes returned to the beige flats near Queensway, then a lively mixed area with shops around the corner open at all hours, and also close to the Ice Rink. Robin was keen to show off his skating skills, developed on Edinburgh's Happy Valley Pond, and the exercise and freedom of movement was a relief from the passive and sedentary life of music and the trials of travelling.

At first Robin fell over repeatedly, as Licorice and I giggled from the safety of the barrier. Mike slithered round slowly and carefully, with great concentration and without spills. Once we decided to join in, I managed fairly well, and Licorice too. She was gifted with grace and balance, unconcerned by the bumps and tumbles around her. With her long skirts and woolly beret, she looked like a figure from a Victorian Christmas card.

Afterwards Joe took us to a fashionable bistro on Queensway, with bread sticks in glasses on every table, red check linen and candles in Mateus Rose bottles. There was venison on the chalk-board menu, and French onion soup with croutons, and it became our regular canteen. Here we could meet Joe and each other without roaming the streets in dissatisfied conflict over restaurant choices. Even before the vegetarian, then vegan, then macrobiotic days, we were not gourmets.

Our choices changed with our belief systems. Robin's Hindu phase ruled when I first met them, shared by all to a greater or lesser extent, as we stuck pictures of Krishna and Vishnu on our walls. At the height of that period, we stayed at an Indian vegetarian hotel opposite the Trade Union building in Bloomsbury, apparently the only place Joe could find in central London with an exclusively vegetarian kitchen.

It was a rabbit-warren, original rooms cut in half by thin random walls, with narrow corridors full of unmatched doors. Curry smells rose day and night from the takeaway below. The consolation of Indian sweets didn't reconcile me to the discomfort, as Mike and I sweated in a narrow bed in a grubby room, with a window that wouldn't open. Robin's room was bigger and at the back of the building, both quieter and less smelly, which didn't improve our mood. But it didn't whip up resentment or open disagreement, and we could laugh about it together, just another small irritation in the accumulated trials of touring.

Determined to find something better, Mike and I moved to a hotel on Russell Square, with English breakfasts and afternoon teas. This didn't last long either. Robin and Licorice came round and we sat together in the lounge, feeling at home and losing the formal reticence Mike and I had till then preserved. When I sat on his knee, that was the last straw for the staff, already uneasy that our appearance and behaviour might upset their guests. We were politely asked to leave, and Joe had to find us another flat quickly.

Be Glad in Wales

Summer 1968

Our UK gigs are overshadowed by growing tensions. How should we live, and where? Robin plans more multi-media work with Stone Monkey. Mike is less enthusiastic. Peter Neal still films us now and then for the documentary. The final weeks filming in Wales are a turning point for the band, and for all of us. We can never return to more settled times.

♦

The routines were swamping our lives, as we became distanced from the people and habits we knew before. Previously, even when at odds, there had been a near-organic interdependence. Now a mutual separation grew as we found new interests and new versions of ourselves, new substitutes and new consolations in all the others who surrounded us, known and unknown.

Mike and I continued for some time to cherish the idea of a home at Roman Camps, returning to it at intervals as a loving couple, if none too tightly bound. As we became less romantic and more workaday, I felt increasingly uncertain how the relationship might survive new faces. The hippie ideal condemned sexual exclusivity and shamed jealousy, so we never talked about how the shared life could extend past the present. Robin and Licorice's arrangements seemed even more fluid and ill-defined than ours, but we never discussed them either.

As far as Mike and I could tell, they were both equally averse to the shared stability of a permanent home. Robin was like quicksilver, easily forming new friendships and passionate interests, spending increasing amounts of time away from any fixed address in Scotland. Licorice went her own ways when the band was not working together, and we knew little of her in those times. Both seemed happier living in the countryside, while Mike and Robin's collaboration across such distances became a practical problem.

Technological solutions were theoretically available. Despite the packing and posting, with cassette tapes we could share and develop material, work out accompaniments and cut down on rehearsal time. We never possessed an efficient tape-recorder between us, though visitors were sometimes helpful here, but Joe could sort that out. To Robin, the idea of regular home recording and interchange of tapes felt wrong and artificial, he said. Not the way music would come to him. Licorice disliked anything that came with an instruction book. She was content with the distances and didn't want a fixed address for post all the time. Taking parcels to a local post office, when she didn't know where they would be living, was going to be an impossible chore.

Mike was prepared to buy and master the equipment, but without enthusiasm, foreseeing that his efforts would be wasted. He did buy a Stylophone and played with it for a couple of hours, but this exhausted his affinity for home mechanics. I bought a cassette recorder, hoping it would help me practice and learn, but we never established a way of working together involving order or routine. We were all too erratic in our daily lives, never quite sure what would happen next, which meant there was no possibility of lasting success for the scheme. As with many of our plans for the band's future, our diverse personalities got in the way.

As Mike and Robin circled around their mutual dissatisfactions, film-maker Peter Neal came up to Roman Camps to film us in our native habitat. He had just made a film about Jimi Hendrix, so much wilder and high-volume, and I couldn't imagine what motivated him to consider ISB. It could hardly be "the stars at home", even if our public lives did arouse curiosity about the private times. The final film would mix interviews, studio time, performance clips and archive film to illustrate the range and variety of ISB music, as well as our lives.

When he arrived in Scotland and settled down with a cup of tea, it became straightaway clear that he understood and was sympathetic to the ISB ethos. This is what he intended to film. We went for a stroll and it rained. I had a black PVC sou'wester and mac, bought in student days. Mike and I walked hand in hand, like the children from the old Startrite shoes advert. I picked a flower and ran back to Mike, clinging to him, overflowing with affection and enthusiasm, a filmed gesture that was genuine and typical. There were many playful times still at Roman Camps, as Mike's bright, childlike fun made the days pass too quickly.

We were in our cottage at Roman Camps when Dick Steele, an American *Newsweek* reporter, came to interview Mike for the film. Panoramic views of the village and its landscape set the scene for the incongruity which followed. Sitting on a cushion on the floor, Steele tried in vain to overcome his general dislocation. We were used to it, but for others the hippie dream clashed with the industrial waste and the ugly workers' settlement outside.

I sat at Mike's side, embroidering coloured flowers on the orange canvas of the jacket I was making for him. The collar of the frilled shirt he was wearing was brilliant white, washed, bleached, starched and ironed for the interview. I had taken heed of the neighbours' whiter-than-white laundry skills. Mike was so stoned he could hardly speak, but I saw no anomaly in his incoherence. That's how our life was, floating in some no-man's-land of rediscoveries and novelties. He could sound oracular in a few words, along with a Heron smile to make up for the silences.

In their parallel interview, Robin and Licorice expose a very different relationship. They stride through the woods separately, wild and beautiful, and Lic's affection is directed at the dog. They visit a suburban instrument-maker, and Licorice disappears. When they sit together, she too stitches away, the proper hippie display of the feminine supportive role.

Then Joe and afterwards Robin told us that he and Licorice were planning to move to Pembrokeshire, to live in the deep countryside at Penwern farmhouse near the Pentre Ifan cromlech. "Somewhere in Wales near the wet sands and the magic stones live the Incredible String Band" began the fairy tale of our stay there. Robin's friends had rented a house, and he told Mike and me that it would be ideal. I knew wet Wales from days camping on its mountains, and I could hardly imagine anything more miserable. The nearest town was down miles of narrow winding lanes and the farmhouse itself too primitive for any but the most committed visitors.

Communal life with Robin's little-known housemates would disrupt our home peace. With touring schedules becoming intense, Mike needed somewhere to escape the inexorable round of events and interviews, and I needed to be able to disappear, for hours at least. Sitting watching creative angst, sewing outrageous trousers, making cups of tea and waiting for an indefinite homecoming were losing their charms. Close contact now and then with Robin and Lic was essential for both of us, but so were comfortable spaces in which to think our own thoughts, to follow the moods of the moment, to play, to write and to read.

New directions

Robin had been dissatisfied with the band's current lifestyle for a while, feeling that his creative powers were not being given full expression. On their second US trip, in May 1968 at the Chelsea Hotel, he and Mike had met an Englishman in New York, Malcolm le Maistre, as well as Rakis, who was anything but English, despite the accent. Typically, Robin had asked them to join that night's performance with a short dance narrative, while he and Mike improvised happily, delighting the audience with the new additions. Now Robin thought of these "counter-cultural trans-media performers" again.

The dancers Mimi and Mouse had already decorated ISB's stages, as had the light shows at UFO and other clubs. Mike and Robin's own paintings, masks and written works were all integral parts of the image ISB had made for itself. Now Robin wanted to stretch the parameters further. Rakis and Malcolm were planning a group, to include a motley crew left over from David Medalla's alternative art collective Exploding Galaxy. They had scraped together money for the rent in Wales and Penwern was to be their artistic commune. With the esoteric name Stone Monkey, they were intent on developing further the friendly association with Robin. They had no clearly defined artistic plans and were very willing to follow him in spontaneous multi-media performances.

In keeping with the times, ISB had already rejected all ideas of musical or theatrical training. Expertise was considered an unnecessary restriction on innate creativity, as my presence on stage confirmed. Neither Mike nor I therefore felt able to make judgements on their performing skills, and with their startling variety of good looks and general pleasantness they were occasional good company. Unfortunately, I felt no great affinity for any of them, or for the communal lifestyle they seemed to have chosen.

With its various residents, the farmhouse also allowed Robin to break out of our current life, as couples staying together in flats and hotels. He could revert to the random times and manners of earlier days, once more floating through aimless yet creative hours surrounded by sympathetic, admiring spirits. He and Licorice moved into the Welsh farmhouse. Perhaps for them it looked like a return to the fluid and productive life at Mary's Temple Cottage, in idyllic countryside free from the impositions of contemporary civilisation. But Mary's personality, employment and children had imposed a tentative order that this run-down house of chaotic, aimless waifs and strays entirely lacked.

Mike and I were pressured to join a household living in excruciating discomfort, accepting the hardship as part of Robin's experiment and new ideas of performance. Neither of us wanted to go, but as Robin had taken the initiative we had to follow. After a long and disconsolate drive from Scotland, the approach to the house was ominous. We were tunnelled up narrow lanes with dark arches of trees and high hedge-banks. The sun didn't reach through the dense and choking cover of leaves, and soon the road was a narrow, mossy, muddy track. Deep silence imprisoned us in an alien landscape and there was no way back.

Culture clash: Penwern farmyard, Pembrokeshire, 1968

Rural decay

In the old grey stone house, with its flaking paint and damp flagstones, was all the furniture and leftover crockery the farmer's wife wouldn't allow in her modern bungalow. Armchairs exhaled the dust of dead horses, their manes and tails stuffing the seats. Cushions whose feathers had been salvaged from Christmas geese failed to soften the wooden frame poking through where the fabric had rotted. Woodworms dropped their powdery remains onto the floor.

In the kitchen, tables gave way at the joints, tops stained and cut by generations, along with an ancient cooker, a cold tap over a chipped enamel sink, and a plywood cupboard hanging tentatively on the wall. A surfeit of sideboards, like coffins on legs, stood in the passageway. Once a kitchen range had warmed the place with its glow, but it had long since subsided into a heap of scrap iron in the corner. Nobody got up very early to light a fire in the sitting room.

The house was cold with the winters that had soaked into its damp stone walls for a century. Surrounded by briars and brambles in that dank hollow, it would never dry out. The bushes dripped with perpetual rain, and caterpillars fell in my hair on the one sunny day. Spiders descended the windows on silky strings. Webs covered every corner inside and out. The active farm work had moved elsewhere, and the farmer visited mainly to gloat at hapless tenants paying rent for what should have been storage space.

Mary's house had been luxurious by comparison. Here in the absence of anything better the diet was macrobiotic, brown rice with carrots and onions, so even food's basic consolations were absent. Physical comfort was each other, and this too failed within a day or two. A diminutive blonde calling herself Mal held Mike's eye. They huddled together in corners, her wide blue eyes gazing up in adoration. They giggled together by the fire in the evening and slipped away very quietly as the night fell outside.

Robin and Licorice were also unable to recreate their beautiful personal oasis of calm. She sat on the windowsill, gazing out at the landscape, at odds with all and ill at ease. This scheme had simply been a personal idiosyncrasy, the dream of a group of unemployed hippies. Return to nature was fashionable, with new imagined communities a desirable alternative to the "doors of the prison-house" that we saw closing on the nuclear family homes of the past.

In the USA, musicians were retreating to the wilds and recording their own music at home. Escape from city life into the back of beyond let creativity blossom undisturbed, with the mystic powers of the earth playing their part. Elsewhere in rural Wales Led Zeppelin contemplated retreat to Bron yr Aur, Robert Plant's childhood haunt. The Celtic twilight, the ancient language, primeval forests, eternal mountains and pure air all made Wales appealing to sturdy souls leaving English cities to colonise the old land again. Scotland had always been imaginatively close to Wales in its rejection of the English imperialists.

But the Welsh language loses its charm when screamed at full volume early in the morning, mixed with bastardised English, by an irate landlord whose pig has escaped. Chatting locals falling into hostile silence in the local shop as the English buy necessities at exorbitant prices confirmed the popular prejudices. None of them would have lived in Penwern at any price.

This was the cusp of a changing time. Only a trickle of escapees from urban desolation had yet discovered the houses the farmers had abandoned, the low property prices and the minimal rents. Those who had lived there for generations knew too well that the slate floors covered bare earth and the thick stone walls radiated a chill even on a warm day. Mike and I learned this at the bed and breakfast we retreated to once the brief nightmare was over.

Loneliness and discomfort can be tolerable in a city with distractions to hand. Imprisoned in a world of green mould, with flimsy wooden

Artistic dissensions: Malcolm le Maistre, Rakis of Stone Monkey and Mike, 1968.
Image © Peter Sanders.

walls not screening out the sounds of the happiness of others, your miseries are exacerbated. Theoretical utopias fall apart away when the warm centre of affection goes cold. Universal love and harmony, and remnants of romantic idealism, couldn't survive this Welsh onslaught. Licorice had always shown a cat's pleasure in the material conditions of her life and was intolerant of irritations, but she never spoke to me about how she felt.

With Robin effectively dominant in matters artistic, his work claimed her attention, but the spool of their joint life was also unwinding. Her straying footsteps no longer swung back to him as magnetic centre, and he too was finding other confidantes. The shrines of their joint life at Mary's were never fully reinstated in later environments, despite the colourful Indian posters, the statues, astrological charts and psychedelic ephemera. Our group conversations became utilitarian gossip, no longer about ideas and ideals.

Moving images

At least the film gave us something to talk about. Robin seemed to think it would follow a story he would write, but what this was remained unclear. The narratives that others discussed were haphazard and ever-shifting. Some days we all came together to make possible costumes, but with the storyline and characters so flexible it was more every person for herself rather than a team effort. Joe had said he would visit, at least while the film was being made, which gave me some hope of a tenuous order.

The three girls in it were the Fateful presences dominating the cromlech scenes: Licorice, me and Ishy from Stone Monkey. Licorice chose Druidic overtones, I tended to the Classical and the minimum effort of unsewn garments, and Ishy just wanted to look pretty in her normal clothes. The crystal ball Licorice found among her own possessions. Daily life with ISB still sometimes had a sense of "meant to be", so this was unsurprising.

But there was little unified or mutual effort or understanding of the film. Responsibilities remained ill-defined, even creatively. The group chaos was amplified by the addition of these new, unknown people. When asked about his plans for collaboration, Robin lapsed into irritated vagueness, falling back as charm or mantra on their former counter-cultural antecedents on London's Balls Pond Road, as Exploding Galaxy.

It was not clear to Mike or me how this association could progress within the ISB framework, let alone how it should be defined in business terms. But we shied away from this discussion, even with Joe. ISB was now a commercial operation, and this larger group needed some attempt at structural formality. Since Robin and Licorice rejected all forms and hierarchies, the venture seemed blighted from the start, and Mike's heart was not in it.

Hence perhaps his latest romance, and why it seemed more important than previous passing fancies. This, or boredom, or the house. I had entered this anarchic world with open eyes, and to dispute the terms of the encounter now seemed petty. But it bothered me, though I was hurt and lonely rather than jealous.

The three Muses: from left: Ishy, Licorice and Rose, 1968

The Penwern bedroom to which I retreated looked like a Victorian garret to die from TB in, picturesquely. Mike and I had never owned a vacuum cleaner, but at least I understood a dustpan and brush. The household had one besom broom, hand-made from local reeds. Mal of Stone Monkey would sweep the kitchen's slate floor, her long blonde hair tucked into her embroidered peasant cap, but she was more intent on making a pretty picture than domestic cleanliness.

As a group, Stone Monkey were no stronger on performance than on domestic virtues. Beyond childhood ballet lessons and an exhibitionist streak, their lack of expertise as a dance troupe became clearer as the days passed. Only Robin's and Malcolm's dominant personalities were driving things forward, against our doubts. Nevertheless, Lic and I went with the flow of the days and took the line of least resistance. I was too aware of my own musical incompetence to criticise others. Lic supported Robin and never voiced open criticism, yet the music he imagined making in response to the long performance would fall victim to the troupe's lack of ability.

Robin always rejected interpretations of his work anyway, positive or negative, preferring to accept whatever form his inspiration chose to take. As far as I could tell, he saw himself as the voice of mystic powers and superior to the pedestrian concerns of rationality. Those who surrounded

him, he believed, had also been companions of his past lives, in the palaces and temples of the last several centuries. This conviction outweighed ability or aptitude.

For once Mike was easy to persuade. Continuing to work with Stone Monkey ensured the presence of Mal, this adoring, compliant, non-dependent lover. The advent of new people willing to follow his lead encouraged Robin's plans to extend ISB's performance fully into musical theatre. The failure to develop a plan for the present work was irrelevant, while raising the issue of financial constraints was devil's talk.

Dionysus incarnate

For me the one bright spot in this morass of personal and artistic dissatisfaction was Rakis. His origins were Greek. Black curls framed a face you might see on a Grecian urn, in a Dionysian celebration. As a romantic teenager, I had stuck a British Museum postcard on my wall and imagined the "*wild ecstasies*" in Keats' *Ode*. Here they were again, live before my eyes. But Welsh misery had chilled me to the bone, and nothing came of the encounter for a while.

Rakis liked warmth, comfort and chocolate, and looked sufficiently miserable to seem a possible ally. He muffled himself up in woolly hats and scarves, several jumpers and a greatcoat, to stomp in his big Wellingtons down the lane. He strode through the woods and across miles of fields to buy chocolate bars and Jaffa Cakes at the village shop, which he very guiltily ate all the way home. I never asked to go on these outings, because they were so clearly a personal secret, even though everyone else probably also knew.

Leaping and stamping half-naked around the Welsh countryside, his trousers precariously tied up with a sash on a cold wet day, this exotic flower surely suffered during the filming of *The Pirate and the Crystal Ball*. Predictably the trousers fell down, heightening the ludicrous comedy of the hapless pirate caught up in a cosmic whirlwind of eternal powers. At least this was a possible interpretation. We never agreed on a single storyline.

Rakis recognised Stone Monkey's performing deficiencies clearly enough. He too favoured counter-cultural theories of spontaneity and innate creativity but he also felt basic competence was useful. He had little sympathy with all the half-understood spiritual pretensions, to which Robin's ideas gave such ample scope. But he resigned himself to it all. Beside the smaller, feebler, more colourless members of his group he looked so vivid and dramatic, the only one able to play the pirate role. He exploited the comic potential as far as he possibly could, with

Robin as some non-specific deity, 1968

pantomime makeup and a painted, stuffed glove tied precariously to one shoulder, masquerading as a parrot. It lurched with his every bound over the rocky landscape and settled at odd angles.

Robin was a white-painted god-priest, seer and arbiter of eternal life. Mike painted himself in gold, with an Aztec-style head-dress, like one of South America's bloodier gods. Both look impassive and deadly serious in the finished film, sitting on their personal and imagined Holy Mountains. Unfortunately the god-like roles seemed to reflect and reinforce their own opinions of themselves in those days.

It was easy for me to look doleful and fatalistic, trapped in false eyelashes. I was aiming for the Biba Betty Boo look, perhaps not very suitable for a Fate, but no theatrical verisimilitude was required. This was a rare gesture of concern for fashion on my part, hoping that the close-ups would be flattering. I needed positive reinforcement right then. The spiky filaments gave me an eye-irritation for several days, leaving me more convinced than ever that artifice was unwise.

Licorice had no apparent doubts about fable or performance and enjoyed her part in it. Apart from the cameras, it was a fairly average day for her rambling round the countryside in floating garments, trailing ribbons and flowers. She generally looked fey and remote. Gazing into trees, skies and crystals and contemplating the Universe was normal for her, not performed.

In Scotland she often had her dog Leaf with her, an Italian greyhound, elegant and beautiful. Walking through the woods she could take on a litheness of step, like a bronze figurine of Diana the virgin huntress rather than her usual lazy stroll. I always presumed she was acting out pictures in her imagination, for her own delight. At Penwern she had reverted to the times and habits of Temple Cottage, staying by Robin's side in their room and largely ignoring the goings on in the daily life of the house, until it acquired momentary relevance for her.

Once Peter Neal arrived with Joe, hours of aimless discussions punctuated the short periods of filming, which only emphasised the lack of understanding between us all. The rain and hunger became too much to bear and Mike and I decamped.

After a night in a convenient guest house, we felt better. We were warm and clean. We both appreciated a fried breakfast in a tidy room with central heating, floral china, a toast-rack and honey in a pot with a bee handle. We started off the next day with a better spirit. Peter had a schedule to keep, and our license to waste time was about to be curtailed. Even Joe had an amusing cameo role, as Atlas, with a mock leopard skin draped round his loins. But the footage was cut from the final film, mysteriously saving his dignity for posterity.

Mike, a gilded god, 1968

As Film Director, arm outstretched controlling proceedings in his cool city clothes, a more typical role, he still looked incongruous in a muddy Welsh field. Malcolm le Maistre ran around as a mythical bird, strutting like a turkey in the yard at Christmas time. Wrapping himself in a sheet to become Herne the Hunter, he glared furiously through eye makeup out of Victorian melodrama. The antlers he attached to his head drooped irregularly and hilariously, failing to look awesome or mysterious. But there was a symbolic appropriateness, given Mike's current romantic attachment.

The truth of the story

Revealing in its understatements, the film was a truthful portrayal both of "ISB at home" and of the band's strengths and weaknesses. Inevitably it was an uneasy compromise between Peter's intentions, what Robin and Mike were willing to take part in, and the limited abilities of the performers. The gulf between flights of imagination and their realisation only widened as more people were involved and egos clashed, but that was typical of the way we worked.

Mike and Robin's diverse talents created great opportunity for extempore creativity, but on this occasion they had handed the performance over to others. As the god-roles imply, they were the creative spirits but even their music for the film reflected the precariousness of the performance. Much of it was roughly cobbled together afterwards to fill up the length of the tale, with neither showing the conviction or the interest they usually devoted to their writing. We sat down one rainy afternoon in London and the two of them jammed for the necessary minutes, overdubbing instruments or voices to fill up the gaps. Lic and I joined in at random; and Joe played harmonium and made what he could of the tapes afterwards.

But ISB fans were always indulgent and willing to think the best of us and the film, with its failings and its beauties, is a reminder of the aspects of the band and its life that hippie fans, stoned out of their minds during the Summer of Love, enjoyed. They saw loveliness in what I saw as deprivation, and their enthusiasm improved my good feelings towards it. "No electronics, perms, peroxide. The girls' hair sticks out newly washed in rainwater, faces newly scrubbed," an unnamed critic, probably male, wrote in *Oz* – and I agree. Much can be said for the unspoiled life of nature, but it hadn't been a happy time for me.

Scotland and home now looked like heaven. But though Mike and I returned to Roman Camps after filming and aftermath were over, our old life was never re-established, nor that of the band. One day Mal turned up on the doorstep, unabashed by my presence. Perhaps Mike

Peter Neal films Malcom le Maistre as mystic bird, 1968

had extended a standing invitation, but her determination to "get her man" was notorious and he may have been as surprised as I was.

After a couple of uneasy days of unspoken negotiations, maintaining hippie cool about who slept where, I had had enough. I was not going to cede space in my own bed, as midnight confrontations had established, and we only had two rooms. I suggested that Mal and I go down to London together, leaving Mike to "his work". It was a face-saving gesture for us, and Mal had little choice but to go along with it. I knew Rakis was in London, which made up for the inconvenience. Neither of us understood what the other wanted or expected, and this was not an auspicious start for a relationship, but it was a time of sweet calm and good nature, his Adonis looks a daily and nightly pleasure, while we waited to see what would happen next.

Back in Wales, Robin's interest in music-theatre was if anything increased by the filming, and he stormed ahead with plans for the next multi-media project. Alone in Scotland, Mike was reassessing the situation. His and Robin's musical directions had already been diverging, and he now saw possibilities of achieving success in different ways. He was probably also preoccupied with resolving his domestic difficulties. He wasn't unwilling to go along with Robin's plans but wasn't sufficiently inspired to burst into writing for them. The contrast of personalities was asserting itself, as each lapped up the adoration of ISB fans whose allegiances centred on one or the other.

The final musical compromise was Robin's attempt to recreate the world in his own chosen images. His inspiration was, I think, Robert Graves' book *Adam's Rib*, a pagan version of the seven days of creation. The portmanteau title *Creation* was sufficiently magnificent, and fluid, to encompass any musical, lyrical or performance elements to emerge before its debut at our next November concert at the Royal Albert Hall. Meanwhile anyone passing through Penwern could be hijacked to take part in the final performance.

Ivan Pawle of Dr Strangely Strange came to visit and was clearly amused and intrigued. The endless brown rice and no chocolatey or creamy sweetnesses made any small pleasure more attractive than usual. I understood perfectly the sudden interest in fungus forays, and a book on British Mushrooms passed hand to hand at various venues. Mike and I did wander up Scottish or Welsh hills looking vaguely for Magic Mushrooms, but neither of us were sufficiently desperate to risk choosing the wrong species. If we wanted psilocybin, better wait till reaching California where we could be sure of getting the shamanic drug we had read about in Castaneda's book.

Robin never needed such stimuli, pouring reams of sententious imagery into his Masterwork, to be sung and declaimed from the depths of his infinite memory. The difficulty was finding accompaniment static enough for group performance. While Ivan and Mike could improvise to suit any sudden flight of musical inspiration, the rest of us couldn't, and the Stone Monkey dancers needed some basic idea of what they were supposed to be performing.

In the event, all the dancers and other passers-by joined the core ISB to perform the piece as the finale to the next Albert Hall concert. Already swept into the ISB world of their expectations by more familiar songs, the audience were wildly enthusiastic. Hordes of people hopped, whirled, glided and stamped around the stage, arms waving wildly or gracefully. Costumes were strange and colourful and we all seemed to be having a good time, while looking sufficiently serious to indicate that something important was going on. Since most of us were in love with at least one other performer, and usually more, we were very willing to overlook performing deficiencies and throw ourselves into the ecstasies of the moment.

We did generally believe in the concept of the work, knowing why we needed to move on rather than become formulaic. The very length of Robin's song had a hypnotic effect, as his voice droned and swooped along with strings of whatever instrument he was choosing to play. Drums and wind instruments echoed sounds of the natural world, and, if it was a good night, we all fell under their spell. If not, it was a piece to sit through, staying awake and trying to remember when the drum, finger cymbals or general wailing were needed, hoping for the best.

Our identity as a band was established by such performances. They helped strengthen the bonds between us four, despite the personal disruptions. There was always a gig to think of and music to play. Shortly after, recovered from the upheavals of Wales, we flew to New York on Air India.

We had already made preparations. We now threw our clothes into old suitcases. An acquaintance of Joe, Dr Sam Hutt, physician to the stars, had called round to our hotel room, very kindly producing a ribbed glass bottle of tetrahydrocannabinol, labelled very properly as cough medicine. It was bright green. We had confidence in his medical expertise and his knowledge of US Customs, and happily packed it, wrapped up in our clothes. This helped a lot when we were dropped off in roadside motels on the edges of towns, with nowhere to go but the nearby coffee shop and TV in the room the only entertainment.

This was our first venture to the USA as a group of four, and we had a good time, giggling at the novelties of transatlantic flight and the other passengers. Robin flicked paper pellets over the seats in front like a naughty schoolboy and commented on the relative merits of the air crew's inflation techniques for life jackets. We swapped sweets and magazines, kissing and cuddling and falling asleep in each other's arms, much to the disapproval of the stewardesses, whose forced smiles faded as they passed our row of seats.

Licorice had taken up chewing betel nut, which dyed her teeth and mouth blood red. I tried it but felt none of the physical or spiritual qualities she claimed for it. Even Air India did not provide spittoons for betel-chewers, but they were perhaps less perturbed by it. Stewardesses in saris served us curry in plastic trays, and we found it all very exotic.

We were off to America and a whole new world awaited.

Mercy, I cry city: New York

Autumn 1968

We once more tour the UK venues we now know well. In November Robin's multi-media *Creation* appears on-stage as part of the Royal Albert Hall concert and *Wee Tam and The Big Huge* is released. We set out for the US, playing Fillmores East and West, and anywhere in between where there's an audience. New York City's hip Greenwich Village and Chelsea Hotel are our hunting grounds. In December we encounter Scientology.

◆

We arrived in the US in November 1968. I had never imagined I would visit New York. Flying the Atlantic was for movie stars and wealthy businesspeople, and the dreamworld of skyscrapers was an image from 1930s art or gangster movies. As Joe navigated the many lanes of freeway into the city centre, I took comfort in his accent and his presence. He dropped us off at the Chelsea Hotel on West 23rd Street, made sure we were settled in rooms, with coffee and buns to sleep off the jet lag, and escaped from his encumbrances. Sometimes his relief was visible.

We felt at home in the Chelsea, its reputation as the haunt of the bohemian avant-garde known even in the backwoods of Scotland. This was no safe and protected grand hotel, but exactly the opposite. Obsequious politeness was as foreign to the doormen and the chambermaids as it was to us. Here was a comfortable relationship of equals, and I never complained about unmade beds or unchanged towels. You knew they were just as uncritical of how we behaved, as long as we didn't get in the way. Whatever mess was left, whatever sexual, alcoholic or drug-fuelled performance was in progress, they had seen worse and were unshockable.

I loved the staircases with their iron banisters and the old, cracked lino floors. Ceilings were high and landings wide. I had a pair of tap shoes, bought in London for their jazzy colour, which still had the metal on heel and toe. They made a satisfying clatter as I ran downstairs, being careful not to slip when I hit the marble levels. And when there was no one around to watch, the banisters were wide enough to slide down like children.

None of the other guests seemed to play like this. Joyful laughter and spirited activity were alien to the city cool that hung over the Chelsea, with its slow, heavy atmosphere. Even Robin and Licorice could be playful, he mimicking some of the more bizarre inhabitants to her stifled giggles. We refused to be intimidated by the decadent sophistication that oozed everywhere.

Mike and Robin had spent little time in the US, and this was a wild and comparatively unknown world, far from even the hippest corners of London. Andy Warhol superstars had been resident at various times, and a cartoonist who had worked in the early days for Disney lived in a penthouse on the roof. Famous artists had paid arrears with paintings. Huge canvases were still in the lobby, at the mercy of coffee splashes and passers-by.

Freakish people passed us in the corridors, as did Janis Joplin and The Doors. Middle-aged journalists enjoying the buzz of a place known to be wonderful and strange. An elderly lady walked her dog down the stairs every few hours. On an upper floor a man had a small alligator, two monkeys, and a snake in his room. Many rooms had pet cockroaches summer and winter.

Once past the shock of dated décor and scuffed paint, I liked our rooms, with their old furniture, historic iron radiators and table lamps from the 1950s. The air-conditioning made an infuriating rattle and buzz when it worked, which wasn't often. When next door flushed the toilet or let the water out of the bath, strange knockings afflicted the pipework. But the Chelsea was all unexplained and random sounds, the hour of the day or night having no significant effect on its activities.

We could wander from room to room undressed and untidy as we were, if something couldn't wait another moment to be played or explained. We could bring in food from the deli or the coffee shop on the corner, knowing it wouldn't be tidied away before we got back. Clothes could be flung on chair-backs or dried over the radiators, and bags left heaped in corners. We relaxed with each other, regaining the private life that tours took from us.

The next summer, we discovered it was possible to get out on the roof and sunbathe. Being blond, Robin got sunburned with a sick headache, but there was a pharmacy handy for emergencies. It also sold coffee and I could chat to the pharmacist for local knowledge. Apparently syringes and anti-parasite ointments were common requests from his regular Chelsea Hotel clientele. Most drugs of choice were available in the hotel,

Up on the roof: Robin sunbathing, Chelsea Hotel, New York, 1968

with addiction levels high. He seemed surprised by the simpler, healthier purchases of a so-called psychedelic group. Reporters hung about on that corner, waiting for the stars, hoping for an outrageous comment. With our English accents they even intercepted us once or twice.

We failed to widen our acquaintance within the hotel's social life. We went out quietly in pairs, or as a group for meals. Despite public perception, we were quite puritan. We rarely drank, seeing alcohol as a commonplace and sordid drug without enlightening powers. We took drugs to open our minds and fire our senses.

Joe took us round the city, and we viewed Manhattan and its attractions with curiosity, as we were driven through the streets. We rarely went uptown together, apart from to the instrument shops where Mike and Robin bought strings and yearned after guitars. Uptown was not welcoming and we needed to be enticed.

By contrast, Greenwich Village was where the Head Shops were. People sat on the high stone steps watching the world go by, smoking dope, playing guitars or sleeping. On hot days tempers might fray, wrong words causing violent offence. But a shopping trip to the

Village was a mutual pleasure, and as we met again in the Chelsea we compared successes.

Joe brought people to the hotel to see Mike and Robin, suggesting other routes for their music without putting pressure on them. Licorice and I were not expected to contribute more than our silent presence and polite smiles. Very rarely a question would be asked of us, but our interests, thoughts and feelings were assumed to be those of Mike and Robin.

There were exceptions. One interviewer in the US wrote: "About this time, Rose, who had been busily eating licorice and joining in the conversation at various points, got up to leave. I asked her if she really had to go. 'No,' she said surprised, and sat down again. 'No one has ever asked me to stay before!'"

The same journalist noted that Lic had nothing to say, even when prompted. She used her powers of influence from behind Robin's throne. At first I copied her, smiling vaguely and looking down with a shy gesture while Mike picked up the thread of a question. I felt that I knew too little about the music scene to express opinions.

By the time I began to have ideas of my own a year or so later, Scientology had claimed the band and I was becoming increasingly uneasy about my loyalties to the band and its ideologies.

Fillmore East

The best part of our first stay in New York was the concert at the Fillmore East in Greenwich Village. We usually performed twice there, two Sunday evenings a week apart, and it was always sold out (until we tried to impose the "surreal pantomime" called *U* upon them). This meant we could see other bands in-between, which was enough to get Mike and I in a taxi and uptown. An interviewer noticed the difference: "Rose shares with Mike a great liking for hard rock... she enjoys running around town and catching the 'heavies' in concert." I did, when I got the chance. If a band was involved, Mike was an enthusiastic companion.

When it was our night to play, we were driven from the Chelsea to the centre of Greenwich Village. Unlike its London namesake, this was neither villagey nor by the water. The wide road we were driven down was down-at-heel and dusty-dirty, and not even busy with traffic or activity. Our name was on the old cracked glass sign over the door, with our psychedelic posters on the walls. A few flowery girls and long-haired boys stood around for late tickets, as we arrived for the sound-check. Once inside, the theatre began to live up to its hip reputation. Mike and Robin were met with a warm familiarity and respect. People knew their music and we all felt welcome.

The stage door opened onto a long back street with rusty black iron fire escapes and swinging ladders, garbage bins and odd characters hanging around, like some cops-and-robbers film-set. None of us went out there on our own, so once we were in we stayed. The staff knew we didn't just want beer and burgers, and that our incense wasn't going to burn the place down. They looked and talked like us, happy to share their time and space. So many UK venues considered performers an unwelcome evil, always wanting something awkward and holding up their work.

Inside was like any Victorian theatre back home, with worn gilding on boxes and balconies and threadbare red velvet curtains. I knew the layout to expect, how to find my way out front without being seen, how to climb vertiginous iron ladders to get to gangways above. Despite lightshows and sound equipment, this was a proper theatre, and that added to the comfort level. I could roam between soundcheck and showtime without feeling lost.

When not needed, I spent hours high above the stage. I knew where to find the lighting box when an engineer offered to show me its miracles, knowing I could get back to the dressing room in time. I discovered what a lighting schedule looked like and how it worked. I worked a follow-spot when another band was playing, learning how a coloured gel could make or mar a face. Knowing the power of a lighting crew. I

Filmore East, 1968

made very sure I wasn't left in the dark on that stage. Nobody shaded me with a green tinge.

Our following in the US was even more exclusive than in England. We fitted into no category. "The most incredible thing about the Incredible String Band," Joe Martin wrote in *Good Times* (June 1969), "is that they defy all normative descriptive categories." We were emphatically British, with all the cultural references thereof, and we neither knew nor fully understood American counter-cultural concerns. Audiences found us strange, but that was also our attraction. We told them stories of a life they could only dream of.

Crawdaddy called us a special taste and a different music: "...ISB people are arty, poetic... Rhythm it has, but not the kind of driving, pounding wham-wham... more the droning, hypnotic kind of rhythm... and it has melodies, but a kind of long-line, non-pop sort that you might almost expect from Benjamin Britten not those rock and roll bands..."

We could be playing our gentle little set at the Fillmore one night and Jefferson Airplane would be there the next. Anyone turning up expecting an English rock band could leave very puzzled.

At the Fillmore we were always on a stage that suited us. The technical stuff was all there, as much as we wanted, but also mats, cushions and incense burning in copper vases. The long low table, with all our instruments laid out on coloured cloths, was lit to form a visual focus for an expectant audience. If they weren't already stoned when they arrived they soon felt they were, absorbing the vibes from those crowded around them.

The next day, the *New York Times*' Robert Shelton wrote: "There was the aura of a trance ritual at the Fillmore East last night as the Incredible String Band from England [sic] gave its first major concert here. The trance was engendered by the haunting and evanescent music of the group."

The American audiences who knew us seemed more willing than English counterparts to abandon themselves to the music and our words, and we responded by relaxing and giving our best. That first concert with the four of us was much more important to me than the Albert Hall. Mike and Robin already had their devoted following, but Lic and I had to face people used to the polished performances of Janis Joplin or Gracey Slick, not two little English girls who didn't play perfectly. Licorice even curled her hair. Electric curling tongs made the process quick and foolproof. Someone put flowers in the dressing room, which was kind and made us feel happy.

The programme was largely from *Wee Tam*. We had both been around for most of its writing and all of its recording sessions, so it was ours. Starting with 'The Half Remarkable Question' and ending on Robin's new piece 'Creation', the set declared ISB's mystic credentials. But we also played a Scottish jig, with Licorice and I on our feet in a gleeful little dance. Soon the audience was hopping in the aisles, as Robin's fiddle skirled and trilled. He was playing extempore, so we had no chance of going instrumental. Even Mike could only keep rhythm on guitar.

Robin's 'Waltz of the New Moon' restored a joyful calm into which Mike dropped the falling notes of 'White Bird', slowing to fragile silence as the morning of the song froze into 'Death not Life'. I always held my breath here, as Mike's guitar began whispering the notes of the chorus, which swelled to chant as life flowed back and we all joined in. By now the audience was living the song along with us.

As well as vocals, Lic and I both had instrumental parts in 'The Iron Stone' and 'Very Cellular Song', and this was less contemplative for us. We had melodies to remember, cues to pick up accurately. The audience would float down the "labyrinthine paths of gentle sounds" (as Shelton's very formal review puts it), until returned to American earth by Mike's country music 'Log Cabin Home'. We tore ourselves away from the applause, Mike and Robin waving and laughing at the audience. "We'll be back when we've had a short break."

Beginning the second half with 'Job's Tears' was a gesture of trust and defiance rare in popular music, a song about the crucifixion of Christ and scenes round his cross. But the audience were now with us and we with them. Robin could confide his thoughts, fears and beliefs. Licorice's high diamond voice told of her longings to be free of all the trivial burdens of life in a body. "*Let me go through*" repeats and repeats as she longs for the 'old golden land.' The old-time homeliness of the words turn heaven into both a remote cottage in which she could be herself or an eternity in which free spirits roam. She and Robin assert their belief in a spiritual world and in each other, yet she also begs for release from the present.

Critics sidelined Mike's simpler songs, like 'Little Cloud' or 'Cousin Caterpillar' as twee or sweet, but they weren't listening. I knew all about transformations from one life form to another. My way had been that of the caterpillar. I was living it, learning to accept the strange things and love them.

'Cousin Caterpillar' hints at the theories, philosophical, environmental and scientific, which place humanity within the natural world, our primal unity with the organic economically expressed. Mike's affection for all his creatures tells us everything. Seeing the caterpillar dragging itself along through his eyes, we are all just worms on the face of the earth. We could contextualise our own doubts and fears – our "what's happening?", our "how can this be?" – through this small creature's body.

Our problems were not worth worrying about any more. We joined in enthusiastically with the *do-de-da, la-la* and *wa-wa* choruses threading through the song. But the white and silky threads of the chrysalis were the beauties ensnarling me, trapping me in tight places where patience and acceptance were the only answer. The final "*One day he'll wake with wings*" is the ultimate understatement, with its delicate reprise of the choruses drifting into silence. We all made our own heavens in the seconds before the applause erupted.

Mike's wisdom was simple and uncomplicated but also very real. He sang what he knew and I believed him, with the rhythms of my little silver drum tripping along behind his voice. I didn't lay down a track governing his melody but instead ran along alongside, sometimes uncertain or even behind – a record producer's nightmare. But the relationships between us all, sung out in the music, were meant to please no one but ourselves, and certainly not aimed at musical perfection.

The song mattered to me that night at the Fillmore, as I sat there on the stage with my little drum between my knees. It was my life and my music on the line, before an unknown world, and I really cared.

The long instrumental that followed had developed from the recent *Be Glad* soundtrack, made in Wales and was not my favourite piece. Mike on sitar was always a lovely sight as he gazed up its long neck, but this also meant me on tabla. I couldn't get the music out of them and crossly wished he had chosen a simpler accompaniment. The changes were quite entertaining, as we picked first drum, then whistle, then bass and back, but they also meant I couldn't settle, always busy thinking of the next instrument needed.

As melodies came and went. Robin's imagination wandered from folk balalaika through India to free-form flute, with Lic on mandolin and me on keyboard, Mike just hoping he could keep it all together with his guitar line. As Robin picked up yet more instruments – gimbri, whistles and flutes, one with a horn-like quality, sarangi – Lic and I stuck to the rhythms, melodies and chords we knew, hoping that we'd all get back in harmony at some point in the future. The wordless singing was a relief, meaning the end was in sight. But no, more assorted percussion and sitar followed, and I must fold myself up around the tabla again. It went on too: 'The Song Had No Ending' indeed. But it was a jolly tune to sing along to, and it gave the audience a chance to join in. They knew by then they could make their own little concerts in the auditorium, swaying along and dancing in the aisles, humming and singing quietly in a sub-chorus to our music. We were all together: "A total involvement of we with they until the very distinction disappears."

Ending on 'Creation' transferred their attention back to us on-stage, as Robin recited his poem over our melodic and hypnotic chanting. The melody's sway carried me above the mechanical business of playing tabla. Nobody noticed much what went on beneath the singing and recitation, until Robin also took up drums, driving the rhythm along. The words and images flew, as he recited his own creation story, and for a few minutes we sang and played a better world into being.

The song changed from poetic to meditative, and back again, ending on a cheerful parody of ourselves. In front of an audience like this the Incredible String Band could be its most serious, most funny, most entertaining. All the tensions and differences melted away. We moved out of the daily into the creative world where all artists make their best art, and even if Lic and I weren't the inspired spirits, we were essential to the creation. Even critics with reservations (like *Billboard*'s) were intrigued: "Though gentle in nature, their tunes are weird, defying empathy and a communicable warmth. But whether not of this earth – or moon music like the lonely whinings of two cats on a fence – the virtuosity of the Incredible String Band is something else."

As we left at 10.40, we saw maybe 100 people lying on the Sixth Street sidewalk waiting for the box office to open tomorrow. "Crosby, Stills, Nash, Young are playing and it's the only way they'll get a ticket," Joe told us.

Piano non grata

A couple of days later I played the grand piano in the Lincoln Centre, home of the New York Philharmonic, on those same long pieces of Robin's. I imagine few less competent musicians than me have been on concert stages where virtuosi also performed. Very shiny, orderly and efficient when we arrived, our stage set-up turned it into a street market spread across the polished floorboards. The grand piano loomed over our rag-bag of instruments, ready for a soloist and guarded carefully by their stage crew.

It was probably not the piano they kept for special occasions, but nevertheless the gilded name of Steinway or Bechstein stared me in the face as I moved over mid-set to sit on its stool. My difficulty with keyboards was locating the correct octave. Once I had done this I was fine, and could play the learned notes quite accurately.

The enormous concert grand's keyboard looked as long as a high street. Overawed by its splendour and size, I couldn't decide where to start and the song set off without me. But I'd got to the piano stool and needed to do something to justify my presence. Tentatively poking, even I could hear that this was wrong and discordant. The next octave along didn't improve the situation. All was lost. My only hope was that Mike might be thought to be venturing into atonality.

I continued with miscellaneous notes and phrases until blessedly the song ended. Comparatively new, its harmonies were unfamiliar to the audience. Mike and Robin probably sang and played a little louder, given my new version of the accompaniment, and Lic too performed with enough verve to lend conviction. Perhaps the person on the soundboard also reacted quickly enough to reduce the piano's volume. I couldn't tell.

In the usual informal flow of the set it didn't stand out, and it wasn't remarked on afterwards. I had played gently and lightly, trying to look deeply concentrated and involved, a technique honed by years in the school orchestra. Everyone applauded and it simply passed into the history of ISB's freedom and spontaneity.

We had a couple of days free, and I had time to explore away from the others. Alone I could move with the speed of the city and feel part of it. Walking along as a group was like dragging a tin can behind me, noisy and demanding attention. I walked up to the Garment District, dodging the dress racks wheeling across the streets in all directions. I had plans for Mike's shirts and found all imaginable braids and embroidered bindings in wholesale haberdashers with shelves from floor to ceiling. Since I didn't know the rate of exchange, I bought what took my fancy.

My trips to museums and galleries were also always solo. The others had their own priorities. It seemed strange to me that Mike and Robin

New York escapes – the roof of the Chelsea Hotel, 1968

had no interest in these remnants of the past, when their songs were so concerned with myth and legend. Robin once explained that in his past lives, playing harp in the courts of Europe, the objects in these glass cases had been part of his everyday life. Why would he want to see them now, old and damaged? This sense of an infinite time beyond the present helped us through the upheavals of time-zones, jet-lag and reversals of night and day. Then at tour's end we went back home and in a few days all was normal again.

Into the Vortex: Scientology

1969

Through 1969, Scientology develops into a major obsession for all, even in passing for Joe Boyd, who is impressed by our new-found organisation. It motivates much of the work for all but me, and the relationship continues for long years after. How many I don't know, as I am free from all involvement once I leave ISB. But for now, Mike, Robin and Licorice have fixed criteria for the band's public expression, dictated by a belief-system which knew no compromises and aimed to control its adherents' entire lives. We spoke as Scientologists or not at all, a situation which was becoming increasingly intolerable for me. After Christmas 1968, we begin a UK tour. Peter Neal isn't around for the hurried soundtrack to *Pirate and the Crystal Ball*, but is still filming, including a take in Sound Techniques of 'All Writ Down'. In February we record the Julie Felix TV show and John Peel's *Nightride*. April-May: we again visit the US, returning in June-July for the UK festivals. *Stones in the Park*, the memorial concert for Brian Jones, introduces us to a new technology.

◆

Licorice had been depressed as we filmed *Be Glad* in Wales. Once back in London she slept all the time and we didn't see her for a few days. I supposed that, like me, she was trying to work out how she wanted to live, now that Mike and Robin seemed determined to plough different furrows as success forced them together.

I thought that perhaps the communal life hadn't worked out as she imagined. Janet Shankman, later Robin's wife, was also appearing more often on the peripheries of our scene, which must have disrupted the erratic flow of his relationship with Licorice. Her solution to whatever unhappiness was shadowing her life impinged heavily on all of us. Though recollections differ about the sequence of events which led her to Scientology, its later effects were only too clear.

We were staying in serviced flats near Oxford Street, so Tottenham Court Road was a daily route to the rest of the town. The Scientology building was by the entrance to Goodge Street station, convenient for commuters, shoppers and the university, with placards outside announcing Free Personality Testing and general self-improvement. Scientologists handed out leaflets and described therapeutic methods to cure all ills.

Licorice was the first to be attracted, at a time when she must have been vulnerable, looking for ways out of her immediate problems. Robin followed, and later Mike and I were curious enough to visit the London office and discover what the two of them were talking about. When we met Licorice there, she looked happy and confident, talking more openly than I had ever seen. She had obviously cheered up and found a side of her personality that I, at least, hadn't seen before. Her transformation was enough to suggest to us that there might be something in Scientology itself.

The London office was light, clean and full of smart, short-haired people in suits. Inspirational posters with dated images and colours promised a better life and freedom from present cares. The tone of their exhortations and the manner of their presentation reminded me of the very conventions we'd been trying to escape over the last few years.

While I recognised the problems of living as part of ISB, I was enjoying myself. I admired Mike and Robin and their work, despite our differences. I liked performing and seeing the world and I wanted to continue, tolerating the band's beliefs even when they seemed outlandish. From the brief explanations Robin had offered Mike and me, Scientology was weirder than most of the religions we had encountered. But Licorice and Robin were certainly easier to get on with since their introduction to it, so maybe it was a good idea, for them if not for me.

As I looked at the posters and the people in the Scientology office, I knew I didn't want to embrace a therapy aiming to turn me into an American provincial secretary or a happy housewife. I didn't want a husband who worked office hours, then watched sport all weekend while I looked after two children in a suburban home. If this was the aspiration, I wasn't interested.

Mike and I were used to the spiritual vagaries of the others by now and unsurprised by any new fad. In common with the spirit of the times, the institutional forms of any belief were anathema to the band's free-wheeling creativity, and we had all been only casual followers of any belief-system. But we had also seen enough of the alternative culture's casualties, and we'd suffered enough disruption to our own lives to realise the need for spiritual support. The religions we had followed so far had not offered the needed fixes for mental or physical suffering.

Drained by kindness

ISB's fast rise to success had had "one of the highest fame-to-obscurity ratios it is possible to imagine," according to Joe. This had caused its own problems. We kept our cool and tried to continue as normal, but the days were different. We played concerts night after night to large audiences, who all picked up on the open friendliness central to the stage-show. They wanted to be our best mates. Robin would chat into the dark auditorium, maybe picking out a face, but really just talking about himself and telling stories, an art-form that has since made him a living.

The audiences that, Joe says, "filled the Royal Albert Hall over and over again, as they did the Fillmore West in San Francisco and the Lincoln Centre in New York," were regaled with tales of 'Big Ted', the Welsh pig, or "what happened on my way to the theatre." The mixture of stand-up comedian and whimsy was amusing enough but above all it affirmed approachable closeness, rather than stardom and indifference. The people in front of the stage responded in kind, expecting to spend time chatting, thinking we would be interested in their own stories. We had never hidden behind security staff, or even protective roadies. No trouble was ever expected at our concerts.

As Mike and Robin enjoyed the pleasures of stardom for a while, I learned how to negotiate the awkward ground of the groupie scene. This was less clear for a woman assumed to belong to someone other than herself, and assumed also to be jealous and resentful of those invading her territory. Mostly I wasn't bothered by the girls who hung around backstage to see Mike. Sometimes I could see why he liked this one or that one beyond the pretty face, and I was glad of the space to get on with my own pursuits.

There were also plenty of good-looking young men, with black curls and blue eyes or Nordic-looking and athletic, or like native Americans with long silky black hair and aquiline faces. Often we just wanted some peace and quiet, to get away from each other and everyone else, to feel free of the oppression of sound and noise and light. Hotel rooms, we had found, were an inadequate substitute for home, and sometimes very desolate after a long day in public. It was easy when we four were best friends, sharing evenings and nights together, and the day's work took up time and energy. But on a free evening or after a concert, I became very familiar with the sense that a party was happening somewhere and I wasn't at it. Or that everyone else had a home, family or friends to go back to and I hadn't, as I sat looking at the walls, too tired to read, too wired to watch TV.

We were each so protective of our own idea of "cool" that we never talked about it to anyone or admitted anything other than perfect satisfaction and comfort with the life which was changing so quickly. We rarely mentioned, or even considered, the physical effects resulting from all the changes in our lives, or the even more disturbing mental scenarios.

With his sheltering presence, Joe had made it easier to deal with the pressures. His long experience of bands on the road had taught him what to think of and how to deal with it. He made sure we ate reasonably by taking us to restaurants where food was good, reliable and interesting. We went on outings purely for relaxation, to funfairs or someone's garden for the afternoon. He introduced us to new people we had something in common with, or whose acquaintance we could at least find some pleasure in. As far as possible, he kept us healthy.

But once he became a remote figure only turning up occasionally, all this dissolved. His substitutes lacked the hands-on experience and the strength of will to confront our temperaments, and to deal effectively with all of us. They were easily distracted into taking sides despite their best intentions and, liked or disliked, their power to control the whole group on a daily basis was limited.

Rigid retreats

The absolute normality of the Scientology office and its personnel was like school or the bank, or anywhere else where behaviour was predictable and boring. It must have been attractive to Licorice, at a time when she was probably suffering a minor mental health crisis. Her previous habits and daily rituals of beliefs were falling apart, as Robin and Mike kept the words but not the meditative lifestyle that went with them. They had too many other demands on their time and attention to sit quietly contemplating the universe or devoting serious thoughts to esoteric matters.

Scientology offered clarity and speedy solutions. It definitively promised clear progress, in terms that allowed no doubt, up a ladder from one stage of enlightenment to another. It could clear all previous diseases and ailments for ever, pledging eternity to anyone committing themselves to its methods. It was an international organisation that bridged the distances between the different loci of our lives. It offered the security of belonging and of being protected by its all-enveloping presence. I guess that behind all the certainty Licorice showed in public, there was a deep and hopeless insecurity.

More important than any practical considerations as the band changed, was the way we each estimated ourselves in relation to other people. I felt I was lucky to be with ISB and hoped my good fortune would hold, but there were always other possibilities, other lovers, other lives in which to imagine a happy future for myself. But I think Lic enjoyed celebrity for itself more than I did and not just its opportunities. Her obvious career asset was her voice, but she would never have accepted the disciplines of being a session-singer, or the trials of making a name for herself alone.

She liked having money and buying things, as I did, but the emotional response to being a celebrity Scientologist was more important. It confirmed to her that the difference she perceived between herself and the world of the ordinary, was due to her superiority. Scientology was only too happy to assure her that this was the case, to offer explanations, and a simple way to extend her powers that didn't involve boring or difficult thinking. All it demanded was to follow the rules and give them the money that paid for the courses offered, on the road to enlightenment.

As a result she grasped Scientology's consolations quickly and wholeheartedly and changed overnight. She became what they asked of her, got her teeth done, went to a hairdresser, sent her dresses to the dry-cleaner and bought new and more conventional ones. She got up on time every day and, in organising these simple things, talked more and with more careful observance of the common expectations of conversation – which was a bit of a nuisance as far as I was concerned. Silence had been easier to live with. But we all could see that the experience was positive for her, and she learned all the jargon that eventually convinced Robin to join her.

Then Mike and I were persuaded too, setting off on the Scientology journey to mental and physical perfection. The doubts that we first expressed to one other were no longer mentioned. Robin and Licorice were more friendly and supportive, and despite my dislike of its forms and its theories, Scientology seemed to be delivering on some of its promises.

Conversational ability, known as "Comms", was the first course we were taken by. Studying at Formica desks looking at Xeroxed folders of information, it took a week to pick up the basic rules of verbal interchange. "Listen to what is being said to you, think, and then reply in terms the listener will understand." This may have been useful for backwoods hippies who had deliberately chosen to distance themselves from such exchanges. But we were out there in the world most days.

Scientology was good at producing ten pages of science fiction story to convey advice so simple that any ordinary business would expect its trainers to cover it. I felt it was an expensive method, but the others had earned the money from their talent, and it was their choice how to spend it. It was also silly to protest. I knew it was always pointless when the other three were united.

The first course we passed successfully, with much earnest congratulation and cups of coffee in the lobby. Now that we were effective communicators we could progress to greater achievements, we were told, as if a successful band had no such skills. Mike and Robin were led to believe that they would soon achieve stages of pure operative spirit, soaring with their special talents above the ignorant earth-bound majority. Licorice and I would follow this lead.

The path was long, with a long-term commitment and a heavy price list. Mike and Robin had already largely abjured the false gods of drugs as a daily habit. Quite soon, the effect on them was the same as it had been on Licorice. Robin rarely did anything without making a crusade of it and his allegiance to the Scientological lifestyle was supported by both Licorice and Janet, a new girlfriend. My clear impression at the time was that Janet's enrolment in the cult had preceded her meeting Robin. The three of them shared its convictions and its doctrines. Scientology was insistent that drugs were a path to damnation and decay, spiritual or physical and preached that clean-living, according to its dictates, was vital for the band's progress and success. Soon, Mike, Robin and Licorice accepted the drug-veto with zeal.

False prophets

The audiences continued as before, however, and expected their heroes to do as they had so often preached through their music, albeit indirectly. New lyrics were still read in a context of chemically induced mysticism, and indeed Mike and Robin repeated the ideas and images of these druggy days in their new songs, while abandoning the convictions which once underpinned them.

The Eastern philosophies and religions they had earlier read and written about had now lost much of their mystique in the popular imagination. Embracing a guru was no longer unusual, and many pop musicians had spent time in an Ashram in India or been initiated into some other alternatives. Hare Krishna groups chanted and chimed their way down Oxford Street every day and the Maharishi Mahesh Yogi sat alongside groups on the major stages of the world. Ravi Shankar's fame was now international.

Scientology was different. The only celebrity Scientologist was jazz musician Chick Corea, and who had heard of him anyway? Once more Robin and Mike were paving a way. It would establish them in the spiritual elite, so they believed, and hopeful fans could follow.

The spiritual benefits were available to all, but at a high price. For those unable to afford the financial burdens of membership, Scientology grudgingly provided an alternative. A system of work in lieu allowed initiates to pay off the cost of their courses and treatments through labour which, if not exactly forced, was certainly undertaken under stringent terms and supervised with rigour. But such voluntary labour was an open-ended commitment. Once hooked into the hierarchy of progression, the desire to move to higher states of being was encouraged. This was the organisation's whole ethos, a business model I saw as dictatorial. It also fiercely condemned anyone who refused the dictates of L. Ron Hubbard.

An endless stream of new proposals for personal improvement followed one another, each demanding yet more money and urgent attention. After the free Personality Test, advertised on the billboard outside to call the curious through their door, the first invoice was not unreasonable compared to most private clinics or psychiatrists. Once initiated, the organisation promised to save you all those expenses, by returning you to perfect physical and mental health. If we followed their courses to the highest level, we would emerge as free beings inhabiting a pure body, untainted by the ills of the world. We would be clear of the legacies of sin and shame, accumulated over this and past lives. These caused every disease we suffered, from colds to cancer, so they told us.

We would be able to operate outside the body too. Robin assured a visitor one evening that he was "going to the cinema in Edinburgh that night to watch a film," while apparently sitting in his own front room at the Glen all the while. No one ever liked to question such experiences or demand a resumé of the plot. It seemed too brutal, and also pointless. Robin would never have listened. If we failed to see his absence this was our blindness.

It is never comfortable to write about Scientology. There is always the lurking fear of a threatening phone call, of the hacker or housebreaker who violates your privacy and weighs down days with worry. Often reported, such after-effects are more than just paranoid.*

Joe dealt with their admin as he would with anyone negotiating a contract with him. But we trooped along like lambs to the slaughter, accepting each new course as a step in our progress towards Nirvana. We followed the same time-schedules we had once despised and abandoned,

---

* When I escaped its clutches and moved away from London, the call from Scientology Head Office was followed by one from Military Intelligence. Both warned me they knew where we were. My baby daughter's father was close to the Peace Movement in Britain and anti-Vietnam war activists in the USA. With Welsh Nationalism on the rise, the military apparently thought it worth a call.

If only Scientology knew how little money was in my account, how powerless and voiceless I was, stuck in the back end of nowhere with a baby, no household appliances and no prospect of buying them.

committing days and weeks to joyless classrooms, instant coffee and soggy sandwiches. We read reams of simplistic psychology and bad science fiction, telling us how the universe worked and how to improve our place within it.

The questions we were presented with, in all seriousness, were the kind you're asked to "win" a competition prize, when the prize is fairground rubbish and the advertiser just wants the entry-fee. Our evenings of "study" were pitched at scholars whose basic level of literacy was not high. Yet talented musicians and writers as Mike and Robin were, they failed to see this. They were unoffended by texts I found insultingly condescending. Apparently the applause of joyful, smiling Scientology faces pleased them.

I was seething with rage and frustration. I saw no improvement in our health or well-being, just verbal justifications for every sniffle, ache and pain. Once we'd just take an aspirin for a headache, but now a lengthy discussion always ensued. The simplest daily activities and social interactions would be clouded with jargon or promptly terminated. Anyone who disagreed with a theory was by definition malignant, to be shunned. A day when things went wrong and we were cross with each other was explained away by the sufferings of past lives.

Proselytizing

In the early days we had taken up and put down faith systems at our own volition, sometimes encouraged or discouraged by the others. Even then Licorice and Robin tended to believe with a zealot's certainty. Now every Scientology office in the world reaffirmed their dogmatic convictions. They could be sure of a shared language and understanding, and the security derived from habit. New phrases arrived amongst us, and the band's daily talk changed. When the non-initiated had to reach for normal language in our conversations with them a quick glance between Lic and Robin and a pause of sympathetic condescension often followed.

From the start of our "journey", we had been taught the necessity of full communication with others, in order to spread the word, and we followed the rules. With Licorice a look of intense interest, as recommended to encourage personal disclosures, became familiar. Similarly advised, Robin soon picked up the officially-suggested questioning tone of approval, along with a look of interested concern. It worked. People thought us more accessible and easier to get along with. They told us how much simpler it was to work with us now. And the surface level of information exchange was more successful between ourselves. Now Robin would wait until the end of a sentence before he lost interest and walked away.

On another course, Scientology office, 1970

The talking-therapy, intended to reveal and assuage all the emotional crises and physical hurts of this life and all the lives before it, was called auditing. As we all progressed through it, Robin and Licorice gained all the affirmation they could wish for. Previous lives rose up from an unconscious past recorded on the psyche, to be liberated into the conscious present. The unique experiences and the spiritual superiority they appropriated for themselves were now sharply outlined.

Both were hard-pressed not to reveal all the new stories they had discovered to anyone willing to listen. But these had to be told with much circumlocution and hesitation, to preserve the secrecy of the auditing-room, or the Confessional on which it seemed to be based. As the Auditor elicited the traumas of an infinite past as well as the current present, the rituals of Christianity were replaced with the pseudo-science of the lie-detector. The power of such traumas to generate present ailments was to be dispersed. Absolution was granted by the motion of the lie-detector's needle.

The first few, half-related accounts favoured historical highlights – from Cleopatra's Court to the Saxon warriors of Sutton Hoo and soon it was neither interesting nor funny. The self-important expressions became annoying, as we sat and listened, looking concerned and involved. It is a great tribute to my acting ability and self-control that I am remembered as part of that happy and reasonable band.

Perhaps for those genuinely in need of therapy this offered a security lacking elsewhere. The various US offices were small-town America at its worst, often surrounded by high fences and shorn lawns. The staff we met were often unpleasantly similar to characters in movies exposing the cruelties and prejudices inherent in the moral confinement of suburban America.

As celebrity guests, ISB were cosseted and at first welcomed, orthodoxy insidiously encouraged but not enforced. It was hinted to us that Scientology had a high success rate battling addiction. It was easy for us to achieve the drug-free prerequisite of membership, but it was very soon made clear that doubt, disbelief or criticism would not be tolerated. Those who voiced or encouraged any such views were, though the phraseology was different, inhabited by evil spirits. Like all cults it separated members from earlier, wider lives, aiming for total allegiance and dedication.

One costly treat was a visit to The Global Headquarters at Saint Hill Manor in East Grinstead, anticipated with eagerness by initiates progressing to the higher levels. I hoped for something to emerge in its rarefied atmosphere that would convince me that my silent criticisms were unfounded. Perhaps the early stages were boring and unimpressive, with something better to follow.

We arrived at what had been an English country-house to find its past beauties erased. Renovated and altered, its individual character was reduced, with Philistine bitterness, to a conformist, pseudo-modern, pseudo-scientific, pseudo-everything image of the modern office. The same trite and impoverished language as the 3 Tottenham Court Road office.

Same smiles, same neat clothes. Same revelations, same Formica desks, same Xeroxed sheets. Perhaps the science fiction was slightly more outlandish. It was no more convincing. But I saw no trace of criticism on Mike's face, just stern conviction, as we all discussed it on the train back to London. I couldn't understand what he could find to persuade him to take this seriously. His imagination was always lively and fantastical, but also beautiful, kind and open, willing to think the best of people, thrilling to the delights of the natural world. Why had he such sympathy with repression, enforced obedience and ugliness? The hierarchy were probably more flattering to him than to me, knowing whose work paid the fees, but this alone didn't account for its attractions.

Still, there was an added artistic problem now for Mike and Robin. As costs of both Enlightenment and touring a larger group rose, the looks, beliefs and attitudes which had made them successful financially were in decline. They were incompatible with the new belief-system they had embraced. Long hair suited both and added to the fairy-tale look, but Scientology disapproved. The dress-code there was more Jehovah's Witness suit and tie than casual hippie.

Certainly it was noticeable that flowing tops, oriental jackets and velvety flares were gradually replaced by plain T-shirts and darker coloured jeans, embroidery more restrained, plain even. As we had never acquired the tidy habits of immaculate dressing, these more ordinary clothes quickly looked depressing, from lack of care. Mike had always been the neater and more harmonious dresser and still managed to look reasonably glamorous. Robin's habitual carelessness turned whites to grey, beige jeans to neutral bags and conventional jackets to shapeless drapes around his slim body, however much Janet tried for sartorial respectability. Stage clothes and daytime clothes diverged, as an ideologically acceptable compromise that suited earning potential and personalities. Both of them enjoyed dressing up, but a game now became a disguise, as daily activities became unacceptable to a large part of their audiences.

To the outside observer, the greater problem was song-writing. They had always written from the emotional truth of their beliefs. They saw Nature as the voice of eternal and universal spirits to be transmitted through their own music. But both had now either abandoned their original ideas entirely, or else warped them to fit into a rigid new form. Scientology offered nothing to fill the gaps. Spacemen and faraway planets were not a frame of reference that came naturally, and repressive formality doesn't make good music, except perhaps marching songs. They were now astray lyrically, the words lacking the conviction that had given them vibrancy and power. Ramblings which previously flowered into moments of brilliance when invested with Robin's personality and beliefs were now often a pointless and derivative meandering.

Licorice's new-found sureness and loquacity, her measurable progress on an agreed and competitive scale, aggravated her determination to play a more equal role in band discussions and work. Regardless of ability, she wanted to play more and more instruments. Scientology had "removed past pain in me so that now I am able to play instruments on stage which frightened me before," she said. Her confidence knew no bounds.

The ties were loosening that had bound the four of us like spider's silk, invisible and indefinable yet fiercely clinging. Membership of the cult suggested greater harmony between us, but also dissolved our commitment to the music. Writing, playing and performing were now the source of necessary income, and no longer the spiritual or creative centre of Mike and Robin's lives.

Communal confusions

The emotional intensity of our performances had already been threatened by Stone Monkey's presence. Now these relationships were further weakened. Stone Monkey had no allegiance to Scientology, and no will to become further involved. Robin and Mike were willing to allow the situation to continue, but it never became a matter of discussion. It was a necessary compromise. For penniless members of Stone Monkey, both the necessary Scientology fees and the voluntary work in lieu would make it hard to continue the flexible financial terms needed for a working relationship between ISB and Stone Monkey.

Most fans were not Scientologists, and the exclusivity of the cult robbed both Mike and Robin of a free-flowing interchange. Prejudice and suspicion had crept into their lives, fear that the evil forces embodied in other people might injure their eternal purity. This increased the distances between audience and performers, as the band's isolation and spiritual arrogance grew. Spontaneity and joy left our lives, replaced with warped imaginings and repressive authoritarianism. Audiences responded slowly but decisively. Politeness and manageability carried a heavy price.

As our money flowed into the Scientology accounts and the band's management conformed to its dictates, I continued to fulfil requirements. I attended the courses while wondering how to improve the situation. A dark stream of doubt flowed under all our bright days, sometimes deeper, sometimes nearer the surface. However much I tried to forget it, it didn't go away.

Increasing estrangement sent me off at tangents. After sitting drinking tea in a coffee shop and making plans for the next Org (like all the cult's crass jargon, the abbreviation itself drove me to distraction), I could head off into a separate life. One night waiting for a late connecting flight at an airport somewhere in the US, we were all perched miserably on a narrow circular bench, tired, cold, surrounded by guitars and luggage, Licorice and I maintaining the bag-lady image.

The Cloisters, Washington Heights, Manhattan – Changing Horses cover, 1969

We were all in sheepskin, the Afghan jackets and fine lambskin boleros of the cold Scotland we had just left behind. Sweeping down the hallway towards us came Crosby, Stills and Nash, all in heavy, wolf-skin coats, a picture of power and prosperity. They waved as they passed. It seemed to sum up our situation, this helpless flock guarded by the unseen sheepdogs of Scientology as the circling wolves enjoyed the chase.

Gold tarnishes

At first, with Licorice and Robin as members but Mike unconvinced, Scientology-speak had been irritating but also easy to ignore. We had the money to get by and could live life in the moment, when not on tour or otherwise engaged. Our real home was transcendental, the love between us as spiritual as it was earthbound. We floated through the days with few cares. "I wanted to show more people how happy I was and so I started playing on gigs and now I just get happier all the time," I told *Oz* in April 1969, despite the shadow of the cult. The adrenalin of performance was an almost daily stimulus, on-stage, in the studio, in interviews or rehearsing. It substituted for other drugs. "Rose has a smile which goes on and on and on. Go down the tunnel of Rose's smile and find Mike at the end with his silver sitar. Been together since the beginning of time and before, as Licorice and Robin have."

These were relationships whose temporality and frailties were now apparent, but I wanted to believe the myth. It was a guarantee of some timeless security when the present looked fragile. Eternity is more popular in times of global instability. It framed our thoughts and contemplations better than terrestrial parameters, whatever the belief system. We were sure that our spiritual and aesthetic path to peace and freedom was better than political solutions. Licorice and I knew very well about Women's Lib, and we were neither of us the protected daughters of aristocratic families, like so many of the pretty girls around us. Our survival technique, in our separate homes, had been to live the words and music of ISB's songs.

The photos for the cover of the *Changing Horses* LP were taken on the Spring trip to New York, out at The Cloisters in Upper Manhattan. The album cover tells of a band in transition, and the title confirms this. Generally this was interpreted as the acknowledgement of Licorice and me as playing members, but this was only part of the story.

Mike is cheerfully proprietorial on the cover, casually patting my face as I sit adoringly at his feet. He still wears the androgynous clothes of hippiedom, satiny flares and our shared chiffon blouse. Robin is carefully posed above us in meditative profile, his more conventional jeans and t-shirt swathed in a floating scarf. A flower-crowned Licorice is arranged at the highest point, gazing determinedly at the camera, unsmiling and fixed.

The tour was just beginning for Mike and me. We had a couple of free days, like a holiday, and we enjoyed the stroll along the riverbanks. The adoration of the Roman Camps days was gone, but on-stage we appeared as "private but close together like new lovers and lit with a clean fire that talks of peace and apple-cheek country weather," as *Oz* described it. We were doing alright, together and musically.

But Licorice and Robin seemed to be drifting apart again. In our hours at the Chelsea, Robin spent more time playing with Mike, while Licorice and I found our separate ways around the city. I suspect she found a Scientology office and spent her leisure hours there, finding comfort in people who were not like her bandmates.

This was our endless round: gig after gig, days passed in studios, hotel on hotel, the eternal service flat. In the Chelsea Hotel everything was available except rules. But things were very different elsewhere, as our travels revealed. In a motel with a neat blue pool and tidy lawns it was unexpectedly hot, and Robin had bought swimming shorts from the shop in the lobby. Sitting in the coffee bar, the rest of us were entertained by the sight of him, now wrapped in a large towel, being forcibly escorted back to his room by the hotel porter, under threat of being arrested for indecent exposure. Without their outer cover-up, the white undershorts he'd bought went transparent when wet, and the gingham-swimsuit ladies round the pool were greatly upset.

In the same motel, on the same morning, Mike was only saved from attack by an enormous American Football player storming down the balcony towards us when I explained frantically that we were just playing hide and seek. I was squealing with amusement, not fear. This was exactly the provincial and repressive conformism we were protesting against.

But on-stage the strains and pains, the boredom and irritations all lifted. Here was our joint home, to share the best of each other free from everything weighing us down. Here we lived our best and happiest times together. And in New York, the Fillmore was home: "I saw the Incredible String Band use the Fillmore Stage for a picnic and turn the Lower East Side into a woodland glade… on a backwards trip to the fields of childhood innocence… How beautiful to find that England shimmering on New York air," wrote the nameless enthusiast in *Oz*.

Not all the audience were so in tune with our playful and peaceful intentions. It could easily take five minutes to change from one song to another as we each found instruments, adjusted tunings, seating and mics, and sometimes more. Roadies couldn't tune an oud or a sitar. Mike or Robin would chat to the audience, especially Robin, who enjoyed the chance to tell a tale or a joke. Lic and I weren't expected centre stage, and were usually more preoccupied finding our instruments.

At one point the Fillmore audience got fed up with waiting. Rustles and murmurs became clapping and whistling: "Come on man, get on with it." We didn't like this. We had no time for these impatient souls. Robin walked very quietly to the front of the stage, then stood there looking out into the auditorium. After a moment he spoke, very gently but clearly, with a clipped English intonation, cold and low-toned: "Our instruments take time to tune. If you want us to play, you have to wait and we need to have quiet." With another gaze which swept the entire theatre, he returned to his seat and continued peacefully to collect his instruments. The auditorium went quiet and we continued as before.

Shortly after, during 'Creation', the usual tumble of instruments and visual diversions had relaxed the quiet intensity this intervention had gained us. As Robin started to recite his poem and the wordless sung melody drifted above his quiet voice, someone in the front row started to argue with his neighbour about a camera. The disturbance was obvious and jarring.

Robin noticed. He went silent, nodded at us and we all stopped singing and playing. Suddenly the argument was at the centre of the theatre's shocked attention and dismay. Robin looked directly at them and said "How can I sing about Creation while you're…?" Discomfited, they went quiet, and we continued from where we left off. The group spirit was still powerful, carrying us through such challenges without great disturbance to the atmosphere.

Next day, on a trip to see *Easy Rider* at the Beekman Theatre in the Upper East Side, we were all four sitting in a nearby coffee shop, waiting to be collected from our outing. We had enjoyed the film but despite our appearance were protected from most of the social troubles of hippiedom that it portrayed. The waiter came over and told us that we should eat what we wanted, as our bill was paid. Overcome by pity and guilt, a very conventional family sitting nearby had been horrified how hippies were treated in the film and wished to prove their goodwill in a positive way. We were grateful and appreciative, but they were gone so we couldn't tell them.

Other places hadn't caught up with the idea of hippies, and venues were unsuitable, with no audience for us: "Although most of [Detroit's] vast Ford Auditorium on May 16 was empty, the stage was filled before Mike Heron, Robin Williamson, Rose, and Licorice came on. An organ, piano, two amplifiers, bass, gongs, sitar and an array of unusual Eastern instruments graced the large stage with the tremendous and gaudy gold curtain…"

We faced rows of empty seats with scattered bunches of free-ticket groups, from the Fire Service, nearby government offices or social facilities. Even if those who did turn up were puzzled and not very appreciative of this strange Scottish band, a free ticket was something and deserved a clap. At least we never faced abuse from them and that was already a success.

The fans that did come were always embarrassed and apologetic about the lack of audience, assuming we would be more upset than we ever were. But this was when we benefited from the mutual support of a foursome. And through the music we still talked to those who understood the themes of earlier days: "They were in person, as their songs and stories are: gentle, peaceful, full of love, concerned about living and understanding life and all that is around them," the critic wrote, "Most of all, they came to Detroit with a message:… learn, create, try all types of music, not 'scholarly' to 'broaden your knowledge' but to feel and know more; more music, sounds, human experience."

Facing the void alone, Robin and Mike would have lost heart, in these venues bigger and emptier than the Scottish clubs where they began their musical careers. Licorice and I filled up the space of the stage and gave the band a family look, like Country and Western singers or down-home folk groups. As we moved round, we made the little comments and smiles that kept us all amused and encouraged. Self-contained and self-reinforcing, we were rarely despondent or demoralised.

Big university gigs were better publicised, to an audience with some frame of reference for the foreign hippies. At Princeton: "Barefoot, wearing shoulder-length hair, dressed in embroidered vests and peasant dresses, they look simultaneously like a 14th century minstrel band and a 21st century family… The Incredible String Band offers a unique musical experience, a celebration of music, myth, poetry and love an invitation to be joyously and completely stoned on the beauties of existence."

Being stoned was a part of the scene that couldn't be acknowledged. The students, more and more middle-class people, from conventional or prosperous backgrounds, were taking to the hippie lifestyle. And as they rejected convention and misused various drugs, the casualties were also becoming obvious.

Lost souls and lost youth: Stones in the Park

Back in London, Joe took us all to the Stones in the Park concert of July 1969, a tribute to their dead colleague Brian Jones. Joe, Mike and Robin greeted friends, but us girls were not always included in the welcoming waves back. Our insignificance was liberating. We didn't have to fulfil expectations, or to be pleasant to boring people. If there was a reason, we could choose to assert our presence, or just gaze blankly and slip away, when some fat, pompous journalist, sweating in the afternoon sun, offended our eyes and noses.

Mike wanted to talk to Roy Harper. We were keen to see the Rolling Stones, genuinely regretting their recent loss. In photographs Brian Jones had always looked like a rebellious sixth-former, more often sullen than cheerful. We all had friends like that. A shadow was on our minds: "It could have been me." It seemed right to mourn his passing, even if we didn't know him.

In the stage area, friendly Hells Angels had taken on crowd-control. It was still early in the afternoon and the prevailing mood was cheerful, despite their studs and knuckle-dusters. We felt protected as they repelled would-be invaders. One or two girls got through their cordons, but that was only to be expected. Grappling a semi-clad girl and carrying her off was a bouncer's perk.

When Mick Jagger came on stage in his white little-girl dress we made no particular comment. The colour seemed appropriate, a ritual mourning for a lost and outrageous youth. Besides, we were busily demonstrating our cool imperturbability, in public as in private. Attacks on convention were met with indifference. Swirling and dipping, his skirts only emphasised the masculinity of his stamps, to the beat of 'Jumpin' Jack Flash'. This play on gender was aggressive and overt, the opposite of Mike and Robin's ventures into blouses, frills and beads.

Echoing the flutter of Jagger's skirts, clouds of white butterflies were set free. Those of us close enough saw that many of them had already died in airless captivity, and the sad white little scraps of death littered the ground. Soon those who survived would devastate any cabbage-patch or window-box within several miles of the Park. The symbolism of souls freed from earthly bonds became one of destruction and corruption.

Mike and Robin both preferred simple songs of lost love and mournful death. Their acknowledgments of hopes deceived and far-away innocence were clean and honest. This flight of half-dead butterflies was like the heavy putrid smell of decaying Arum lilies. Violence ran below the surface of the Hells Angels' friendly stewardship. The unnerving clash of sweet dress and erotic dancing, and the finale of 'Sympathy for the Devil' made a bizarre memorial for Brian, but maybe an appropriate one also.

While not insensitive, we were in holiday mood. It was a sunny day, a concert that everyone wanted to be at, the Stones were rocking and we were in the front rows. I was never even sure that Robin and Licorice enjoyed rock bands. Mike and I liked to stand near the speakers and feel the vibration, but they tended to fade into the background, or stroll away. Joe had also wandered off to talk to people.

He came back in great excitement to tell us the event was being recorded. "Video" was a new filming technique that could be played back straightaway, and we were invited to a showing after the concert. We stuck it out through King Crimson's seemingly endless set then left. Walking with Joe through the city, we were like recalcitrant children on a school outing dawdling behind the purposeful teacher.

When we settled in a hotel viewing room with others, equally inquisitive, we were amazed. The images were a bit uncertain and the syncing of sound and picture not perfect. But despite its imperfections, we recognised that it was a clear and instant recording, as we had been promised. Talking about it afterwards rang alarm bells, but also the promise of new possibilities.

By making filming more casual, video suited ISB's spontaneity and playfulness. But instant replay also meant little editing, and Mike and Robin could be very obstinate. When we heard that Hoppy Hopkins

'U' at the Roundhouse, Licorice, Rakis and Robin, 1970

wanted to video *U, a Mystical Pantomime* at the Roundhouse in 1970, they were both enthusiastic. The result was a mixed blessing. Where live performances had been received with rapturous applause in London, the video showed up the show's weaknesses. But Mike and Robin were now so entirely committed to their own ideas of music and performance that criticism was met with indifference and withdrawal.

There was a particularly British acceptance of post-war "make do and mend", along with a delight in the home-made and the amateur. This had merged into counter-cultural rebellion in the UK, but abroad met a more frigid response. In the US at the time, and to later audiences accustomed to high levels of technical and financial investment, the amateur levels of presentation and performance in ISB's multi-media productions are incomprehensible. Fragile moments of beauty seem lost in a welter of uncertainty. That first night after the Stones gig, the video of future performances was what Mike and Robin talked about. What would it be like when our performing mixture of superb expertise, hopeless incompetence and genuine fun was frozen into a form over which we had no control – to be played again when performers and the world had changed? We never intended that degree of scrutiny, or chose to concern ourselves much with what others thought. Joe never acted as controlling manager of the band's legacy.

Woodstock: an Aquarian Dawn?

August 1969

Festival time in the US and the Woodstock Festival of Peace, Love and Music should have been a launch pad for a glittering if unusual career, perhaps even our finest hour. It is not. We tour through September and meet Crosby, Stills, Nash and Young at the Big Sur Festival.

◆

As one of the few women who can still say "I played at Woodstock", my vivid memories are those of living it, and the immediate impressions of a physical experience still seared on the mind. To have been on-stage is to have been at the centre of something iconic. For ISB, it is also the "if only" used to explain our failure to make an enduring name, and the fortunes that go with this.

Yet at the time it was just an interesting-sounding Friday evening gig conveniently slotting into the tour. For all their lasting effects on subsequent careers, the decisions made during those 24 hours were simply part of the way that the ISB worked. It was our bad luck that, for once, they really mattered.

We were scheduled to play the first evening, with a late-night gig the following day, at a folk festival at the Singer Bowl Stadium, Flushing Meadow Park, NY. Upstate to Woodstock then coming back to the Chelsea was not a long drive. The first indication something out of the ordinary was afoot came from our tour manager, Walter Gundy. He had been surprised when the freight handlers at Kennedy airport shouted, "Right on man, we'll see you there," when he told them where we were heading.

"You mean you're gonna drive a hundred miles to see a concert?" he asked.

"Hell YES, gotta make love not war, brother; gonna cop us some hippie chicks, smoke dope and dig Hendrix ALL night long."

Joe had decided to drive with us, hoping to dash back to town very late that night, but we were still far away from the site when the traffic hold-ups began. At every junction, more cars joined the river of people heading in the same direction, every type of vehicle and mode of transport we had ever seen. There were VW surfer-vans painted with bright flowers and peace-and-love slogans, open-topped sports models driven by preppy girls and boys with shiny hair, battered retro roadsters with excited young faces under ancient Stetsons, and one old lorry with children looking out of open packing-cases tied on the back.

Soon every lane was grinding to a halt in the sun.

Bikers with Hells Angels Chapters on the back of their leathers wove between students in college T shirts and hippie couples strolling hand in hand along the roadside. Some tried hitching lifts, but the cars were crawling no faster than the walkers.

At first, we were just curious. It wasn't our problem. On tour we were portable property. Our responsibility started when the stage lights went up and ended with the applause. But time was passing and tensions were rising. There were raised voices and occasional angry outbursts when some small accident frayed tempers. Most people waved and laughed when Walter told them that we were on-stage soon, as he tried to manoeuvre through the vehicles blocking our way. But rumours started to fly back from the festival site and even Joe looked worried.

It was impossible to know how many people were on the road and what would happen when they all finally reached Yasgur's Farm. We were unusually subdued. Three o'clock came, check-in time, but we were still stuck. We saw a motel with a paper sign saying Festival Headquarters. Relieved, Joe told Walter to go in and find out the latest news. Cowboy boots and all, Walter waded a ditch and entered a lobby full of roadies, musicians and managers.

When he came back, he called Joe out of the car "to show him something", so they could talk without us hearing. Bobby Neuwirth, one of Dylan's "travelling companions", had advised him to give up and join the party in the motel: "A million more people than expected are streaming in. Lay back and let the promoters deal with it." Neuwirth was a party animal, but Joe and Walter took matters more seriously. We were all beginning to worry what was awaiting us when we got there. We were not heroic, and it occurred to all of us that it might be better if we never reached the festival. Certainly it would feel safer out of the crushing tide of people.

Some families were setting up impromptu camps wherever they could find space. Others were trying to turn vehicles round and go back but that was equally impossible.

By the time we arrived on the outskirts of the event itself, Walter had arranged for a helicopter to fly us into the backstage area. We took some of our equipment with us and Walter drove the rest in the car, slowly, very slowly. In the performer's area we had the luxury of space to breathe, with picnic benches and plastic cups. But it was not looking good. We had escaped the bedlam, but there was little order here. And we were small fry.

Staff at US festivals always seemed so cool and laid back, drawling "OK man" and "Sure, no problems." Now nobody would stand still long enough to talk to us. The main promoter was riding around on his off-road motorcycle but had nothing useful to say when Joe grabbed him. Like air crew on a crashing plane, everyone had general reassurance but no real information. The general suppressed nervousness was clear, as well as disconcerting. We felt increasingly helpless.

Joe couldn't tell us where our instruments could be kept safe in the melee, when we would eat or how we could get out of there. As for playing a set at some point, that was far over our horizon of concern. We found a place to sit and wait, talking to each other as if it were a minor delay at the airport. The obvious magnitude of the problems facing those dealing with the pandemonium went unmentioned. Robin was cross that no meal was available, Licorice withdrew into silence, Mike deflected his annoyance onto Joe in quiet grumbles.

We were all grumpy now, and also hungry. We were unimpressed by the return to the land which seemed to be happening out front. We were protected in the backstage area, but also cut off and dependent on hearsay and rumour. The stage crews were desperately running around rigging the stage for an evening show. Luckily champagne and strawberries seemed to be available in unlimited supply, easing the mood for all of us. Robin liked to meet new people and before night fell he was getting very sociable.

I was daring enough to climb the stage rigging, to get as high as possible. The view was difficult to understand. All over the fields and hills, up to the visible horizon, temporary dwellings were springing up. tepees thrown together from branches and sheets of plastic, tents made of blankets strung over ropes, even the odd small geodesic dome. I asked a passing rigger what was happening about the evening programme, but he just muttered. "Dunno, nothing to do with me man." I asked him if there was going to be any food anytime. "Get someone to go outside, we've only got soda and chips," was his surly reply.

Like Joe, those managing the festival had all become less hippie and more forceful. No room for English reticence when so much had to get done so quickly to save the day.

Marooned at Woodstock, August 1969. Image © Henry Diltz.

'By the time we got to Woodstock we were half a million strong'

In the huge natural bowl in front of the stage, a vast audience had collected. They sat on the ground or stood around talking, smoking, forming little knots of people then drifting apart. They too were trying to get comfortable, and to work out what to do next. Soon they wrapped themselves in blankets and warmer clothing, if they could find any. Many had been there a while. Afternoon was turning to evening and it was getting colder. We couldn't imagine the numbers. It seemed important to know, a fact in a world of uncertainty. Audience size defined success.

Mike grabbed another member of the stage crew and asked. "There's half a million of them out there already and God knows how many on the road," he replied. We could believe it.

We were billed to play after Melanie, as part of an evening of gentle, thoughtful music. We still had hopes of escape afterwards, but Joe was beginning to hint that we wouldn't be able to get off the site. This couldn't be true. None of us strayed too far away from our picnic table, in case we missed a chance at freedom. It reminded us of food and home, and we clung to it like flotsam in a shipwreck.

Licorice was wandering around nearby, seeking out any comforts available from other sources. Mike was more concerned with the amplification for his guitar, given the makeshift stage electrics, set up in a hurry. If we couldn't get away, if the festival was indeed going to happen, then we were going to have to play. And rain was threatening.

We knew well enough about people being electrocuted on-stage by faulty equipment. Childhood horror stories had impressed upon us that water and electricity were a fatal combination, we were all afraid. Mike was unwilling to take the risk, and kept telling us that Joe needed to be impressed by this priority, as if we could do anything about it. Every time Joe re-appeared, Mike told him again. We shouldn't even think of performing as planned, he said, without cast-iron guarantees that everything was earthed and there were no live wires around. "Look, it's like a madhouse around here. God only knows what's being wired to what."

Robin was now disinclined to rouse himself. He had put aside all thoughts of having to play, so any good reason would do to put it off. We all agreed that the best thing would be to get away from this bedlam. We'd had no chance to speak to anyone else supposed to be playing that evening, so we had no idea what they were thinking.

We were too preoccupied with our own problems to concern ourselves much with the greater spaces beyond our corner. We were still concerned for the safety of our instruments. We relied on them being laid out properly, with all the cloths, keys and impedimenta that we needed to make ourselves at home on-stage and keep things in tune. There didn't seem much chance of that.

We were told the sound-systems were doubtful, and as night began to fall the noise from the audience seemed even louder. Lighting rigs appeared unfinished and we were convinced we would be invisible as well as inaudible. We would never hear or even see ourselves clearly in the darkness of the stage. This wouldn't do. We needed to be able to glance at each other and chat as we moved between songs, or even within them. What made us different, as some American critic had said, was the "English drawing-room atmosphere."

At best our set would now start late, and the air was getting damp. Tuning the instruments would be difficult, if we could even find them. Mike was convinced that amplification could not be safely used, and reluctantly, Joe finally agreed.

If we had understood the importance of the event we could have played an acoustic set. Certainly Joe had some idea of the festival's importance by then. When challenged by Production Coordinator John Morris, who asked him to get Mike and Robin on-stage as an acoustic folk duo, playing old songs, Joe was doubtful. It had been a long time since they had played like that, he said, their songs were quite different now, depending on richer and electric instrumentation. And then there were the girls, and he stood up for us.

In the *Re-tying the Knot* TV documentary Joe says that he suggested the acoustic set. Had that happened, Licorice and I knew the old material well enough to sit around, join in on choruses and look happy with tambourine, finger cymbals, fiddle or drums. But the outcome would have been unpredictable and possibly disastrous, as Joe well knew. Perhaps this is why (as backstage recordings at Woodstock confirm), it was Joe who asked, "What about the girls?" Robin says he is willing to play the acoustic set. Mike says nothing. Joe swings the balance, recognising that we girls were by then central to the ISB performance. If Mike and Robin charmed audiences through musicianship, looks and personality, we completed the picture, reinforcing their chat and jokes with our smiles.

Amongst ourselves, we had no sense of being called upon to respond to a challenge. We were cross with the world and unwilling to make inconvenient and unprepared adjustments to our programme. By then Joe was no more cheerful and dynamic than we were. An acoustic set would require a good spirit from all of us. No one had the positive energy to get us out onto that wet stage with dodgy electrics and instruments that wouldn't stay in tune.

Worst of all, we now realised that we were not getting away that night, which was an unthinkable disaster. Even getting from the stage area to the edge of the audience was a major expedition on foot. "It can't be that bad," we told each other, but Joe insisted there was no transport to get us anywhere. Roads were now even more hopelessly blocked. Someone said even New York was now feeling the pressure, but this had to be ridiculous.

We missed the exhilaration spreading through the audience as they realised what was happening around them, and that they were part of something going down in history. Opening the festival, Sri Swami Satchidananda had told them they were the "entire youth of America" and that "Music is a celestial sound and it is the sound that controls the whole universe, not atomic vibrations." He ended by asking the whole huge audience to join him chanting Hare Krishna, consecrating the festival's celebrations. All America, they now knew, was watching them, and maybe the world.

We were too disgruntled to take much notice. We were British, when all was said and done, and hype was easy to ignore.

Yet the sentiments of these hours of Woodstock were those ISB had always celebrated. How we looked, the stage-presentation, our instruments, the songs Mike and Robin wrote and sang – it all perfectly illustrated the Swami's message. Had we played soon after he spoke, this twilight crowd would have heard their youthful utopia sung back to them, as they watched through a haze of marijuana and good-fellowship. We sang about myths and legends. Robin and Mike had both created some of their own. This audience was looking around at themselves, knowing they were part of a legend too. This great gathering of the tribes of hippiedom would become a mythic event.

Disaster zone

By the time Joan Baez was on stage dusk had fallen. The audience was lit by faint lamps, torches and candle flames. Flower-wreathed heads had disappeared under blankets and waterproofs. The rain had started to fall, and people moved towards the woods for some shelter. John Morris gave warnings from the stage: "The rain's a hassle. There is a problem that can get a little heavy. We're all here and there are more people who have joined us, more people than any of us ever thought were possible… There are water pipes not buried terribly deeply… Please be careful of those pipes, they are our water supply, yours and mine."

The fragility of the life-support system was already clear from announcements about supplies of insulin, ailing family members and lost children. Even taking to the woods for the night, for primitive shelter, demanded guidance, as John continued: "It's getting fairly heavy. Those of you who decide to move up into the woods, please do so slowly. Please don't go back. Let's move slowly to the side. Remember there are people there. We'll take our time."

We knew the problems of the now-drenched crowd were ours too, if things got worse and goodwill was lost in fear and panic, as John explained, in no uncertain terms: "More people than any of us ever thought were possible" had found their way to Woodstock, he said. "We all have to make some kind of plans for ourselves. It's a free concert from now on."

There was a smattering of applause, but the mood was reflective. Still, his slightly parental tone was reassuring: "That doesn't mean that anything goes… What it means is that the people who are backing this thing, who put up the money for it are going to take a bit of a bath, a big bath. That's no hype, that's truth. They're going to get hurt. What it means is, these people who put this thing here have it in their heads, and it's worth being grateful for, that your welfare and their welfare is a helluva lot more important, and the music is, than a dollar."

This was language we understood. It sounded real and cool when he continued: "Now let's face the situation. We've had thousands and thousands of people come here today many, many more than we knew or dreamt or thought could be possible. We're going to need each other, to help each other to work this out because we're taxing the systems we've set up… The one major thing you have to remember tonight… is that the man next to you is your brother and you damn well better treat him that way because if you don't then we blow the whole thing."

The ground was now wet, but we all knew that a bad cold was the least of our risks. Still, the Swami's blessing hung over the field like a dove of peace. Candles were held high and waved with the flow of the music, when Baez lulled us with well known songs and shared emotions. The feeling of togetherness that would mark the whole festival was beginning to establish itself, peacefully working through mutual discomforts as one.

Those out front knew to stick together and help each other through cold, wet and hunger, and they did it. People divided what they had with others, which was often very little. It was the Sermon on the Mount without loaves and fishes, but the people were showing that they didn't need a Messiah to be good to each other.

We were too concerned about the rest of the evening to relax or to respond with admiration or generosity. We were wondering uneasily about the performance we had now definitely refused. *This is all fine*, said our tone, *if you like a pow-wow round a campfire in the rain*. But none of us had ever joined the Scouts, or volunteered to join a peace-movement protest. Nor were we about to start. We used different words, but our expressions conveyed our thoughts to one another well.

Joe had now been away for some time and we felt cut off from the rest of the world, oppressed by crowds and aware there were no contingency plans to deal with this level of disruption, not for us, not for anyone. In the dark and rain, it felt desolate and far from any kind of comfort.

When Joe came back it was not good news. We were going to have to perform the next day at five, get a helicopter ride to Monticello airport right after our set, then be flown straight to La Guardia. It sounded grim but that was tomorrow. We still had today to get through.

We were past caring what we ate by now, as long as something turned up. Joe made sure we didn't starve, promised we'd be taken to safety at the earliest opportunity. The audience was not so lucky, but we didn't think of them. They too were stranded, without the dimmest hope of a next meal or ever being dry again. There must have been innumerable crises, with errant children or spouses unable to get home to cover their tracks, personal medication running low and pregnant women worried about their babies.

Many festival-goers had been on protest marches against the war. There was real suffering in Vietnam, but this was just a fun weekend of peace, love and music. Until with no warning they found themselves in what was now said to be an official disaster zone. They knew to expect very little sympathy. We were used to being unpopular with straight people.

Now that we saw how many people had turned up, we understood why locals had feared for their peaceful, tidy homes.

Walter returned looking drawn and shaken after a foray into the chaos, which frightened us even more. His roadie-cool cracked as he told of a near-accident that would have ended the festival in death and destruction, killing him and some of the stars, perhaps even us.

National Guard helicopters were landing and taking off non-stop near the stage area, trying to deliver and rescue personnel and survival essentials. As one approached, lights had suddenly blazed from the stage, blinding the pilot. Walter could see that he was flying directly toward a rope of cables stretched between the stage and a power pylon. "Thank God the cue was brief," he said. The lights had dimmed in time for the pilot to see the wires. Maybe he had perfected instant responses learned in Vietnam. He flung the helicopter upwards and averted disaster.

There were also rumours of disease in the mud, with a fair risk of illness and infection spreading in the cold and wet. There was no way, it seemed, that a bunch of hippies could cope with running this great encampment of people with all access to the outside world cut off.

We weren't afraid all the time. The novelty was also exciting, but we felt as if we were walking on very thin ice. What we really wanted was someone to convince us it was all going to be alright, for everyone. All the music and dancing seemed a bit like fiddling while Rome burned. But if these hippie organisers – who looked and talked like us – could pull it off and the festival could be made to work, against the odds, then the hippie ideal would be proved right.

We had plenty of time to think about all this, as we sat waiting through the long hours with nothing to do and nowhere to go.

At some point, John Sebastian of Lovin' Spoonful emerged from the hectic turmoil around the stage, took up his acoustic guitar, walked across to the lonely chair in front of the mics, and played. It seemed to happen by chance almost, as if someone had just asked him to while away a few minutes while they got organised. He had no backing, stage lighting or visual effects. Just a quiet man with a quiet guitar, talking and singing as if we were all friends safe and happy together. Along with thousands in the audience, we were soothed and carried beyond ourselves by the music.

It felt like a triumph of the lifestyle we all pretended to, immediate and very peaceful. In those minutes he made us believe in all the good things we hoped for, and that we had been singing about, bringing out the best in us for a while. The systems of the known world had disintegrated into a vast sea of mud, but his voice was something to cling to.

It was a time to create new folk tales and make songs and sagas to tell of great deeds. Some were discovering strengths they never knew they had. Others were facing the demons of their black night, but they had new friends to help them through.

There were meant to be security guards in red jackets, many of them New York policemen earning extra money moonlighting. But I didn't see any, and there was clearly no intention any longer of enforcing state laws. With so many people in difficult straits and unable to escape, the only safe way was to avoid grounds for conflict.

The smell of marijuana was everywhere, as people shared joints and pipes. Some slept where they sat, in front of the stage, in order not to lose their place for the next day.

In the mysterious way things happened for us, we found ourselves shepherded into a tent late at night along with others, nobody I really knew. Joe's care for his band didn't extend to keeping us warm through that night. It was only a day-in-the-garden tent and the rain came through. I never knew who was lying alongside me and didn't care enough to look. We had no waterproofs, sleeping bags or even coats, just a few covers Joe had cadged.

It was a miserable night and a lonely one. We each withdrew into gloomy silence, our way in most adversities. Licorice had the best of it, sharing John Sebastian's goodwill. Later, Walter shared a pipe with him, trying to get warm and get some sleep in a borrowed car. I just kept my head down, hoping to doze and waiting for the morning light to tell me the night was over.

A new dawn

There was no romance about that daybreak. It rained again during the night, and the sun rose on a churned-up morass, even in the comparative luxury of the stage area. Dazed mud-covered figures staggered around the rest of Yasgur's Farm, which looked like a film of the trenches in World War One. With no immediate prospect of salvation, Mike and I wandered off. We knew Joe would need to find us at some point, but we had lost faith in his promises. We were still planning to leave, disconsolately looking for escape routes rather than building a new social order.

Gleeful shouts and splashings attracted us to a pool surrounded by low banks and reeds. We stripped off and joined in, sliding down the banks into the water and fooling about with the early morning skinny-dippers. If anyone recognized us they never said, and we were only too glad about it. The sense of being cut off and abandoned disappeared for a while. We were part of the crowd, brothers and sisters together, as John Morris had told us to be the day before.

But we had work to do, sooner or later. As we walked back, drying out in the sun, reinvigorated and regaining hope, we saw the Hog Farm commune cooking vats of food with such cheerful intent that it looked like they could feed the world. Miracles were happening. A new social order was forming in front of our eyes.

Despite the optimism and the busy activity we were still a bit afraid, knowing things could still go seriously wrong. There was no escape, and the field was awash with unknown drugs, where from nobody knew. A minor incident might well erupt into violence. We trusted this mass of people who looked like us, but the worry hung in the air.

We saw small incidents of rage as we walked around. A boy in jeans and caftan came back to his patch to find a bag was not where he had left it. He blamed the neighbour, and a small group gathered: "Cool it man." A girl was panicking and they said it was the drugs. Her friend was found and wrapped a poncho around her, cuddling her until the sobbing got quieter.

We wanted to go home, not queue for a bowl of rice and a veggie burger in solidarity.

It was not our finest hour. Joe had arranged a helicopter-ride and as it landed, with rotor blades still turning, we ran to it. We knew how from the movies. We were determined to get on, no matter what. It was amazing how fierce and fearless we gentle people could be when it came to it. We threw ourselves into the hold area. Licorice was struggling to hold onto her scarves and skirts, and Robin did lean out to pull her in. I think I'd left mine behind in the morass.

There were no seats. The helicopter was not personnel transport, and we never discovered its normal purpose. Perhaps a crop-sprayer, we didn't care. It could get us out of there. We swung upwards and across the site, staring down over the whole of Yasgur's Farm, only then realising how gigantic the festival had become. And it was still growing. The landscape was covered with people, its colours changed from green to mud-brown and rags of rainbow.

In a few minutes we arrived back at the "Festival Headquarters". Our joy at seeing this bland motel with its dingy coffee shop was extreme. One day and night had been a serious shock to the system.

Here in this unlikely place were all the stars of world pop music, collected on the far outside edge of the battlefield. None of the euphoria could be felt here, and rumours of riot and plague felt worse. Managers and roadies worried about groups, equipment, personal safety and financial loss.

We were not about to volunteer to return. We had missed our set through no fault of our own, we said. The stage was unsafe, we needn't put ourselves or our instruments back in the danger-zone. Joe was saying we should go back but we were not prepared to listen. He had got us into that mess and the least he could do was to get us out of it.

The Who were also in the room, waiting for something to happen. Most musicians were keeping out of the way, grabbing a rest or a smoke while their managers made decisions. Pete Townshend was wearing his white boiler suit, immaculate and stark against all the jeans and coloured clothes. As the arguments rose he became our Henry V rallying the troops. It wasn't quite Shakespeare, but the speech worked the same. In other words this was our St Crispin's Day, and we owed it to the kids to get back and do what we could.

He shamed us into it. The masses had been sitting for a day in a swamp, and we had to face them and perform. Once The Who had decided to brave the difficulties, the rest of us followed. Pete's charisma convinced the waverers.

We were fussier this time about the helicopter's air-worthiness, less eager to race out to it, but we were flown back and dropped off. The airlift continued as we changed into stage clothes on the scaffold-rigging. With so many naked bodies around it didn't matter.

Myth-making

ISB still had no idea that the Festival was the most important gig they would ever play, an event which could have gained them an international following way beyond that of 'an English cult-band'. We didn't much mind playing after a rocking Keef Hartley Band to an audience buzzing with frenetic energy, as long as we got it over and got away. We were still uneasy, haunted by the fears of the previous night. Luckily, we weren't watching while Walter Gundy set up our equipment. The stage was still soaked. Plugging a cable into an amp, an electric shock knocked him off his feet and he slid on the puddle that had grounded him.

Our performance was further postponed while the Lighting Director, the megalomaniacal Chip Monck, wearing his disgracefully genuine lion-skin cape, gave one of his public service updates over the PA. "Hey folks, do not take the brown acid; do NOT take the brown acid, it's a real bummer."

The interruption improved no one's mood. Robin and Licorice, crusading drug-abstainers at that point, looked out at the audience with disapproval.

Our mood was discordant and Joe's querying our choice of songs didn't help. In most group decisions we were unimpressed by reason. Naïve, uncalculating and uncompromising, we rarely reached group agreement but instead went along with the most determined voice. So we carried on as usual, refusing to change our set-list or adapt our performance style to suit circumstances. On that day of insecurities, familiar, comforting songs might have been better for us as well as the audience. Even for me, Mike's latest songs lacked the easy attractions of earlier ones, those idiosyncratic tales of hedgehogs or amoebas which had woven their meanings into our lives. That day, as always, Mike and Robin wanted to play their most recent compositions, even ones not yet recorded. Robin and Licorice were both thoroughly committed to Scientology and determined to spread its doctrines in at least one song. We usually overcame personal disagreements in the highs of performing in front of an enthusiastic audience but on that day this wasn't so easy. When we got the nod, Robin stalked on-stage looking detached and indifferent. Licorice gazed blankly at the crowds and even Mike failed to reach out with his usual all-embracing smile.

It was disconcerting to walk into the bare bones of our normal playing area. All the vivid colour and softness, the gleams from mirrored textiles or shining strings, the patches of colour where stage lights caught the mics or made pools of brilliance on the floor, none of this welcomed us. Stage crew were working all around, we had no performance space to make our own, and none of the usual homey atmosphere. I felt like a doubtful guest rather than a welcoming host.

Robin started the set with his poem 'Invocation', calling upon fellow nature spirits to join his song. In the dark space of an auditorium, this could create an intense atmosphere of magic and mystery. I loved the words, which at their best cast a spell which transported us all, band and audience, from the everyday world outside into the enchanted space of music and theatre. But on that day, in daylight, with roadies, stacks of amps, lights and scaffold draped with heavy cable all around, his serious voice and expression sounded irrelevant, pretentious and boring. One verse would have been enough but compromise was not his way.

Mike's song 'The Letter' was more good-natured and up-beat, a typical ISB crowd-pleaser and reasonably well-received. Everyone could imagine that "*Maria from Illinois*" might be one of those strangers beside them. I wondered, as always, what Maria had written in her letter and if she and Mike had met yet, or ever would. That wasn't important. The song reminded me of waking up to a quiet day with Mike back in Scotland and the rare excitement of the postman arriving. On that day of all days I hoped Maria would hear her song.

Unimpressed, Robin and Licorice played their accompaniments, Robin's piano line was more random than usual and Licorice's drumming dutiful rather than lively. But her sideward smile when Mike got the lyrics wrong was sweet. His mistake revealed a hidden tension, obvious to anyone who knew our usual laid-back shows. There was none of the usual flow of sympathy and friendship back and forth over the footlights, and we made no attempt to break the impasse.

With its images of the eternal pilgrim seeking the truths of the universe, Robin's 'Gather Round', just sounded feeble on this day of screaming guitars, while the charm and light humour of Mike's 'This Moment' was lost in repetition, too long-winded for an impatient audience.

The audience wanted to carry on rocking and we wanted to escape as soon as possible, but our instruments were damp and tuning was hell, as Robin told the crowd. They were restive, especially when we wouldn't respond to requests for old songs. Instead we played stuff that hadn't been recorded yet. Mike did apologise for this refusal: "It's nice for us to play them and we hope you don't mind that." But he sounded strained and his voice lacked conviction.

Even Robin was unusually hesitant and awed when he said, "I've never been to anything like this before and the thing that surprises me is how many of us there are. It makes me fantastically happy, I'd just like to say that."

Out there was a whole world of hippies, waiting for a rock band. If they were bored with the songs, so was I. I suspected that Mike too would rather be among them than up here as resident mystic. To be there, to be one of that huge crowd, feeling that a new world was hatching, was a reason to be joyful, and I wanted people to know I felt it when I stood up and looked out at them, trying to embrace the thousands in a wave.

The set finally wandered into the interminable drone of 'When You Find Out Who You Are', with its labyrinthine preaching of Scientology and Robin's endless reiterations for doubters. Mike mostly kept his head down, concentrating on the piano, hardly looking towards the audience. Then Robin's "We have to go now" was a strangely abrupt ending to an uncomfortable set. The applause was feeble.

The best, most valid excuse for our failure to entertain the audience was that the tone for the day had been set by the greater volume and energy of rock bands. The audience needed strong stimuli to take their minds off their other problems. Waves of euphoria had rippled over the field when Jimi Hendrix played. Communal ecstasies of rhythm and movement and the exhilaration of massive numbers in harmony together carried everyone along. Bands that could reach out and make themselves one with that had a unique and wonderful time. We were too quiet, too self-absorbed and we lost our chance. But we had also seen it all with our own eyes and been part of it.

Back to the old world

Our mood when we left the field was very different. The helicopter shuttle was now a service more than a mission and it landed on the small area near the stage. Volunteer medics who'd just worked 24 hours straight were first in the queue, then us. "This'll be the last one," the pilot's mate said, "we haven't been paid…" We all threw ourselves in but Lic was elbowed out of the way by a leather-clad rocker, took offence and refused to board. Robin jumped down beside her, then Walter. As Joe, Mike and I lifted off for the nearest air-strip, they were left standing below.

Another babble and confusion, then Joe crammed Mike and I into a tiny plane which he had found from somewhere. It felt very claustrophobic as we sat bent heads crushed against the ceiling. We had to leave the road cases behind.

It was a clear dark night and swooping in over the brash lights of New York City was a glorious relief from the fear of the previous hours. When we touched down at La Guardia a van was waiting to take us to the venue, its driver desperate to know about what we'd left behind. "Half the band and much of its equipment," we said. Now he felt part of the excitement too and the evening programme fell apart until Joe decided that Mike and I could fill the space. Robin, Lic and Walter arrived just before we had to play. We didn't have time to talk as we were scrambling into our now rather grubby stage clothes.

Walter had found someone with a flat-bed truck willing to drive the three of them off the field over a forest-trail. Another chartered plane and there they were. When journalists asked how it had been we were non-committal. It was too soon. There was a new mass of faces in front of us and another set to play. We too were curious to know what had happened and what was still happening out there in the countryside.

This new audience was made up of teenagers whose parents wouldn't let them go to Woodstock. They felt they had missed out on an epochal event, with their Flushing Meadows concert a limp compromise. But our Woodstock-related delay turned their night into an adventure, as Mike described what was happening upstate as Joe and the stagehands set up the gear round him. The young audience was delighted. Now they were connected to history.

The Woodstock event was now the focus of all news, raising serious political comment as well as media excitement. Joe pointed out some of the more negative aspects and marched us off next day to a clinic in the city for a dose of gamma globulin: "Just in case you've picked up anything nasty on that field of mud." We remembered the jolly pool we'd played in, the water and the reeds.

We had little idea whether gamma globulin was a necessary or an appropriate measure to take. I was attracted by its name, which suggested some fat drop of magic rays. But it was more from superstition than conviction that we took it. It had no effects that we noticed and we didn't get ill. As the media frenzy continued, we began to realise that we had disregarded the festival of the century. Today Joe admits that his failure to encourage us to play that wet evening was one of his major career mistakes.

The festivals after Woodstock absorbed its success and its compromises. At the Texas Folk Festival the Chief of Police in his official uniform brought salt tablets round in person, urging us to take them because the day was going to get hotter and we weren't used to it. He made sure we had all the water we could need, telling the crew to make sure we drank it, a fatherly gesture of goodwill.

Perhaps he had a child who wanted to flout Texan convention and wear coloured flares. Many young people in our audiences escaped from behind respectable white picket fences to see us. In their Indian shirts and beads they braved parental disapproval and neighbourly outrage. Although we understood for ourselves what it meant to choose peaceful rebellion, we had little thought for those to whom every day brought such confrontations.

TOP: Rose climbing at Roman Camps. BOTTOM: Rose on tour, 1968.

TOP: Mike playing the guitar. BOTTOM: Christmas at Roman Camps, 1968. OPPOSITE PAGE
TOP: Robin with Puppies, 1968. OPPOSITE PAGE BOTTOM: Roman Camps, sunrise.

TOP: View from the window of the Chelsea Hotel, 1968. BOTTOM: Mike, New York, 1968/9.
OPPOSITE PAGE TOP: East 23rd Street 1968, Sister visits us on tour, from left, Robin, Licorice,
Rose, Mike and Sister. OPPOSITE PAGE BOTTOM: Sister comes with us to the gig, from left,
Licorice, a fan, Rose and Sister.

TOP: Mike, waiting, just waiting – Chelsea Hotel; reading 'High Priest', Timothy Leary's psychedelic autobiography, 1968/9. BOTTOM: From left, Licorice, Robin and Mike, New York, after seeing the 'Easy Rider' film, 1969. OPPOSITE PAGE TOP: Mike, serviced flats and flights of fancy, on tour, 1969. OPPOSITE PAGE BOTTOM: Robin, Licorice and fans.

OPPOSITE PAGE TOP: Duel on the dodgems, Mike at the wheel. OPPOSITE PAGE BOTTOM: All the fun of the fair – Rose with ice cream. THIS PAGE TOP: Mike and Robin meet a fan – polite acknowledgements. THIS PAGE BOTTOM LEFT: Robin and Mike. THIS PAGE BOTTOM RIGHT: Mike.

TOP: Motel lobby, Rose, Maria Muldaur and a fan, Robin dancing in the background, 1968/9.
BOTTOM LEFT: Mike and Sitar. BOTTOM RIGHT: Mike and Robin in radio studio, US, 1969.
OPPOSITE PAGE TOP: Outside the Scientology office, Tottenham Court Road, 1969. OPPOSITE
BOTTOM LEFT: Wow, a limo!, leaving for the US, 1969 (Rose & Mike in car). OPPOSITE BOTTOM
RIGHT: Licorice getting into a limo outside the Tottenham Court Rd Scientology Office, 1969.

Live at Woodstock, August 1969

Earth, Water, Fire and Air: the fair garden of Glen Row

October 1969 – February 1970

When the US tour ends, we move to Glen Row in Scotland, its cottages now housing ISB and Stone Monkey, as well as many visitors. We write, learn and rehearse Robin's musical-theatre project. Each band-member has a separate cottage, which keeps us close while leaving scope for personal lives outside the group. *Changing Horses* is released in November and we play tracks from it on our long US-Canada tour. In between UK tours to re-establish group finances, *I Looked Up* is recorded at Olympic and Island studios in early 1970.

Jumping Jack Flash

We never worked out how to maintain the balance between the exhilaration of cities, concerts and touring and the quiet peace of our normal rural lives. Life had cast Mike and Robin as psychedelic celebrities while expecting us all to be the simple souls of the Scottish landscape. In America this ambivalent disparity was forced upon us like nowhere else.

I was in awe of the New York star groupies I'd heard stories of, and when I encountered one in a lift, her style, appearance and conversation confirmed what I'd heard. These were not the sad girls who crawled up the ranks of roadies hoping for a chance with the musicians. They were like courtesans at Louis XIV's Versailles, beautiful, intelligent, the most confident and independent of women. So I counted it a personal success when I was taken for one long enough to reach the Rolling Stones in their suite at the Plaza Hotel.

On tour the Rolling Stones lived very differently from us. We flew into New York on the same day in November 1969, but they were scooped up and whisked to a whole floor of the Plaza Hotel near Central Park. We got taxis round to a couple of rooms in the Chelsea. They were playing at Madison Square Gardens, on the bill with Ike and Tina Turner and Big Brother and the Holding Company. We wanted to be there. But at short notice even Joe couldn't find tickets or passes.

We knew where they were staying, so we were already a step ahead. We got a taxi uptown, and as the glitzy social whirl of New York buzzed in and out of the Plaza's lobby, I too went in. I sailed across the foyer in my black velvet dressing gown, pea green sandals and paisley bonnet with purple velvet ribbons, my current travel outfit. By talking nonsense to genuine guests as they walked past security, I made it up to the Stones' floor. Then it was easy.

The Stones knew us. They had tried to sign Mike and Robin to their label in 1967. Passes for the show were found, our welcome assured, and I returned in triumph to the taxi, its meter still running. We laughed together. We had won the game. It was a great evening. Joe appeared too, with none of our difficulties. If he was surprised to see us, he didn't admit it.

Change was taking place around us. Along with a growing audience, the band was rapidly gaining status and prestige, and people were more deferential. Mike and Robin were taking themselves and their success more seriously, and sometimes this showed on-stage as well as off.

A reviewer in Montreal understood our intentions: "Hope and love and beauty… their experience with the wonders of this and any other world." He could discern failings that went beyond the girls, the usual target of a discontented critic, to the whole group: "In a word, it was sloppy. Self-indulgent. They evidently feel a lot of feelings but they betrayed them, in my view, by countless amateurisms. Simply, the singing was pretty awful, whiney, uncontrolled, bereft of any sense of drama, timing and pace… They state the obvious, which is fine in its way, but they do not make it worthwhile hearing because they drown these simple everyday revelations with a posture which dictates, 'Look here, this is the inner light,' or to quote a particularly gushy line, 'I swear you have the power as the angels do'… The Incredible String Band pluck and strain away taking themselves and their thoughts far too seriously to be believed…"

We had plenty to encourage us towards self-importance, including a proper touring crew, if a smallish one. Joe now delegated day-to-day affairs to others, and Mike and Robin began to see him as our record producer, a recording industry employee, rather than as our guide and guardian. Although he turned up to gigs when around, he no longer helped resolve group dissatisfactions.

As we were away from London most of the time, we were no longer familiar visitors to his office. We could no longer drop in to leave our coats or borrow a few pounds. Other artists took up his attention. His personal interests in America were becoming more pressing. Increasingly confident, Mike and Robin didn't miss his presence. They were managing their own success, making the decisions they once happily left to him. Enthusiastic, uncritical audience approval outweighed the measured response of those few who saw problems in the direction the work was going.

Both were also losing the previously stable points in their lives or changing them. Mike was more distanced now from his family and long-term friends, and the names he had once mentioned with interest dropped out of his conversation. Neither expressed regret, but I knew from my own loss of friends from home that new acquaintances did not replace the old.

Neither had ever admitted that financial stability was important to them, or publicly shown any great interest in the money they earned or might earn. As long as Joe gave satisfactory answers to occasional queries and they had their comparatively few immediate wants supplied without difficulty, this had satisfied them. Their lack of concern had allowed Joe to make decisions for them, but it gave them more latitude to reject offered work and to resist managerial pressure.

As we played night after night to full houses in large venues, it now occurred to all that the band must be making money. More people were taking active responsibilities for organising our daily lives, but we were increasingly out of touch with management and its expenditure. This was very convenient when it meant that we could get someone to do odd jobs or run errands, but we hadn't much wanted to be taken to the airport in limousines.

The hotels became bigger and better, the airlines more prestigious and the post-show guests in the restaurants more numerous. All more for the crew's benefit than ours, it seemed to me. "Getting and spending" had never been integral to the band's daily lives, but there was occasional frustration now when Mike or Robin wanted to do something and lacked instant funds. Yet neither were willing to raise the obvious financial questions openly. Indeed their willingness to listen to practical or creative advice seemed to diminish daily. Licorice and I were very definitely on the sidelines of all decisions, and so less affected, but even we occasionally wished to know more about plans for our future and the band's. Fun days together were not as carefree as they had been.

There was no decided rift between the four of us or our management, more a group unease. But minor dissatisfactions were magnified by the arrival of new lovers less interested in band unity. In later times, Susie and Janet took more active management roles. Inevitably, the interests and enthusiasms of the partner dominated their thoughts. Susie supported Mike and Janet Robin and management became a divisive factor. Whichever of us were left out of the dominant partnership at any given time, Mike or Robin as well as Licorice and I, were more doubtful and disturbed by management decisions which affected all our lives. Still we preferred to avoid discussions. To all appearances, things carried on much the same.

In the States we were still staying at the Chelsea but discontent had spread there too. Mike and Robin grumbled about its deficiencies, Robin about its moral tone, as being "sodden with drugs and traumatic lives." I heard him telling Joe that they wanted to stay at another, more civilised hotel in future. He tried to entice Mike towards greater luxury. I knew then the whole ethos of the band was changing, and for the worse.

On one Spring trip to New York, flying into JFK in the early morning we found it was Passover and that this year it had coincided with another holiday. As we drove into town along the quiet freeway the whole town seemed to be closed down. It felt like childhood Sundays, with that foreboding sense of a long gloomy day in which nothing happened and hours passed slowly. In the very centre of New York the street sounds were muted and the tempo deadened. And even the Chelsea had to recognise public holidays. Its lobby was quieter and a deeper drowsiness than ever had descended on the corridors and landings.

We rarely ate in its restaurant. The hotel's general shabbiness didn't augur well for kitchen hygiene and we steered clear. But today we would gratefully have taken the risk as we sat forlornly in the lobby, cross with ourselves and with each other. Visions of eternity and ethereal sounds weren't much good to get us through a long dreary day.

Maybe Joe felt the same because he soon joined us, taking us uptown to a dairy restaurant and lots of cream buns. We may have acted like spoiled children but days like that were genuinely difficult. We were tired, cut off from all the routines of home, with no mental or physical energy to throw ourselves into work and with no healthy diversions. Drugs were one escape and I vividly understood why the Chelsea addiction rate was so high. We were lucky, someone would come along tomorrow to tell us what to do next, to cheer us along and make sure the bills were paid.

Robin pointed out that in a "decent" hotel the day would have been easier, and in late 1969, we abandoned the Chelsea for better things. Interviewing us, Bud Scoppa noticed the difference: "The Fifth Avenue Hotel, just up from Washington Square Park, is flat out baroque and boy Robin Williamson, Mike Heron, Licorice and Rose belong there. Like Hummels on your grandma's knick-knack shelf." Hummels were cutesy kitsch figurines for the most elderly and reactionary mantlepiece. If that's what we had turned into, then our counter-culture credentials were blown for good and all.

As we recorded *Changing Horses*, we had been discussing the idea of ISB living together long-term in some loose communal arrangement. It didn't seem particularly pressing when we were on the move all the time and we had so far done little to resolve the practical problems this presented, even after the miseries of the Penwern experiment.

Home-hunting

Joe felt a London flat might be easier for keeping track of us, arranging for us to view one in Battersea. As a material possession offering some nominal security, the idea appealed to me. Surely we could work out the living arrangements for the time spent there? But the others weren't interested. We walked through rooms as Joe pointed out their advantages, each making claims to the most desirable spaces. Nothing came of the plan.

As Mike and I grew further apart, and the band swallowed our lives, Roman Camps no longer felt like home. One day we left together to go down to London, and I never went back. I left the usual household impedimenta, and also small possessions I treasured – the pearls my father had given me for my 21st birthday, my sewing machine, the green shoes of the *Stones at the Plaza* outing. These were a sacrifice to avoid the greater pain of dismantling the dream of the little house.

After weeks living out of suitcases in serviced flats followed by touring, we all turned up together at Glen Row on the Glen Estate in the Scottish Borders, to a row of eight estate workers' cottages. Mike had found them, so that ISB could carry on working together, and also accommodate Stone Monkey. He and Robin both had reasons for wishing to maintain Stone Monkey's proximity.

We officially moved there in October, but only finally took possession when we returned from the American tour, unpacking bags and baggages and starting to work out new ways of living. As next-door neighbours with a cottage each, we would experience the least possible aggravation from living so close together. The row looked like something from a book of fairy tales, especially in a hard winter, with icicles hanging from the elaborately cut eaves over the thick stone walls. With snow on the hills all around, each chimney had its own thread of smoke rising into the sky, and the windows glowed from the fires in the hearths.

The two couples were now fragmenting permanently, though Mike and I floated amicably between our two cottages. Janet moved in with Robin, and Licorice had a cottage of her own, although I could never quite accept that they were not together as before. Janet seemed too straightforward and decisive to meet Robin on the deeper levels of his capricious personality. The new relationship only thrived, so I imagined, as long as both were also orbiting around Licorice.

A group spirit persisted amongst the four of us, the "*Occult Quart*" as Robin called us in 'Waiting for You', all mutually loyal to the ISB's original nature. We were the Earth, Water, Fire and Air signs, of Capricorn, Scorpio, Sagittarius and Libra, as predicted in Robin's 'Koeeoaddi There'. We were met together in that fair garden and very definitely bound in skin and bones.

Enquiring someone's star sign was a standard introduction at the time, and astrology was part of the everyday hippie language, sometimes genuinely believed, sometimes with amusement at its pretty pictures and stories. As a time-honoured anchor in crises, its explanations could resolve doubts and fears, and provide answers to questions, along with the *I Ching*, Tarot cards, runes and crystal balls. We all had horoscopes cast and charts written, to confirm our hopes and prove this was the right way for us all. However flippantly applied, however little credence they were given, the modalities of the astrological elements were a convenient framework for the ideas we formed of ourselves.

Stars aligned

Mike was a Capricorn, the earthy one of us all. He revelled in earthly delights, though I never saw him as a goatish Pan figure. I preferred to see the romance in his pursuits of pretty girls. He had plenty of choice once the band had made a name, but appearances were sometimes deceptive.

We had been keeping ourselves to ourselves at Max's Kansas City in New York until late, listening to Lou Reed's monologues. Mike was by a very beautiful tall blond, I felt of indeterminate gender. Mike clearly didn't share this doubt, and they left together shortly afterwards. As Robin, Lic and I left the Chelsea for breakfast next morning we met Mike on his way back. He looked shaken but never told the story, quickly rallying good humour over French toast and syrup. He had been the only one of us to risk a close personal encounter with any of the Warhol group. I always watched them mesmerized but uncomprehending, too naïve, and too conscious of this, to get involved. If Mike was reckless, I was impressed by his daring, if unconvinced it was a sensible choice.

Tentative contacts with the Velvet Underground at the Chelsea also led to Nico's offer to perform with us for UK and US concerts. Mike and Robin were both pleased, Licorice and I less so. I felt challenged by her looks and reputation, while Licorice just ignored her. Nico ignored both of us, talking only to Mike and Robin. She played an Indian harmonium at a couple of gigs, lending us the gloss of her notoriety. But we failed to match her expectations, and she drifted back to Paris.

Earth-bound he may have been, but country walks, outdoor activities and nature study were low on Mike's list of pursuits. Songs like 'White Bird', 'Hedgehog Song', 'Cousin Caterpillar' and 'Puppies' show more affection than intimate knowledge. He was a city boy who admired it all from a distance, enjoying the aesthetics of landscape without needing leaves in his hair or dirt on his hands.

He was not impractical and had shown himself capable at Roman Camps of useful household tasks, but had no interest in DIY. Playing instruments was his manual labour, writing songs his creative and imaginative contribution. A balance of these achieved his happiness. His morning ritual was picking up the guitar without thinking and playing a while.

But his lyrics are rooted directly in the real world around him. They lack none of Robin's spiritual or emotional depth, but are less blatant about it, without the vague intimations of immortality or symbolic pretensions. They are more often sensual, compact and energetic, as he was physically. When Robin introduced him in 'Waiting for You' as "Black Jack Davy on the steam organ" it was a good-natured recognition of a being very different from himself.

Small daily incidents fired Mike's imagination. One morning we were sitting together on the Roman Camps floor and an Elektra record with tracks of South Sea music was playing. The sun was blazing and the music appropriate, but we had things to do and couldn't doze away the morning. Of course we had painted the window closed when we moved in, but now we forced it open, so that the warm breeze streamed in. I went shopping and when I came back Mike had picked up one of the melodies on his guitar and was humming words into it. It became 'Air', a much-loved song, simple but with a meaning everyone could understand.

When in New York we could choose LPs from the Elektra store room to take home, a selection both wide and random; Mike was always good at organising their delivery, but Robin would lose interest in the heap he'd pick out, and leave them in some hotel room. Like the fire-sign he was, his enthusiasms flared up then died, but as long as he cherished any belief, his devotion was extreme. He rarely argued for his viewpoint, but if you failed to agree he looked at you in derision, or just turned and walked away, Licorice following him in silent withdrawal.

Both Robin and Licorice claimed illuminating flashes of insight and intuitive powers of judgement. There was no argument with such assurance. Robin's dreams delivered entire stories that he wrote down when he woke, claiming transcendental origins for them. They arrived in a state of perfection, he said, with no need to rewrite or edit. He was simply the scribe for their spiritual originators. Production techniques and commercial judgements were therefore of limited relevance to him.

Robin's mercurial quality we all attributed to his Sagittarian sign while Licorice, as a Libra, reflected balance in mediating gestures which helped reconcile Robin with the world beyond his skin. The vaporous qualities of an air sign were hers, as she appeared and melted away like mist. Her pale pensive face was the slow steady moon, with a hidden but definite power to influence the tides of our lives. Robin's sunny blondness was more brilliant when the two were in harmony.

Her Air sign also fanned his Fire sign, sometimes encouraging him in opposition when he might otherwise have given in through inattention or boredom. Together or apart, their relationship looked like two spirits orbiting around one another in a force-field which fixed them in space. Each claimed a relationship across the recurring times and geographies of past lives, both firmly convinced of the specific details of their encounters. With this absolute faith in their inner guidance, both were determined to get their own way. They often seemed unaware or uncaring of the emotional impact of their actions on others, whether friends or strangers in the audience. Believing in their own spiritual powers, they were both ready at times to break up the band rather than compromise. If Robin was seer and prophet, Licorice had formed an idea of mystic womanhood whose powers were equally worthy of expression.

The combination of an Earth sign and a Water sign is auspicious, and the meeting of Mike's Capricorn with my Scorpio was essentially happy. Earth contains the emotionality and fluidity of Water, shaping and directing the flow. My pleasure in theatre, performance and needlework were given outlets I never dreamed of.

Water softens the fixed forms of earth, breaking barriers, nourishing and making fruitful the solid ground. I hope I did that for Mike, for a while. Sometimes water is dammed and earth washed away by flood, as the varying phases of our relationship showed, but the positive interpretation was also true.

Robin's Fire and Mike's Earth sign are generally antipathetic. Earth is warmed by fire but then dessicates and crumbles. Fiery energy is extinguished by earth's solidity. My Watery and Lic's Airy nature contribute little to each other's wellbeing. Astrology was one of many ideas we played with, in varying degrees at different times. "Acid opened my eyes," Robin told *Oz* in an interview. "You name it I've tried it. Like the mysterious ancient things. Tarot, magic, astrology."

Living the timeless life

We had wanted to avoid the rules and work patterns to which most people conformed. We wanted to choose our own times, to find harmony within our own diurnal rhythms and the greater cosmic ones of night, day and the seasons. But trains and planes enforced their own schedules and compelled us to spend miserable hours of sleepless waiting, powerless in face of the leviathans. One night-long delay at the airport in Dublin when storms kept us grounded, I crocheted much of a cushion cover, with wool I had brought along, but it wasn't much of a consolation.

Such disruptions in strange places forced us into a "timeless life" we hadn't bargained for. A comfortable timelessness was having no clocks in the house and never wearing watches, though Mike usually did. Or sitting on a mountain-top on a summer's day, gazing down at the busy ants in the town below and congratulating ourselves on being free of all that. But now we were finding that routines are comforting. Reinventing the course of every day is an exhausting way to live.

All business travellers become very familiar with airport shops and coffee bars, all the food we called "plastic" but ate because it was there and we were bored. But we found it intolerable for our daily lives to be governed by the demands of an imposed work ethic. To express a wish Mike or Robin would sometimes, in a parody of Scottishness, say "a body needs…" We were finding it to be true, and our bodies began to grumble about the inordinate demands we put upon them.

We rambled along in the apparent insouciance of freedom, but we also needed home-time to go back to, now that the excitement and the experiments of the first ISB days together were over.

Once established at the Glen, each having a cottage to oneself encouraged home making again, although the time spent in our own houses varied with the flow of relationships. We arranged our cottage our own way, insisting on the right to exclude the others when we chose. But the downstairs rooms were a semi-public area. We rarely locked doors and often had good reason to go into other houses, to find abandoned clothes or instruments. Upstairs was the more private area and I never saw the upper floors of most of the row.

Scientology also imposed its restrictive moralities on the group life. In an interview Robin waved the banner of its dogma in words which confirmed an entire change of vision: "In the commune, Scientology provides a practical set of rules which we can use to deal with each other. The little things that come up from day to day, like someone stealing someone's sugar or something on that level, can be worked out with the proper tools of communication."

We had never before thought it stealing to share common resources. We had laughed off the small confrontations or taken quiet time out rather than discuss small incidents. Nor did I accept the definition of Glen Row as a "commune". It was just somewhere we lived along with friends and other people, not a structured or formal arrangement.

I organised my life as seemed right for me without asking anyone what the rules were. I chose to keep a bedroom downstairs, recreating the two-room area and the habits of Roman Camps. It was important to me to have the same freedom for Mike to come and go, hanging on in some way to the life that was gone. But I also arranged it so that I could use all of the upper floor as my personal home, with the dormer windows looking on the hillside. There I could dream.

The sloping ceilings reminded me of a tent and I painted them bluey-green, with scallops on the short walls beneath, like tents from the Duc de Berry's *Books of Hours*. I imitated the low couches of the Baghdad restaurant with heaps of oriental pillows, cushions and mats, hoping to conceal the utilitarian mattresses below. Impressed by Claude Picasso's laser lights slicing through the New York skies I tried to find a domestic equivalent. I painted the walls very dark blue and imported revolving coloured lights from America. These could be linked up to a stereo record-player and were the most cutting-edge lighting technology I could manage, a very unsatisfactory result.

Around this time I bought a *Teach Yourself Electronics* book and a *Make-Your-Own Transistor Radio*, to find out something about the mechanics of the business I found myself in. I'd struggled with 'O' level Physics so I wasn't too hopeful, but it seemed worth trying to establish some mental ownership of proceedings. They didn't help me much and I never finished the radio.

The primitive kitchens in the Glen cottages were not exciting but by then I'd given up on the endless vegetable chopping and obsessive grain storage required by spiritual dietary demands. Every year's Shooting Season on the Estate saw pheasants fall onto our roofs and into our gardens. A flurry of plucking and gutting followed, but with no freezer on the Row that was of limited benefit, and I was the only one willing to face nature in the raw state of lead-riddled birds. Susie Watson-Taylor showed me how to make game chips to go with them, and to stick the tail feathers back into the roasted birds for a flourish when someone came round for supper.

Susie had turned up with Joe one day. At first she was his London PA, he said, but her role quickly changed. Once he had effectively moved back to the USA, she took over much of his management of us. She was a very pretty blonde, sweet-natured, competent and exuberant, and

Smiles with Susie, from left; Rose, Mike, Susie, Robin and Licorice, 1969/70

Mike married her eventually. She was also the iconic Sloane Ranger, driving around Chelsea in her Mini, one hand on the wheel, putting on lipstick for some important meeting with the other. An endless array of shirtwaister dresses in Liberty prints saw her faultlessly through business days, into concert evenings and long nights of travelling.

Stone Monkey distributed themselves as best they could among the vacant rooms in the neighbouring cottages. One of its members, John Schofield, made me a bed platform. He had never seemed at home as a performance artist and was better at woodwork than dancing. We had all discovered that mattresses on damp floors ended up covered in mould. Most of our furniture came from the local auction room. The textile artist who lived in no.4 for a while, dyeing silk scarves, found some strange tall chairs in a sale and we laughed at their oddness. But they were genuine Rennie Mackintosh and she later sold them for a fortune.

We chopped wood and lit fires in the fireplace, like proper peasants, but since the bills mainly disappeared into "the office" we could always use an electric fire. The finances of the cottages were the usual mystery. We didn't know who paid their expenses or where the money came from.

The children that arrived with Stone Monkey and their friends made the Row at least seem like a family venture. But it was not. Lives became even more complex and relationships even more disjointed with more doors to disappear behind. Much went unacknowledged, and exactly who was with whom was never clear. There was no stability in the relationships, and we never asked the names of fleeting visitors, or kept any track of their comings and goings.

The same faces appeared at Mike's door, so he seemed to be making more lasting relationships. Susie was a friend and companion I was always glad to see there, as well as during our working days. But if any one of us hoped for a peaceful life with a faithful partner who came home every evening, it was a life of constant deception and disappointment. I had given up that idea along with the dutiful cooking.

Freewheeling sexuality had always been a defining feature of the artist's life, as we all knew from Hollywood scandals and lurid tabloid accounts of the pop-star lifestyle. To question it would have been the height of "uncool". The occasional visitor would applaud the political necessity of fragmenting the nuclear family, that building block of oppression. It augmented the violence of state and nation, we were told. We didn't pay much attention, but our parental families had seemingly reinforced rather than disproved that pessimistic view.

Scientology's insistence on playing by the rules finally helped quieten the early sexual chaos of the Glen, although ties remained unstable.

The Glen Estate

All around the Row, the farm, grouse moors, river and forestry of the Glen Estate created the work which made the Big House and its land into a little world of its own. We walked past the farm buildings on the way to the cottages and saw people working, but we were not part of the estate's routine, and didn't want to be. We were living in a feudal system which had no relevance for us.

In summer, our residence coincided with that of the Family. We would see the boys sometimes down at the lake, with its boathouse and landing stage. They were at Eton and had already learned the appropriate behavioural restraints without being old enough to also know how to flout them. That came later but, when we knew them, they were exceptionally pleasant and polite, very willing to lend their boats to us for the afternoon.

When Robin's canoe overbalanced and he fell in the lake they wanted to help. We all found his discomfiture hilarious. He didn't often volunteer to do things he wasn't already good at. They offered to share their picnics, but they were only little boys. We were the grown-ups and a bad example we set them.

We only visited the Big House at Christmas or Hogmanay, when their guest-list extended beyond friends. Even then, despite the friendliness and hospitality, we were aware of being objects of curiosity. But how could it be otherwise? The good-looking Glen Row men were generally more welcome than us girls, more attractive to rebel royals or Scottish Lady Chatterleys who enjoyed a handsome face on the sofa or as partner in a song or parlour-game. Robin came back one day telling of a circle dance around the grand piano, with Princess Margaret playing 'Always Look on the Bright Side of Life'. A Lady invited Rakis to be Hogmanay First Footer one time, but he failed to realise the benefits of the year-long freedoms of access which this automatically conferred.

We also heard of more lurid scandals and saw photographs of the wilder members of the Family's past. Seeing the house as a repository of tales of course encouraged the telling of more, with the tabloid press only too willing to print the recent ones. We valued our tenancies and our own privacy and made sure it wasn't us or our visitors that told them.

The Glen Row children formed links with the local community, including the House, and were probably less tactfully reticent than us. One day, when the children of the Family were home on holiday and there was to be a children's party, a couple of nannies appeared at the small gate which closed the Row off from the driveway. I happened to be sitting nearby. The two little Glen Row girls were playing in front of the houses, the smaller one wearing an unusual Aztec hat. One nanny asked them to find Mummy so that an invitation could be delivered and commented on the "pretty hat". "It's because I've got nits," the little girl explained. The nannies retreated fast.

Visitors did bring their problems with them. I was at Mike's when a couple of roadies stayed in my cottage for a few days in-between gigs. They left a predictable litter of beer cans and greasy chip packets, and also used my beds. A few days later, Mike and I went down to London, where we stayed in a hotel. We discovered that we had inherited a legacy of parasites, as small black creatures sidled across the spotless white bedlinen.

We recalled the Chelsea Hotel pharmacy, with its vast array of anti-lice creams, lotions and sprays. London had these too, but the invasion took longer to get rid of than to acquire. Every garment, textile, cushion and mattress needed disinfecting or disposing of. You could remain anonymous in a London hotel with a nearby dry-cleaner. But at the Glen, discarded heaps of cloth bore false witness to our personal hygiene standards, an unpleasant and inconvenient footnote to the ideology of communal living and the virtues of indiscriminate hospitality.

But there were also artistic benefits from living together. Mike wrote 'Queen Juanita and her Fisherman Lover', a long story-song that overlaps Robin's *U* plot with its mermaid vision as it wanders into a world below the sea. Like Robin's work, the variations of melody, tone and length allow for endless dance or dramatic interruptions.

But it was also a cheerful parody of itself, begging for multimedia interpretation without being overwhelming, showing off all ISB's skills, diversity and sense of humour.

On-stage Robin could invent new fates for Juanita's pet octopus, or pastimes for the queen and her fisherman. Licorice and I laughed as we sang our insistent choruses, which could last as long as any dancing or other dramatic intervention required. Friends who happened along were invited to join us. We improvised with lots of vocal effects, any instrument to hand, an occasional mermaid with a golden comb or a passing hippie with a trident posing as Neptune. Licorice wove seaweed strands in her hair for a while, and wore shimmering turquoise scarves. Mal, the little blonde from Wales, was always ready to waggle a silky tail and gaze in mirrors as an excuse to come with us.

Vashti Bunyan turned up one day with Joe but avoided the hippie chorus. She took up residence for a while at Glen Row when her gipsy caravan became inconvenient, although the Row house was hardly more luxurious. She already had a musical career behind her but she rarely mentioned it, nor the near-misses and unforeseen failures of her early singles, nor the big names that had recognised and supported her first endeavours. To us she just seemed another pretty English hippie musician that Joe was favouring with his time. He liked her music but then he liked her too.

We were never sure which won him over when he produced her first LP with Witchseason musicians. Robin and Mike thought her sweet but were by then fairly dismissive of her music. She seemed to represent a pastoral feyness they had largely put behind them when they embraced Scientology. It all harked back to that toytown world, where rich kids bought gipsy wagons and country cottages with Daddy's money, as toys. We weren't envious, just weary of games that had lost their meaning for us.

As a holiday venue for city folk, the Glen was attractive and ensured us informal house-swaps in London on several occasions. Susie and I stayed round the corner from Harrods for a while, and found that their Food Hall was no more expensive than the supermarket. She was Mike's girlfriend by then, and the relationship between us was almost sisterly. That stay came to an unfortunate end when one of our guests flooded the bathroom, which brought the ceiling down in the room below. We weren't invited back again.

Such accidents encouraged us to reconsider our living arrangements, becoming slightly more careful, orderly and even conventional. Once so unwilling, we eventually acquired hoovers and fridges, chairs and tables.

The four of us were now mostly drug-free, following Scientology's dictates. For others on the Row, living in the country with no transport limited experiments, though visitors brought the drugs they assumed assured their welcome. I kept clear of most of the informal evening gatherings, having little interest in the miscellaneous company. Once Janet was in residence, Robin was also mainly a home-bird, and Licorice kept her own mysteries.

An old climbing friend of mine from York came up to stay one January weekend, evidently finding attractions in ISB Rose he had failed to notice when I was merely a fellow student. Now I was a name he could casually drop in his searches for adventure with arty London girls. I recognised my new position of advantage and didn't want to lose it by revealing the weakling I'd become. I remembered tales of "Bolivian marching powder" on expeditions to the Alps and the Andes: ideal for getting me up a few winter hills fast and in excellent condition.

My friend was unaware of this explanation for my storming energy and, after a long and rapid snowy walk, felt a plunge into the mountain lake would prove his toughness, and cool him down. A few minutes in freezing water were enough to threaten exposure. Shivering and shaking, he couldn't manage to climb out of the lake, and panic began to set in. Holding onto a convenient tree branch, I tugged at his outstretched hand. He must have been amazed by a sudden strength that my fragile appearance denied. I lent him my down jacket to warm up while we walked back to the Row. I wasn't feeling the cold much.

We all had visitors from our other lives and didn't always introduce them into the ISB circle. It was a diverse and unsettled way of living. There was ample scope for misunderstanding between Glen Row and the rest of the Estate community, yet there were remarkably few disasters. When some male Glen Rowers took up night poaching, tickling trout and hauling salmon out with a gaff, it was more for the pretence of danger than any real threat. They knew they would get away with it if caught. And anyway they could afford to buy fish if they wanted it, so the justification of "living off the land" was phoney.

I never found out how successful they were. It was not the illegality but the cruelty that would have made me turn away any offered catches.

With Robin as their Chief Executioner, or so I heard, peace and love had vanished. Apparently his beatnik days in Edinburgh had also involved sheep rustling, including an unskilled butchering of the trophies. I preferred to disbelieve this, but most other Glen Rowers were startlingly incompetent in practical matters. So perhaps there was something in it. As always with moral dilemmas, we turned blind eyes on each other and never asked whether the stories were true or not.

Car crash

In real life, driving was perhaps our most dangerous activity. The vehicles which were left with us were often doubtful and unlicenced. Anyone who could pilot one down the road to the shops became a driver. As ever, Mike was the most legal and the most organised. But with him at the wheel, in a car with no seat belts, on the way to a gig in Edinburgh, we skidded on mud and hurtled into a tree.

Robin and Licorice were re-living their teenage dreams on the back seat. They hit the windows. Mike and I hit the windscreen. I regained consciousness curled up under the dashboard, where I had slipped on impact. Here was a new version of the psychedelic state: the journey from the darkness of unconsciousness into the light required an effort of will. But shocked and semi-conscious, we didn't have much time to think about it. The concert was imminent.

We managed to stagger down to the Estate gatehouse. The family there found us a taxi, and we walked from it straight onto the stage, just in time. I grabbed the microphone to tell the audience that we had just had a car crash, because Mike and Robin still seemed dazed and unsure.

Our audiences were kind, so it was easy to ask them to wait for a few minutes as we collected our thoughts and our instruments. We were still in a mild haze and tuned the instruments as habit-driven automata. We drank a calming camomile tea, hastily made from the tea bags Licorice had with her and made it through the evening with no further ill-effects.

Mike and Robin had lived the crises, trials, discomforts and displeasures of impoverished musicians on a club circuit. Fragile and decorative they may have looked, but they had the survival skills to build a life around the music that welled up within, demanding to be heard. That tuneful spring had forced them on, through all the adversities of a life in the music industry. As they both told many interviewers, they had no other choice but to flow with it.

All our three lives were also bound to Licorice, an unknown quantity surrounded with enigmas, but certainly resilient. Even Robin, who knew her better than anyone, was often disconcerted by her ways, and puzzled by her contradictions. Music must have driven her too, since she had clung to it through the different backgrounds of her life, but she never talked about it to me.

From left, Rose, Mike, members of Stone Monkey, Robin in the centre and Licorice far right

Licorice Allsorts

1967-72

Licorice is part of life with the ISB from the minute I meet them to the day I leave. Every journey, every concert and most of the days in between are influenced by her thoughts and moods.

◆

Long after the ISB years I met Licorice's sister for the first time, on a train from Devon. She recognised me, and we talked as the countryside passed by, sharing memories of Licorice.

Her sister had lost touch with her some time before, and I had even less information. I had cut off almost all ties with my former life. Some years later I met the sister again, at the launch party for the *Be Glad* book. Nothing had changed, Licorice was still missing, and the rumours and unproven sightings left an uncomfortable feeling, that this story's final chapter was probably not a happy one. People say they know where she is now and have definite proof that it is her. If she wishes to stay hidden, leaving all her former life behind her, so she should. Nobody can dispute that choice.

It was like the Licorice I knew to disappear without trace. She never gave explanations. Her choosing to do something was always the only justification she found necessary, and her conviction carried people with her. 'Secret Temple', her last ISB song, was recorded for *Earthspan* in 1972 but not used, as she then left the band. Adrian Whittaker dug it out and mixed it for the 2009 compilation *Tricks Of the Senses*. From start to finish, the lyrics and voice are the Licorice I knew, seemingly addressing an archetypal lover and the eternal problems of being in love, but all in her own head. The firm simplicity of *"Yes I'll believe you"* is her all over. No complications or prevaricating once she had decided what to do.

The lover is part of herself as well as a body beyond her own. This was Robin when I met them, if not always the Robin who sat beside her in crumpled trousers rolling a joint. He was often *"in trouble"*, as she sings it, his visions clashing with a material world which wouldn't play the game. The lover whose soul is the secret temple is the Robin whose soaring imagination met hers in a rainbow universe somewhere.

Her voice is strong, almost harsh, as she orders the temple to open its doors. She would never wait on the threshold for someone to carry her over it. She claimed her universe and insisted her claim be recognised. In the refrain *"how long"* is a plaintive disappointment at delays she never accepted or understood. Nobody saw the world through her eyes and she wouldn't look through theirs.

Imperfect strangers

I was probably one of those she couldn't understand but, while we occasionally found one another inconvenient and wearing on the nerves, I liked her to be around. I had no confidence in her decision-making or reasoning, but I knew none of this was important to her. Her values and priorities were not mine. Her calm, quiet presence was restful, and often more persuasive in winning a disagreement than the torrents of words from others. I admired her instinctive musicality and her high clear singing voice, so essential in many of the band's songs. I wished I had a voice to match it. I envied her ability to sail through the days with no sign of the doubts and uncertainties that bothered the rest of us. I never knew what she felt about me because we avoided conversations that might lead to revelations. I imagine she often found me unsympathetic and inharmonious, but we never clashed for long. It was a sad sight when I eventually saw Mike and Robin playing without her.

Certainly, we had little common ground, but we were each too concerned with our own lives to bother with as strong a feeling as "dislike". If we had, we would not have got through the years of very close proximity that band life forced upon us. Neither of us was particularly good-humoured with or tolerant of other people, and neither accepted much interference in our own pursuits. We established ways to get along and avoid friction. I was intrigued by what went on beneath the surface, and curious how someone so different from me negotiated the times we lived through together. It was usually far from obvious what she was thinking, whether she was happy or sad, and I never knew where she was or what she did in all the hours and days when we were not together. I only discovered 50 years later that she went to the USA with Mike and Robin in 1968, while I was left behind in Scotland. No one had mentioned it. I read about it on a CD cover and had to change the detail in my memoir.

If this gulf prevented understanding, it also hindered conflict. We were often on very good terms. I enjoyed her quirky humour, her little-

girlish response to a funny hat or an odd person. As with a child, I felt protective when I guessed she was hurt. Yet she was far from childish, with vulnerable moments rarely expressed. Once or twice, when emotions were high and we had retreated tearfully behind an amplifier on-stage, she accepted a pat of sympathy, but that was all.

I knew little of her personal life as she never spoke to me about it, but we shared much time together, which allowed me to reach conclusions about her. I felt that much of the time she expressed her imaginative inner life through her outward appearance, her costumes a better indication of her intentions and ideas than anything she said. She wrote notes for herself, but never explained whether they were songs, poems, stories or a diary. What remains as marks of her presence are her songs, the photographed images and the clothes she wears in them.

She had a very definite idea of how she wanted the world to see her. In the snaps I occasionally took on tour she was always aware of the camera, when the rest of us ignored it. Never caught off-guard, she looks straight into the lens or poses in profile. The picture-record describes without betrayal the things she may have thought too delicate for the world to know. I hope that she would at least recognise herself in the words I write.

I never knew where she bought her clothes, but I wanted to. When I first went to Scotland, I looked everywhere for those soft flowing skirts she wore, in lovely fabrics, so old and curious. The Indian import shop in London had the beads and cotton shirts, but their skirts were heavy and coarse. Still, I bought one, and it stood up well to housework at Roman Camps. She knew places in Edinburgh and Glasgow to buy garments that I never imagined: crepe afternoon dresses from the 1940s, tunics brought back from India and China in Empire days, silk scarves to make even the woolly jumpers of a Scottish winter look exotic. Her headbands had floating tails and beaded ribbons tied around her brow, which looked impossibly uncomfortable to me but never seemed to cause her any difficulties. It wasn't that we competed or tried to outdo each other, we just acknowledged the great distances between us, even in little things, and didn't try to bridge them.

She had a pale blue peasant dress with red embroidery which I coveted and even managed to borrow once when my suitcase got lost at the airport. It was fine cotton lawn, almost transparent; we didn't own a petticoat between us. But there was something prim about the garment, with its high frilled neck, long sleeves and skirt covering the knees. Perhaps this is why she was indifferent when Joe asked if I could borrow it. After the first few weeks, we rarely swapped clothes. Everything she touched took on shades of herself and thus became alien to me.

Her penchant for silver extended to rings on her fingers and bells on her toes. Long before anyone else she found the Indian foot-jewellery we had seen in books of Indian miniatures. When all she had to do was sit around as Robin's muse, never far from the mats of their room, the weight of jangling silver was fine. Once we were touring, her jewellery became more refined and restrained. Moonstones were her favourite: she saw herself and her femininity mirrored in their milky pools. She knew all the ancient lore of gemstones and chose what she wore as much as an expression of her star-formed nature as for the outward aesthetic.

She never wore trousers when I knew her, whatever the weather. Nothing affected how she chose to look, not practicality, not fashion, not the opinions of others. But she possessed modern mini-dresses as well as hippie drapery, and we both wore one when we went to a local village hall hop.

Someone's friend was on holiday at Glen Row, and desperate for any escape after a week of rain and boredom. Licorice and I must also have been finding times oppressive enough, to go out in a group of girls. She joined in the jiving and twisting with enthusiasm, transformed from dreamy hippie to giggly dolly-girl, as another unlikely creature emerged from the unseen depths of her life. Our dresses were so short and flared that I had found some fabric that more or less matched and, ever aware of audiences and watchers, made a pair of little shorts for myself. They added to the outfit and preserved the moral tone as we twirled around.

The dress Licorice brought out, which she afterwards wore in other photos, was quite different from the sharp mini-dresses of Twiggy or Mary Quant. It looked like a schoolgirl's Sunday-best, puffed sleeves, gathered skirts and floral cotton with a buttoned cardigan over but there was never a hint of Lolita. It was more a studied reflection of artlessness and naivete. She claimed a sort of single-minded innocence and maintained it throughout a life calculated to destroy it. Her singing voice reflected this determined simplicity. Bare feet and a cavalier disregard for clothing propriety and underwear was common to all four of us, but Licorice's absolute lack of self-consciousness was a statement of unconventionality that I was not prepared to make.

I was always interested as she changed looks and styles, obviously putting time and effort into selection, even as her hair remained much the same. We often saw someone strolling down the Glen with hair in a polythene bag as the henna paste soaked in, deepening colour to red or black. But Licorice stayed plain brown, with plaits for occasional convenience when we couldn't find a hairbrush. A photographer asked once what to do about her missing front tooth. We laughed: it was part of her child-look and she was content to be photographed without it. None of us found it awkward or thought of it as something to be hidden from the world.

Fantastic finery

How we dressed helped define the eras of the band's existence, as a public display of what we were thinking and how we wanted to be seen. I noticed from my early days with them that they insisted on choosing clothes that didn't fit any easy definition. While "hippie" covered every look that was colourful, eccentric and unusual, they had no intention of being classified and labelled. Robin and Licorice definitely believed they stood outside such limits, and claimed uniqueness.

In the West Coast head shops we bought perfumed oils to burn in our rooms and to dab on ourselves. One time I bought honeysuckle oil, delighted by this early summer English smell, but after a day with it on my skin I felt sick with its cloying sweetness. It lurked in my nose for days and the smell of perfumed oils has carried that undertone of nausea ever since. There were oriental oils with strange and intriguing names and the romance of infinitely exotic symbolism hung around sandalwood, frankincense and myrrh.

Licorice was always perfumed, but the smell was more elusive, much lighter than either oils or more conventional perfumes. Perhaps it was the accumulated scents of the incense burning for hours in the rooms where her clothes were hung. I never saw her bedroom at the Glen, but we always had incense burning somewhere. All our clothes must have picked up the mixed aromas. But hers were different, mysterious.

From the time I first met her at Temple Cottage to the day I walked away from the band with no goodbyes, she had always been very quiet but with a steely determination to live according to her own lights. If this impinged on anyone else's freedoms, a silent battle of wills ensued. She was not one to waste words. Her influence was as powerful as it was undefinable.

When Robin sang about the first girl he had loved, imagining her as *"married now, kids and all... turned into a grown-up female stranger"* he was thinking of someone very different from Licorice and from most of the women in his daily life. We were all actively avoiding the domesticity that made our mothers' lives a misery. If being a woman meant being defined by houses, cars and possessions, we'd stay as girls. Much as I liked Roman Camps and the Glen, they were not going to be my prison. Licorice showed even less desire for home-making.

She seemed to teeter uneasily between incorporeality and sexuality, her ways obscure. As she strode through the door with Leaf, her dog at her heels, she claimed the image of a spirit from the Scottish woods with a certainty that repelled questioning. All the wayward heroines of Scottish ballads, who ran off with gypsies or rode wildly across the moors to their lover's arms, formed a part of her picture of herself. And some of this mythic quality she retained to the end, despite endless dressing-room niggles and hours of studio-time wasted. Our wills were stubbornly opposed on many occasions, our beliefs about life and how it should be lived adding a wordless clash to the crosscurrents in the band's existence. Both of us must surely have swayed the opinions and actions of Mike and Robin but Lic would never compromise when she was roused. She preferred to leave the field rather than accept defeat, until Scientology ruled with its iron fist.

Did she ever think back to the Christianity which had been an active part of her school-life, as with all of us? She might have been a convent-girl rebelling against past impositions or searching to replace the discipline she had lost. It could be that she was haunted by some left-over conventions and moralities that still demanded her observance.

The books, gurus and cults that influenced Mike and Robin and 1960s counter-culture were all around her home spaces. I imagine she had collected her own ideas and ideals from these sources and was

Licorice and Robin in the cottage at Penwern, Pembrokeshire, 1968

pursuing them in her own way. Mostly her life seemed to be set aside from that of ordinary people but there are a few photos of her laughing or licking an ice cream. Even when we shared hotels and houses she hid her comings and goings better than I did. Maybe she visited family or friends and had fun. Perhaps she went to parties or music events, but I couldn't imagine that.

Her pearly-pale face seemed mostly to be dreamily gazing beyond the world immediately present. This rapt expression, caught in photos on- and off-stage, was more her usual look than any lively flashes of recognition or response to the outside world. But she was not grave or humourless. If something appealed to her playful sense of fun, she giggled, looking like a mischievous fairy in a story book. On the rare occasions when she got overtly angry, the wicked fairy took over. She needed no magic wand to convey the curses she wouldn't utter.

Fairy footsteps

Though never thin or wraithlike, she often seemed to flutter and glide, consciously graceful, quiet and light on her muddy feet. You can't keep feet white and hands pale when trying to sense the earth's vibrations as bare feet touch the soil. Stroking the friendly bark of a tree (yes, we spoke to the spirits of the trees) or embracing the velvety smoothness of moss for a cool cushion on hot days, means getting dirty, as we all knew.

When her dog Leaf failed to follow us, we automatically shouted commands, but she called him in tones of quiet friendship. We were all horrified and distressed the day Leaf dragged himself home, poisoned and fitting from something on the grouse moors or the farmyards. But Licorice disintegrated into tears and panic. I never saw her in such a human state of raw exposed emotion before or since. With no car immediately available, it had been hopeless trying to get him to a vet in time. Only Robin could approach her, so we scattered, knowing there was nothing that could be said to make it easier. Shock and grief blacked out her days, and I didn't see her for a while.

Her life seemed to always run along unthought paths of physical being, and perhaps Leaf was a better, more understanding friend than any of the rest of us, sharing an instinctive flow of life. When he rested his head on her shoulder and looked up to her face, the loving dependence was as touching as her hug in response. His cheerful pursuit of a ball or a fly made her more obviously happy than anything we did. She would laugh out loud as she ran with him.

She was kind and gentle with children, only playing their games for a very short while but always as one of them. I could never imagine her as a mother, but perhaps Robin hoped. *"I have a sweet woman now,"* he often sang in her presence: *"Maybe someday she'll have babies by me."* She could be any abstraction of motherhood, Madonna, Gaia, Isis, all these, but washing nappies in the sink like Vashti, or getting fractious kids to school every morning, was not how I saw her. Ghostliness was her way, not the clearing up of blood and guts.

She and I never did anything together that women might be expected to do in the enforced intimacy of a tour. We never shopped together or talked about clothes. When we did a photoshoot for American *Vogue*, we went in off the street just as we were, a severe challenge for the photographer, to create a polished image of Scottish flowerchildren from our genuine and untouched disarray.

None of us were innocent or naïve in the usual meaning of the words. I knew the stories of her beatnik life with Bert Jansch in Edinburgh. But more than any of us, she seemed to live in the moment, the past a closed book, the future wide open. She gazed out of windows, wrapped in pictures we couldn't see. She could gaze at flowers *"for hours,"* as she wrote in a song to some unknown lover, or perhaps to herself. If she'd said she was talking with them and could hear their little voices, I wouldn't have been shocked. What in me was a personal indulgence was for her an act with a spiritual significance, revealed only to herself. When I picked flowers it was for interior decoration; for Licorice, the blooms were small friends visiting from a fairy world.

She knew nothing of botanical "facts" and her wilful preference for arcane knowledge prevented her distinguishing between a poisonous plant and others that looked alike. She failed to identify the plant growing by a damp meadow's edge in Oxfordshire one midsummer afternoon. We were visiting academics with an interest in the counter-culture that extended to encounters with its exponents. They were planning to celebrate Midsummer Night, when, mythically speaking, the borders between the human world and that of the spirits and faery is at its most permeable. So perhaps we had offended some wood-sprite, who called upon the most familiar of us to do its will. In the spirit of immersion in their counter-cultural interests, the family encouraged us to make ourselves at home. Accustomed to the kaleidoscope of rooms and strangers a touring life produces, we did just that.

Licorice was in a macrobiotic phase, preoccupied with the balance of yin and yang, trying to create some harmony from the chaos of our lives. While we both enjoyed each day's randomness, it probably disturbed her more than me, rooted as she was, and wanted to be, in the Scottish countryside. The relative yang-ness or yin-ness of tomatoes or potatoes was a real concern to her at that time and she chose to make the meal for all.

We had just discovered the delights of macrobiotic tempura vegetables. The inevitable heap of soggy brown rice was slopped into the very beautiful craft-pottery bowls, as we sat round the stripped-pine table, with wild flowers in the centre. Lic then brought in a big dish, full of the battered carrots, potatoes and onions that we expected but topped also with unusual and very decorative florets, suggesting a culinary refinement that surprised us. Luckily, before we moved from admiring to consuming, Robin, more familiar with her factual understanding of flora and fauna and thus more suspicious, asked what they were and where from. She had carefully battered and fried up cow parsley, she said, "to give the vegetables a bit of taste," as there was no soy sauce. There were some untouched flowers still on the kitchen sink, and academic rigour established their classification and origins. It was hemlock.

We waded through the edible portions of the plates and thought no more of it. Our hosts, less resilient about facing death at the dinner table, seemed to be losing faith in the all-seeing abilities they had attributed to us as nature-spirits. A certain disenchantment had fallen on the evening.

We wandered around the garden, sat by the bonfire or fell asleep uncomfortably in a corner of the dining-room. Some students made an appearance, in kaftans and beads for the occasion. Realising that the wine-drinking of the older generation was not our way, one of them produced a very large bottle of Collis Brown's cough medicine, an opiate concoction familiar from some of our childhoods. Like the gripe water we swilled down in our cradles, this had maintained some drowsy calm in our infant brains. But now, we preferred clear sight and a quiet evening to drug-fuelled investigations of midsummer woods.

Although they were more or less my own age, the students seemed very young to me and I watched them with the resigned detachment of age. As dawn rose over Oxfordshire, sounds of vomiting were heard behind the bushes. Sobbing and coughing, one would-be hippie was now wishing she hadn't left the safety of the college refectory. She wanted to be taken to hospital. Unaccustomed to the fuzzy haze and sickness which went with drinking too much syrupy cough medicine, she was panicking. Someone calmed her down, persuaded her to drink a lot of water and put her to bed to sleep it off. These things happened, and it was nothing to make a fuss about.

The hours of her recovery were probably more tense for the hosts than for us. We just wanted to get back into town for a shower and breakfast. Licorice had already given up her active part in the proceedings. For all we knew, she'd left during the night, or else was sleeping somewhere in the house. We knew she'd turn up when she chose.

A different girl

Later Licorice would slip out of this random, dreamy life towards the more worldly. With Scientology in her life, she became more specific and vocal about the need for money, losing much of her set-apart quality. She also became more talkative and open, without that vague sweetness that helped me like her, even when her remoteness was hard to deal with. In those more rational and calculating days, she still retained her soft voice, with a stronger Scottish accent to my ears than either Mike or Robin. Occasionally, she became shrill or loud, with the odd fish-wife moments, but these didn't last long. Generally, she seemed to enforce her will by obdurate quiet and a blank refusal to be diverted by arguments, chatter, or any signs of anger. "Stony silence" conveys the impenetrable, unalterable resistance with which she met the arguments lapping hopelessly against the cliff-face of her resolve. I think she always believed in her own certainties, remaining unmoved by the arguments of others.

I enjoyed playing with esoteric theories and their implications, but never tried very hard to apply them to my own life, or to how I saw myself. From snippets of overheard conversations, Licorice appeared to genuinely believe that she was one with all manifestations of a cosmic energy, from the flowers and birds to the music of the spheres. Her body was the body of Mother Earth and contained the earth's powers of healing and making good. Sex was part of this healing process, and thus a benefit to be widely shared. This was not how I saw my everyday worldly existence, seeing no need to veil immediate physicality in the esoteric. But for a while at least, Licorice constructed a lifestyle out of the transcendental beliefs that seemed to work for her. She never tried to force this on me, however, or suggest that I was somehow failing in my womanly destiny.

Her assumption of unworldliness got her more or less happily through the ever-varying trials of lives lived in the wake of the fluctuating characters of Mike and Robin, as did mine of worldliness. In her role as a Fate in the *Be Glad* fable, she was barely acting as she gazed into the crystal ball of future and past. She undertook this rite with the certainty and conviction that comes from belief, however often the scene had to be repeated. Sometimes Licorice seemed to live inside a crystal ball herself, stepping outside it only to see what the soothsayer was peering at. Her real home was within, looking out from those crystalline depths at the strange colourful happenings in the human world, happy to flit in and out of them, but essentially unconcerned.

From left, Rose, Licorice and Ishy, the three Muses, 1968. Image © Peter Sanders.

America the Beautiful

1968-1970

Success in the US was the aim of all European bands, a confirmation of international recognition. ISB was so British and its work so novel and complex that an easy reception was never assured. I experienced the highest highs and the lowest lows in that country where everything seemed possible. Absolute warm freedom and freezing repression were only a short flight from each other and we met both. We were embraced as family one day then felt the threat of armed police or leather Angels the next. Every season of the year, through all its internal and political crises, we were dragged around a land with different dreams and other ways.

◆

Touring the USA had always been the most fun and the most challenging, and not just because of the distances. If Britain was now "swinging" and "hip", for its post-war generation the USA had always represented progress and modernity. Hollywood had shown us that everything there was bigger, better and more exhilarating than our small island, weighed down with its history, could manage. As the ISB's reputation spread and our travels took us to all ends of the continent, our familiarity with the US grew.

We arrived in places we had never heard of before and we refused to adjust for audiences who, at best, would only know us from old recordings. We rarely chose to play audience requests for the popular numbers: 'October Song', 'First Girl I Loved', 'Hedgehog Song' or 'Painting Box'. Upbeat numbers like 'Black Jack Davy', 'The Letter' and 'This Moment' were usually well received everywhere – but, much to my surprise, so was Robin's 'When You Find Out Who You Are'. Audiences identified with this direct message to themselves. They felt the world had gone wrong. Times were threatening, and Robin told them that they could put it right by believing in themselves.

Mike's Juanita epic was as popular in the US as the UK, with its endless opportunities for audience involvement. Adrian Whittaker's sleeve notes for *Tricks Of the Senses* quote an "incomparable" ISB gig in Philadelphia. After the show "500 people [were] walking down Arch Street holding hands with friends and strangers, singing the chorus from 'Queen Juanita'."

There were also always mis-hearings and misunderstandings. A Wisconsin reviewer wrote: "During the last song, a meditation about a girl and an octopus called Anita [Juanita] I saw people around me lost in contemplation of the band's story. In the song, after hearty choruses of foghorns, the beautiful maiden is rescued by the virtuous fisherman and GOOD as always triumphs. The song ended with a joyous smile and the band walked offstage."

The sound may have been obscured by an audience with an unusually high proportion of "under-15-year-olds, who had bought half-price tickets." Their parents must have been sold the programme blurb of "the new romanticism. Pastoral tales of love, life, death rebirth and the countryside... The songs are filled with European mysticism and seem to be relics of the time the world was young and chivalrous." The reviewer from the local *Evening Times* was doubtful, but delivered a positive judgement on music that had a "fragile and sometimes esoteric beauty." Expecting lady musicians, he was baffled by me and Licorice, but had to admit: "The ineptness of the girls... helped provide a simple, almost rustic touch... This reviewer kept having visions of 'shepherds and their flocks.'" So, as far as we were concerned, the music had worked, taking us all out of the industrial present into an Arcadian past.

But the imagined pastoral idyll was far away. Joe took us for an evening drive in a convertible down a country road in the more rural South. We wanted to see rattlesnakes and other night animals as they emerged, and he drove along gently, pointing out strange sights. We did see a rattlesnake, and slowed to hear its rattle. A police car dashed up behind and stopped us. We cowered in the back seat at the sight of uniform and gun. After some unpleasant moments of threatening voices and demands we shook ourselves down by the roadside while Joe found all our passports and the paperwork that assured our freedom. It was a threatening time to be a hippie in the boondocks and we were glad to be back in the hotel.

Yet it was also in the South that we played a local but very welcoming ballroom. We had never been here before, and facilities were primitive. The stage-level was hardly separate from the audience, a small platform for a country music band playing dances, and our gear spilled out over the floor, cables trailing and cases piled high behind us. Whole families came, with children nearly at our feet, babies in arms, even grandparents. We were encircled by people dancing to our livelier rhythms and swaying appreciatively to the quieter numbers. It was impossible not to respond to their close and friendly presence, and we enjoyed it as much as they did. We returned the following year to the same enthusiastic welcome.

Afterwards, chatting in the carpark, enjoying the warm night, we saw an armadillo scuttle across into the vegetation. A man gave me a small rock with tiny opals on it, from Australia he said, another a string of beads with dried mushrooms threaded on it, and a dessert spoon bent to make a bracelet.

I didn't like to take such gifts, in case I was taking something precious to them. I didn't want to be put on any pedestals, or to cast shadows over their hopes and dreams. I did value and keep the things but I made promises I couldn't fulfil and later felt wretched. I lost addresses and couldn't send postcards from Scotland. I forgot who had given me what.

I could only hope that my genuine appreciation and gratitude was obvious on the night, and that they kept whatever illusions they had, which were better than any reality I could offer. We said our goodbyes and drove off. Only the tour list would tell us where we had been.

Portable packages

In towns where we knew no one, we were taken from house to house, sometimes feeling like hunting trophies, at others like uninvited guests inflicted on the hosts by Joe and his friends. Joe's own enthusiasm for a new and challenging experience was the stimulus for our ever-expanding social horizons. We were hitched to his wagon-train, in pursuit of new music or the best of the old.

We visited Van Dyke Parks, a name everyone knew that I failed to memorise, being less interested in him than the view. We had been driven up to mountain heights overlooking a city, to walk out on his balcony and see all the bay lit up at night, like a tourist postcard. Licorice and I spent most of the evening out there in the cool of the night, as our presence indoors was clearly irrelevant. This was the meeting of a well-established musician with credentials and Young Pretenders from a different world. It was strained and uncomfortable, a clash of styles without common ground. If the pretext was a social visit where Mike and Robin expressed admiration, Joe had seriously misjudged their inclinations. He failed to forge new connections and none of us were cheerful as we drove back to town.

Head of Elektra Records Jac Holzman wasn't at home when we stayed at his place. I guess he had enough houses not to mind musicians spending a few days of out-of-town recreation in one of them. What Mike and Robin really wanted to see was the Moog synthesiser in the music-room, a great excitement for Mike, who usually played the Hammond organs we requested for concerts. He spent hours talking to the technician who set it up.

In our bedroom there was a water-bed, the first one I had come across. Once we got used to the swishing noise and how to turn on its heater, it was enormous fun. We bounced and pillow-fought as the pool beneath us washed around in its rubbery case. Back home I wondered if I could make a DIY version from an air-bed but decided the risk of flooding the cottage was too great. It was damp enough in Scotland already.

More prosperous members of the counter-culture had established small islands of alternative lifestyles, large wooden houses where the old frontier met the new. Inside, the latest audio equipment, outside acres of land and virgin forest. We were dropped into these oases without having to traverse the cultural desert surrounding them. Counter-cultural utopias they seemed, but then we only stayed there for a few vivid days.

Between gigs on the East Coast, Walter found us a place where we could free ourselves from the touring treadmill with an acid trip in the green of peaceful woods. Everywhere was absolutely quiet, enough to revive the soul. Golden pinewood walls shut us off from the rest of the world, with understanding neighbours nearby if we wanted them.

The acid was good and joyful and when we were hungry I cooked porridge in a saucepan and watched the simmering oatmeal bubble slowly then burst into rainbows. We found orange spiced tea and that was our day, gently sliding into night with no need to move from the cushions.

The next day visitors took us round to the schoolroom run by the community for its own children. The blackboard and teacher's desk at the front were like those from our childhoods but we had windows that were too high to look out of. We dreamed away lesson-times gazing at the clouds. Here, forest branches leaned in through the open panes, there were amplifiers in a corner and guitars leaning against them. Back in Yorkshire we grew mustard and cress on face-flannels. Here cannabis plants flourished beneath the desks.

There were no rules and the children were independent and self-reliant from an early age. Some families gave LSD to their children, convinced that its psychedelic effects cleared the mind of the dross of civilisation, leaving them out in the summer woods to rediscover their place in the natural world. We never heard what happened to the enlightened infants but the children we met were engaging, willing to involve us in their pursuits of the moment and pleased to see us, just like Mary Stewart's back home.

Some of their older siblings were less cheerful. We were in St. Louis before Thanksgiving in 1969, about to fly to Madison, Wisconsin, when

Mike swimming, pines and the river, New Mexico, 1969

our flight was cancelled. After frantic phoning, Walter the tour manager found an alternative route via Chicago, but we were now running late. On the second leg, the plane was taxiing to the runway when it was called back to the gate, fraying our nerves even more. An FBI agent boarded with an urgent message for Walter. His girlfriend Linda, from one of those "alternative" families, had been stabbed at a party and was close to death in New York. Walter threw his briefcase at the roadie and fled to her side. Miraculously she survived and refused to press charges against her friend's brother, who had been eating peyote buttons and Morning Glory seeds all night. Walter was back to mix our sound a night later, after we pointed out the roadie's failings.

It was Linda who had introduced me to dungarees, a useful cover-all that also seemed playful and ironic. I found a workwear pair in Philadelphia with the brand-label Red Ball on the bib. The others greeted them with heavy disapproval when we met out shopping, so after that I only wore them at home. Leather was as far as I could acceptably divert from folksy-pretty where the band were concerned, but it was good for all weathers.

Even in a Los Angeles August, with pavements hot on our bare feet and streaming eyes from traffic fumes, leather tops and jeans kept us surprisingly cool. Inevitably, Robin would make some jokey-dismissive comment on stage when I appeared in them. They were standard wear for a rock bass player, so I could have no claim to them. But I no longer cared what he thought.

The best leather could be rinsed out in a bedroom washbasin and the skins, slimy with hotel soap and water, would dry out in the sun, sweat-free if less flexible for a while. They also made a good gift for any particularly obliging roadie who came along. They weren't all giants able to carry a Hammond organ easily up the back stairs in Oxford Town Hall, and a leather shirt, even a bit small, was a luxury. Towards the end of my ISB career, when I discovered the novelty of thick soft buffalo-skin trousers in a leather shop on the West Coast, and bought the current Road Manager a pair, I was guaranteed the very best on-road service, all wants supplied and all secrets kept.

Back to the sink

Joe had many acquaintances in Boston from his college years and Mike and Robin also knew some of them, including the musicians from Jim Kweskin's Jug Band. We visited them at the Fort Hill Community, in a poor neighbourhood of Boston, where some of them were staying. Joe thought we'd like to see an urban hippie commune.

It was a cheerful day and a lively house full of people and music, but Licorice and I soon felt uneasy. She disappeared and I washed cups in the kitchen sink as coffee circulated among the chatting men. They showed all the vitality, enthusiasm and openness I admired in Americans so Mike and Robin were soon absorbed, but the women were quiet and undemonstrative. The Fort Hill community had embraced the drug culture early, we were told, and fostered freedom and creativity. But the women were excluded from its liberations.

Joe's good friend Geoff Muldaur was passing through, with his wife Maria, who seemed shy and silent. She visited us on her own in our motel some hours later, when she was affectionate and lively. Joe was surprised by my first impression of her. He had seen her fiery temperament at first hand – she once threw a heavy glass ashtray at him during an argument, from a staircase high above. Luckily it smashed on the floor rather than his skull.

As I talked to him, my discomfort with Fort Hill was explained. In this apparently happy communal life, run by its charismatic leader, women were effectively coerced into domesticity. I'd seen it before with "hippie" men. Brought up in households with mothers they viewed as domestic servants, these long-haired sons preached liberation and equality while expecting women to look after them. We hippie chicks were also considered sexually available, just another male perk.

Mike and Robin had never oppressed Licorice and me with expectations of domestic perfection and had always encouraged us to join in with their creative work.

We heard horrific stories about other bands. Young girls were routinely and ruthlessly mistreated and humiliated by stars and hangers-on, and this was just seen as a joke. Mike and Robin never exploited their position to degrade or abuse the many eager volunteers for their favours, and nor did those who worked with us. None of ISB were angels but we took no pleasure in hurting people and liked to leave happy faces behind us.

Some women got their own back. In the US the Plaster Casters had a queue of stars waiting to plunge their erect penises in wet plaster for posterity. It was the vain men showing their assets off to the world who looked foolish, not the girls, who turned a pretty penny from their trophies. In the 1970 film *Groupie*, we watched Joe Cocker being played like a fish by a groupie while he thought he was being cool. But more often it was a tale of regret and drug-hazed doubt, with girls led astray and wondering how to get back home.

The ISB had never been going to lead the way for Women's Lib. No surprise that Mike, Robin, Joe or his management team never once discussed paying Licorice and me for our part in the band's performances, or even considered it. Mike willingly shared his bank account with me, cheerfully accepting my moderate demands on it. This ensured my easy welfare. But both of us knew it was his money not mine, and I had no personal source of income. Endless days with the band had swallowed my life and I enjoyed it thoroughly, but it was also work.

With the advent of Scientology, the money question became important. Licorice, then the rest of us, now needed regular and significant sums to pay for our Scientology courses. Till now we had got money when we needed it, a casual arrangement that seemed fine to all four of us. In our utopian vision, vaguely coloured by what we imagined as the rejection of a corrupt world, value judgements based on commerce and capitalism would be replaced. It was the greater, eternal spiritual values which dignified daily life rather than degraded it that mattered.

I accepted that I was a freeloader on Mike's talents, and anyway I never had ambitions of my own as a musician. Being occasionally treated as handmaiden and dependent was fair enough as long as I got my own way when I wanted it. There were established roles for women in popular music-making and Licorice and I fulfilled none of the requirements, nor were we the long-suffering wives and girlfriends or glamorous PAs.

We made friends with none of the few women on the same stages as us, and never talked together about women in popular music. It wasn't only our lack of professional status that seemed to affect attitudes towards us. Joan Baez, The Grande Dame of folk music, made it more than clear what she thought of the band, especially Licorice and me. If she saw Mike and Robin as purveyors of fey and whimsical irrelevancy, she disdained us girls as too stupid and ignorant to meet her standards of moral integrity.

Mike and Robin she would talk to with that conscious diva smile, but we girls she blatantly cut dead. What other conclusion could we draw? Her vaunted interest in the welfare of the common people and other women's lives didn't extend to us. She sang protest songs against poverty and racism, evoked equal rights and damned the evils of capitalism with a dark, serious look that just annoyed me. I saw her with her chorus of black girls towed along behind, parading through Big Sur no different from any other Prima Donna. I looked enviously at new turquoise and silver "native American"-style jewellery in the little shop while she bought original antique versions at rock-star prices. And who knows how they had been robbed from their original owners?

Other women that we encountered were usually interesting and pleasant enough. I met Janis Joplin across the clothes rails at a store in LA where I bought old dresses. She was as free and blowsy there as on the stage, loud and impatient, cursing when something ripped as she roughly pulled off a silk top. A genuine icon of the times, she didn't claim special treatment and was never pretentious or dismissive. We shopped for leathers where Gracey Slick bought her fringed tops. Foot-long strips of thin fine suede hung from our sleeves too, and we enjoyed the same dramatic flourish as they swayed like the sea with every gesture. But it was less fun than hunting through old-clothes shops to find a peasant dress or silky camisole no one else had.

Sick headaches

Touring also meant too little sleep, strange meals, too much coffee and a life unstable in all its aspects. We got sick with nagging pains not important enough to diagnose but still demanding treatment. One morning I was reluctantly taken to a small clinic where my searing earache was diagnosed as an abscess. Joe leant over one shoulder as the doctor told me it would be agonising for a while but would heal quicker for being lanced. Except I'd be on a plane in an hour, where the normal discomfort of changing pressures would be magnified. "Just take more painkillers and it'll be fine when you land." It was awkward on stage that night, with the music sounding far away and indistinct in one ear. Habit and close observation got us through.

When Licorice was really suffering she stayed in bed as long as possible, seeing no one, or else disappeared like a poorly cat to find her own cures, or oblivion in places we knew nothing of.

Robin treated illness as a passing unserious aberration in the context of infinite lives. That was no help when I developed some strange symptom which seemed to threaten catastrophe. Every counter-cultural group with any pretensions to literacy had to be seen to visit the City Lights Bookstore in San Francisco. There I picked up a book on Hinduism and read a few pages, as the others looked for travel reading. The convincing statements of recurring lives horrified me so much that I fainted. I had to be picked up off the floor and revived. Possibly exhaustion and lack of protein contributed, but it was triggered by the idea of having to start again and build another life in another time. Better angel harps on clouds than reincarnation.

California matched all the expected clichés of glamour and gloom. Sad blondes with dreams of stardom really were serving petrol at gas stations and waitressing in coffee shops, still discussing failed hopes and high aspirations. We ate breakfasts at Barney's Beanery and spent afternoons at pool parties where any drug you might fancy was available.

Stoned bodies lay around on sunbeds, while a favoured journalist might attempt an interview. It was better to watch than join in, and we were not sufficiently famous to attract much attention when Jefferson Airplane or Grateful Dead were in town. Every girl seemed to be a tall, sun-bleached blonde or a sooty silky brunette, with Barbie Doll faces, lightly draped in Indian muslin or brilliant silks.

A journalist who'd written a definitive book on pop music moved his sunbed across to mine for the afternoon. He surfaced after concerts once or twice, in New York and again in London, but it was a mutual curiosity about colliding lives rather than any friendly understanding on either side. During a drunken moment he confessed he usually stuffed a compensatory sock down his swimming trunks, an unforgivable idiocy in my eyes. Afterwards I could never escape this image even when sturdy jeans hid the evidence.

In the hotel lobby our paths crossed with The Doors and Jim Morrison, turning the moody photographs of album covers into real life. We shared a record label but never sought acquaintance. At Roman Camps Mike and I had played the first two albums often, admiring the bizarre street scene on one and Morrison's sultry face on the other. We had been thrilled by the mysterious anarchy of the words and the trippy atmosphere. This was psychedelic rock and they were city freaks, but we felt we had something in common. But we knew there was nothing to talk about as we neatly ate our sedate breakfasts at Barney's Beanery, glancing over as they sprawled across floor and tables. We sat shiny and showered, enjoying the novelty of cornflakes with strawberries and bacon with fried plantain. Their slurring and

Mike playing guitar outside the cabin, New Mexico, 1969

drawling conversations, rumpled shirts and grubby hands made it clear their night was still unfinished.

They stuffed down piles of syrupy pancakes. Abandoned plates of beans and bacon, and beer cans accumulated on their tables, and on the floor around them. They made loutish comments to pretty waitresses. If Mike wished he was one of them, he never let on. Joe pulled the car up at the kerb, sounded the horn and we left obediently. They were still there, no different from any of the other sagging faces lined up at the bar.

In LA we were delivered and collected by car rather than free-roaming, which always tried our tempers. Joe took us down to New Mexico for a break, to stay in a real *"log cabin home"*, as in Mike's song. Peering out of a small plane from Santa Fe, we were surprised that the desert resembled the scenery in Hollywood cowboy films. As our tourist guide, Joe pointed out the crimson slash of the Grand Canyon.

It was strange to land at small airports where red-faced men in jeans and cowboy shirts wore Stetsons as the habit of a lifetime, not for dressing up. They had dusty old cowboy boots with sharp pointed toes, stacked heels and fancy stitching, all scuffed and creased by daily wear. Shirts with embroidered yokes and cuffs, like stage-clothes for Country and Western singers, were for sale in airport shops. I bought a black one with red roses. It never saw an ISB stage, but it was fun to own.

The New Mexican cabin itself was an old settler's dream, iron stove in the corner and chimney rising up the wall through the shingle roof. The sun was blazing so we didn't light a fire, but we saw the logs piled up neatly in their shed waiting for the winter snows to arrive.

In the daytime, the stream coming off the mountains was icy cold, and Mike and I spent happy hours sitting on the pebbles with the water bubbling over our feet. It was too hot for Robin and Licorice and they preferred to pass the days inside or in the woody shade near the cabins.

When Joe's brother joined us, we hired horses and went trekking along mountain trails, with trees protecting from the sun. Bored with our leisurely progress and half-hearted chat, Robin was soon impatient to get back to his cabin and whatever work he had in hand. His moods were rarely concealed, and his horse picked up on them. It set off at speed, with Robin looking like Don Quixote, long and thin under his broad-brimmed hat, thrown from side to side and kept safe only by the solid armchair-mass of the Western saddle.

When we too eventually arrived at the entrance to the stable, he was aggrieved by our lack of concern. Licorice had laughed with us. She enjoyed the quiet countryside morning away from touring and towns, and was always surprisingly good at physical activities when shaken out of the quiet inertia of her life with Robin.

Eventually the band's success demanded a glitzier base in San Francisco, but before this we stayed at a hotel pretending to be a Mexican hacienda, all fake plasterwork and curly wood with ancient doors made yesterday. This was conveniently near tram-lines so I could get around town without asking for help, which was always good. We shopped in the market together for peasant shirts, or the little painted clay figures that reminded me of the drawings Mike's sister made. We bought ocarinas to take home to musical friends, a sake set with small blue and white flask and tiny bowls, peacock-feather ear-rings, jade jewellery and turquoise and silver from Mexico. A bark cloth from the South Seas would make a good tablecloth, batik fabrics made everywhere more colourful.

By contrast, during winter in Canada we bought Mukluk boots and furry hats during an unusual few hours of group togetherness in a square in Montreal, as children sang carols. We enjoyed snowball-fights in a landscape covered in snow thicker and whiter than we ever saw in Scotland.

Such small events show our changing relationships and the way we behaved on tour better than factual accounts of "what happened" or the more interesting and exciting memories. The previous year Joe had taken us to his parents' home for Thanksgiving, and their very American kindness and hospitality had been repaid by our immediate transformation. As we jostled into their parlour, we changed from untidy and unruly hippies to well-behaved and polite young people in a family circle. This reminder of gentler and more relaxed times together was good for us.

We were all used to the alienations of cities, but with no time to build familiar niches within the barren space or to construct the protective barriers of friendship, the daily indifference is more oppressive. So our behaviour changed for the worse and our self-importance, fostered and increased by evenings of adoring audiences, exacerbated our jarring sense of a world out of joint.

Weeks into touring, we became jaded, sullen, confrontational and ever less willing to compromise. The naïve beliefs informing the earlier work of Mike and Robin – about universal harmony and good fellowship – were tested by every small irritation of enforced closeness.

Robbed of simple escapes into personal time, the overriding need to write and play tormented both Mike and Robin. For me it was easier. The Victorian novels I brought with me were a welcome diversion, as were sightseeing outings into the shadowy silences of churches or museums.

Shopping was even fun alone. A sharp interchange with a shop girl at Woolworths on 23rd Street, who told me mini-skirts were a bad choice with my legs, kept my feet on the ground. I could take my knitting anywhere. Its simple mechanical activity was restful. Licorice also found sufficient relaxation to maintain her usual self-contained placidity. But for all of us, weeks of life seemed to be led entirely in public, the boundaries between on- and off-stage eroded, the vanities and illusions of the performance spilled over into our daily relationships.

Gradually everything had changed. We had relied on the intense physical intimacy of four people whose strong individual personalities often jelled and our closeness was protected by what was not done or said. Over long periods of time we shared small spaces, through all the heightened and diminished awarenesses of drug-taking, travelling and performing. This interdependence is felt rather than described, creeping into all the senses. And it remains: every old photo carries for me the remembered touch, smell and sound of Mike, Robin and Licorice. Like any family loss, the erosion of this shared life was a process of bereavement. We stubbornly failed to recognise or to acknowledge any problems and others followed our lead, rewriting the story to fit their own parameters.

Rose by the river, West Saugerties, New York, 1970

Studio Times

1967-1970

Recording sessions are time set apart from the outside world. LP follows LP in a fixed pattern. Mike and Robin write and play the new songs to each other, and work out the accompaniment together. Lic and I are listening from another room, until we're brought in to play our parts, with whatever instrument best suits. When enough material is available and Joe Boyd could get the studio time, recording of the next LP begins.

Joe Boyd

Once tours were over, the major demand on Mike and Robin's time and talents, and on all our lives, was recording. The cycle of our year matched the seasons. Summer was a lively rainbow of festivals. We'd snatch a few weeks at home in the UK, then leave again in Autumn, like the birds. First we'd go round Britain, then America, and home for Christmas. After Christmas we were off again, with weeks in between for recording. The choice of studio was mainly Joe's. Whatever reasons he gave us we believed, but we preferred to record where we felt at home.

ISB were not good at dividing work from the rest of life, a distinction we tried not to make. As long as we could get away with it, we maintained that work should also be play. This meant the job of record-producer was not an easy one, extending in ways that were not obvious beyond the studio itself into the whole of the band's together-time. When Joe was around London with us in the early days, we would go out as a foursome after a day in the studio, which helped bolster group goodwill and co-operation.

Joe's attention pleased Robin and Mike and distracted us all from personal wrangles. He took us to see the shocking new musical *Hair*, with its on-stage nudity. It preached peace, love and hippiedom and the actors looked like us. We saw our own lives set to a different soundtrack. We all got stoned and went to see *2001: A Space Odyssey*. We could find our own amusements very well, but they tended to be divisive. Unifying us was part of Joe's record-producing skill, making sure we turned up in the studio the next day cheerful and willing to compromise.

If there was a schedule it was never clear to Lic or me, but we arrived on time and stayed as long as we were welcome. We knew when our presence was no longer needed, and Joe was good at politely throwing us out: "We just need to… and we'll see you later on at…" John Wood and the engineers left band-liaison to him. Generally Joe didn't bother being tactful, and just didn't comment, but in the studio he had to play the game, to nurse the music along. Exhaustion increased as the hours went by, but conflict mainly took place outside, in quiet bitter words and blank faces before or after.

The record company relied on Joe to produce a saleable sound from Mike and Robin. As the overseer of their earlier transitions he knew them both well enough to give them free rein, until one or other asked how, why or if the music was working. Low-key intervention helped them to clarify ideas and resolve differences without resentment.

But diplomacy didn't always work. Sometimes there was no happy solution. Mike was usually responsive, considering comments with a calm face, replying to Joe's "What if…?" with a quick OK, his rising tone turning the affirmation into doubt. Mike was willing to try for agreement and generally repressed irritation. But if he blanked the suggestion, turning away "to look for something", this meant his mind was fixed. He too could be steadily insistent when he chose.

When Mike's face looked detached and disinterested, I knew he felt we were wasting time and money. He wouldn't admit this, but his guitar playing now became aggressively accurate, yet blatantly devoid of expression, until the music caught him again and his face brightened. Concentrated studio time without distractions suited his way of working, doggedly and patiently in pursuit of the musical dream. It took serious dissension for Mike to lose interest for long.

Similarly quiet, Robin was less amenable to criticism and more clearly adamant. His shoulders tensed and it seemed likely he would walk out but he didn't. On the very few occasions he was faced with a united front, including Licorice, he shrugged his shoulders and ceased arguing. He didn't bear grudges. The new thoughts and images chasing through his mind pushed the old ones to the side. The unspoken fall-back position was that the song-writer made the final decision and everyone accepted it, for the moment at least.

Dissension wore us all out, so we avoided it, but sustained dissatisfaction occasionally turned to apathy. Even Joe gave in when we all fell into torpor, collapsing on benches or the floor like zombies. Sometimes Mike returned to the studio in the evening, after everyone else had gone home, to talk to Joe and mix an improvement. But Joe was usually glad to get rid of them both and carry on undisturbed, to make the best of the recordings.

Joe's managerial role with ISB changed as other interests took precedence but by then Mike and Robin had more confidence in their status and experience and were content to go it alone. His place in the recording studio remained unchallenged. There was no substitute for his expertise and understanding. Getting a good record from such capricious musicians demanded ruthless determination, sensitivity and enormous flexibility. When he finally moved to Warner Bros some of the wonder in our lives, and in the music, faded.

Joe's contribution was as much about public relations as it was technical and aesthetic skills, or nearly. He was the peacemaker, creating an environment in which Mike and Robin were as comfortable as they could be. He couldn't always resolve disagreements or mistrusts, but he could ensure both felt their voices were being heard and their wishes attended to, personally and musically. Unless both were reasonably content, the friction in the studio made it difficult to achieve a result which would survive subsequent arguments.

It wasn't just the music, he had to catch the personalities too, the idiosyncratic voices that conveyed the physical charisma of Mike and Robin. The people sitting at home spinning their LP wanted to imagine how Mike and Robin looked and lived when their voices entered the room. Joe built all the bridges, between the musicians, the music they made, the mechanics of a studio and the record company. Years of enthusiasm and experience, sensitivity to the spirit of the times, admiration and respect for the musicians, all went into that studio time.

In the replays he would point out details they might not have noticed. Was this instrument accurately tuned? Was that fumble a playing fault or a recording failure? He had developed a fine ear for tuning, he said, by sitting underneath his grandmother's grand piano as a child, listening as she played.

What everyone wanted to hear on record was the musical conversation between two song-writers, as each brought out the best in the other. Only Joe could identify how this worked in the playing and singing of a take. Even when the words and notes stayed the same, small variations of tone and style told the stories to the world. If Robin wasn't committed to a song, or was bored on a bad day after too many delays, it was usually obvious in his music. He sounded as if he didn't care and his singing mirrored the blank, absent expression on his face. His mind was obviously elsewhere, and Joe could hear this even when we, tired or distracted, couldn't.

Repetition quickly dampened Robin's mood. It was always easier if a song was comparatively new and interesting. A much-performed song guaranteed an awkward recording session. There was a down-side to his insistence on playing new material on-stage, if recording it was delayed.

On-stage his longer songs could be so tedious that I frequently began to daydream. In the studio, despite length, multiple takes and over-dubbing, Robin never lost concentration on these lengthy pieces, whatever the rest of us felt. He was spilling out his soul and wanted all the shades and colours to be heard. Sometimes it seemed he would prefer to play it all himself, picking up instrument after instrument and improvising to get the sound he wanted, as the rest of us sat around and waited. On-stage he could change the music instantly and spontaneously to embrace a new thought or emotion, and Mike could follow him. In the studio he had to be more thoughtful, becoming totally absorbed in the process of working and re-working and leaving Mike behind. Any interruption or attempt to interfere with his creative flow only made the wait longer.

I never knew how much John Wood contributed to the process of recording ISB. He set the tone of the studio and its sound-engineering originality, playing a major part in our studio life through his working relationship with Joe, but his presence was enigmatic. He didn't dress like a hippie and seemed to be from a much more serious world of work. People talked as if he lived in the studio, and I often wondered if he had a home or a family. If he looked as if he'd slept on the floor in a corner somewhere, he probably had, supported throughout his 24-hour days with whatever stimulants were available. Most were, just out on the King's Road.

Sound Techniques

John Wood's studio, Sound Techniques, housed in an old dairy on Old Church St in Chelsea, was a familiar space for us, with the pastry shop around the corner. The engineers usually looked worn-out and irritable as we arrived, all in various states of disarray, hauling in whichever instruments were currently in favour.

It was the ethos at Sound Techniques to nurture the creative lives of its clients rather than impose anything organisational or technical on their work. Home studios were a wild dream only available to the most successful bands. Sound Techniques offered an alternative, its atmosphere free and relaxed, with few interruptions. We weren't overwhelmed with slick efficiency or needless formality. If we had to switch chairs or adjust microphones they slid in and kept it quick. Mike and Robin got tetchy if they thought anything was prioritised over the music, if a change

"I'll just try it with a pick-up:" Robin goes electric at Sound Techniques

interfered with how they played, or a chair was uncomfortable, or they couldn't see properly. When they sulked, it wasted time and goodwill. But they trusted Joe.

The studio atmosphere was often much less fraught than in the forced rehearsals at home as tour dates loomed. Technicians provided some audience stimulus, and concentration on the work in hand lowered internecine tensions. The neutral atmosphere of work in progress made up for the lack of any applause or visible approval.

The studio had dark DIY walls and was not much tidier than our own houses. Different types of sound insulation, some not far removed from egg-boxes apparently, seemed to have been stuck on as they came to hand, without a master-plan. The room was dim, dusty and grubby, its black concrete floor pitted and scuffed. But all this just added to the sense of laissez-faire, like the Chelsea Hotel. Whether we were gloomy, stoned, squabbling or excited and wildly in love, here we would be sheltered and encouraged. It felt like home.

Like all Joe's musicians, we depended on his presence at the mixing desk, always glancing up at him through the glass after a take. A clear if unspoken distinction existed. The control room upstairs was the hallowed ground we only entered by Joe's specific invitation.

There we listened to replays, all four squashed onto an old couch with cigarette burns on the arms and collapsing cushions. With its knobs, sliders and lights, the sound-desk was like the controls of a spaceship. Tapes spun round in their cabinets, and the engineers' talk was all technical asides. Joe would glance across at Mike or Robin occasionally, to check that they were paying attention. Seeing everyone so engrossed, I knew these skills were something to be learned, another way of playing and making. Talking to an unseen audience through the machines. I wanted to know how to work them but I couldn't ask, it wasn't my place.

A day in the studio

Mike and Robin never made a fuss about preparing. We all understood that the studio was more important than the stage. There were no tantrums about time, place or session musicians. We chatted and sat around drinking coffee and reading odd magazines left behind by earlier visitors. When the sun was shining on our world and we were happy with ourselves and each other, studio time was a total pleasure.

The King's Road shop windows we walked past, before turning down the narrow alleyway, generally meant purchases had been made. We would drop our bags of shopping on the floor as we went in. We girls made cushions of coats, collecting our belongings around us to establish a personal corner in the big dark space. Here we could sit quietly when not directly involved. We sat near Mike and Robin and watched them, sometimes feeling part of the music. Our lives were in the songs as well as theirs, the days and times and places they wrote about. Lic remembered Robin come back from a walk, with 'The Iron Stone' *"that came from the moon"* in his hand and thoughts. I hadn't been with Mike long when 'The White Bird' on the lake calmed him after a night of storming, tormented thoughts. All had been shadows and confusion indoors. I too took a walk that morning, wearing Mike's clothes for some unaccountable reason. I saw a blackbird in the topmost branches of a tree, singing its heart out to the rising sun. The day was better for both of us after that.

Technicians hope for calm, hush and deadened sound. After sleepless nights, lovers' tiffs or internecine disputes, we were often wayward and unwelcome. Their hearts must have sunk as we came through the door, wearing full hippie regalia in the early days, creating innumerable little noises every time we moved. Rings clicked on microphones, bangles and bracelets jangled, beads rattled as we turned our heads or bent over the strings.

We were noisy also because we were careless, dropping things and shifting feet and chairs around to find them. The many instruments, their cases, cloths and stands were obstacles to be negotiated. Quiet movement was unlikely.

Made in tropical climates with primitive glues, the instruments themselves generated problems when being recorded, issues that Mike and Robin had never considered when they saw them in a shop, a market or a souk. Gourds and skins might arrive in the studio already affected by temperature change, with strings broken and tuning pegs loose, or worse. Robin's lute was unpacked in pieces after a winter flight across the Atlantic.

Many of them, Western as well as Oriental, had sympathetic strings, resonating to particular frequencies. One night Mike and I stayed in the house of a sitar player. His music room, where we slept, had sitars and other instruments hanging on the wall. In the silence of the early morning it was alive with their sounds, a low, varied buzz and hum with creaks and cracks as the temperature fell or draughts caught the fat gourds. In a daytime studio our own instruments made their own particular music. This too was part of the ISB recorded sound, adding to the atmospheric quality for anyone with an ear to hear such subtleties.

In times of adversity Licorice or I had to run out for coffee or fruit and snacks, to quieten rumbling stomachs and grumbling musicians. Cakes always meant good humour, especially in the cannabis-munchies days. Later on, when our closeness was disintegrating, I thought of Mike's song 'Warm Heart Pastry' as an unconscious comparison between the present-day *"sour lemon"* grimaces, and earlier, more domestic and harmonious times.

"This is how it goes:" Mike and Rose in a TV studio, 1969

That track was recorded for his *Smiling Men with Bad Reputations* LP, with Pete Townshend and Keith Moon playing as Tommy and the Bijoux, Ronnie Lane on bass and John Cale on viola. Their volume made the point more powerfully than Mike alone could ever have done. He was always hesitant in expressing his dissatisfactions, but here, backed by the rock heavies, I could tell he meant the words as he sang them. We didn't take it too seriously. It was only a song after all.

Nevertheless, we all knew that something different happened in the studio space. There, freed from the physical presence of its writers, their changing moods and varied performances, the music took on a life of its own. Once the tape was made and out in the world, the music was fixed and frozen, beyond our control or intervention. It was on that single performance that critics would make their most lasting judgements, and around which fans spun their ideas of who we were and what we were doing.

Music mistresses

Licorice and I could aggravate as well as assuage Mike and Robin's woes with our presence, and with our lack of musical skills. Lic's voice varied from delicate sweetness to a piercing edge, which was so vital to 'Painting Box' on *5000 Spirits*. Joining in on random percussion as took her fancy on-stage set a precedent for recording. Neither she nor I had a drummer's feel for rhythm, but we more or less kept up most of the time, fine in performance, not so good on record.

Her whispery tones are heard on 'A Very Cellular Song' and 'Minotaur's Song' on *The Hangman's Beautiful Daughter*, and she is credited with finger cymbals. In those days she wasn't always there, but as she drifted in I bet she joined in more than that. Joe probably didn't encourage her and Robin probably didn't object.

By the time of *Wee Tam And The Big Huge* we were both a constant presence, active participants in the creative and the home lives of Mike and Robin. Lic had been written into Robin's songs for a while and 'You Get Brighter' was sung to me on the phone from Scotland one night as I stood feeling like a stranger in a strange land in my parents' hall. By contrast 'Log Cabin Home' was musical fun, a traditional string band song with a chance for me to join in on fiddle. I contributed authentic folk amateurism while Robin made the real fiddle music. I knew how it was meant to be played even if I didn't succeed. Practice had mastered the stress of getting the notes right and that was all that was needed. Robin played his complex fast improvisations round my basic melody, and his skill made me sound good too on the play-back.

My Syrian drum accompanied 'Cousin Caterpillar' on record and on-stage, and my tabla pursued the hectic rhythmic interventions of 'The Iron Stone'. On-stage and in the studio, my heart would sink when I was called upon to play them. Played properly, tabla are melodic and rhythmic. I liked their shape and feel, and the ritual of unpacking them from the padded bags I had sewn. They looked so good, sitting on their little padded rings with the lights gleaming off the metal bodies and the thonging of the skins. I made rough attempts at tuning the skins with the little hammer that came with them.

A few hours spent with an Indian musician in London persuaded me that tabla are best left to those brought up with them from the cradle. But I was stuck with them, because any new instrumental possession was another tool for Mike and Robin and had to be used somewhere. Robin the multi-instrumentalist likely realised their complex subtlety and was unwilling to risk being beaten by them. But all I could achieve was dull thuds on the one and a slightly higher tap on the other, which made for a poor and very unsatisfactory sound on the recordings, embarrassing me on-stage.

Licorice's voice earned me credits that were mainly hers as we joined in on many choruses, but she also played Irish Harp on 'The Iron Stone', and miscellaneous percussion we never thought to mention. If we were in the studio when Mike and Robin were recording we often joined in. If someone put a mic in front of us then it was counted. If not we were still there.

Only with *Changing Horses* were we formally acknowledged as being in the band, which was long after we had been integral to the stage show. I didn't always see that as a gain. It had been more fun before. When they were forced to take us seriously, people began to be more demanding. The idyll of minstrel life was losing its simplicity. What had been spontaneous now had to be organised. A mic sat before me every session, and responsibility was ever-present.

Changing Horses was not a critical success and I could understand why. I never liked 'Dust be Diamonds', officially written by both Mike and Robin to demonstrate our new-found togetherness. *"Happy happy all the time"* felt more ironic every time we had to rip though the words on-stage. When we recorded it, the electric instruments jarred and jangled, never merging comfortably into an ISB song. On-stage, with Lic and I on guitar and bass, 'Big Ted' was a jolly romp, as Robin added jokes and pantomime asides and Mike grunted along with it all. But with its floppy rhythm section, and visuals that couldn't come across on record, it was never for the studio.

The same can be said for some of 'Creation', a very long track whose beautiful and haunting introduction ought to have promised a feast of ISB. On-stage, the colours, lights, and drama held attention, as Robin's vocal incantation faded into hypnotic repetitions of melody. As notes and rhythm fragment, our changes of movement and expression held it together. Our performing presence was needed to carry the listener through the shifting musical references, and to keep the unity of the song.

Left to my own devices, my bass lines were at best basic. When Mike wasn't interested – as with Robin's 'Mr and Mrs' – he left its bass line rudimentary, and Robin couldn't be bothered to improve it. Robin's concern was with the lyrics, and the backing track remained nondescript and uninspired.

My fiddle-playing for 'Black Jack Davey' was not much better than the schoolgirl violin on 'Log Cabin Home'. I had hoped to leave all that behind me, along with the smiling girl in peasant blouse with peasant fiddle in the photos, but this was a recurring picture that people wanted to see. By then I preferred the leather look. I was surprised and not best pleased when Licorice laid claim to bass on 'Davey' but we couldn't be exclusive with instruments.

Mike's voice on 'White Bird' was always exquisite, with its bending, yearning tones alongside Robin's flute. As it flies over the quiet peace of our accompaniment, it beautifully captures the image of the morning swan. I never thought the guitar solo was too long, though Robin sometimes got impatient. The bass line that Mike wrote and I played was more cheerful than meditative, an undercurrent of optimism

From left, Robin and Mike in Sound Techniques studio

and, as the melodies resolve back into the theme it's a rebirth after cold death, a return to life and warmth and being together. When we painted the little pictures for the album sleeve I tried hard to put that in the image but in vain. Painting wasn't my thing either and I couldn't catch the feel of it.

The record as a whole was not a happy choice of music to introduce me and Lic to the public as band-members and the outtakes were better. I managed my little riff efficiently on 'Waiting for You', where I was presented as that "famed Oriental bass player Miss Fenola Bumgarner… first time in captivity". This came out on the *Be Glad* LP, just after I left the band, as did 'Come with Me'. I was pleased with myself on this. I'd learned descant recorder at school, as we all did, but playing tenor recorder was my idea and a new venture. It fitted in well beneath Lic's high pure voice.

I Looked Up was an important LP for me because I played bass on Mike's 'The Letter' alongside Dave Mattacks, at that time the drummer for Fairport Convention. Compared to the Woodstock version, this bounces along, tight and strong. I could make it work with the drums alongside me, and it felt good to hear myself when we played it back. I hadn't created the bass line but I did play it, and without letting the drummer down. I felt I'd earned a sulky pose in leathers, bass slung across my body – but nobody was there to take the picture. My leather hat and shirt on the LP cover was a gesture towards this.

As time went by, Licorice insisted on taking a greater part in the recording process and in deciding how Robin's songs should sound. Joe's disgusted face soon made clear his point of view as he retreated into the office, leaving Robin to sort it out. Understandably, Joe was less tolerant of us than of Mike and Robin, and less concerned to hide his feelings. One standing discomfort was the lack of a good drummer and bass player to lay down confident, certain rhythms rooting everything above them. Neither Lic nor I achieved this, and at the time there was no electronic way to compensate.

I couldn't even sing in tune much of the time, with no natural ear for tone or harmony and my previous singing limited to hymns in school assembly. Joe's tactful editing erased the worst errors and engineered the sound of the rest without destroying what little self-confidence I had. I remained ever-willing to join in on choruses, and even to risk the solo vocal of 'Walking Along With You'.

Many times Joe suggested that in the studio Mike and Robin should play all the parts themselves or get session musicians. The recordings would then be stronger and more effective than anything relying on Lic's efforts or my own. But Robin and Mike would not accept his judgement. They always insisted that records should be as near as possible to the genuine and authentic sound fans heard when they came to see us. Joe did his best, but was often dissatisfied.

Mike and Robin's rivalry may have been the issue here, with Robin always following Lic's will, and Mike unable to respond differently. A change of personnel for recording would not have offended me. Joe could have arranged a compromise, but even when take after take failed, Licorice would assert her rights and Robin stuck with her. Mike would hit his limits, with cold looks all round and few words spoken.

Happy times

But Mike and Robin working well together were a joy to watch, Mike transported by the music, concentrated and thoughtful, Robin caught up in the sounds of whatever instrument he was playing, intent on the strings, hair falling over his face, then glancing across at Mike and seeming to gain new energy from the contact. They talked very little, communication was made through the instruments as melody initiated response back and forth. Emotions bent and soared as fantastically as the lyrics they sang.

A first take was for engineers to make their necessary adjustments as we found our way into the session. The work began after that. By the time Licorice and I were actively involved on most tracks, we had the luxury of running through the song again as one or other of us made mistakes. This was comforting. For me the aim was simple: to get through with as few faults and re-runs as possible. If I failed, I hoped judicious mixing could overcome the problem. There was no question of me adapting, changing or responding. I was trying accurately to repeat a learned piece. I played as well as I could, essentially concentrating on my own part with no deviations, just as I did on stage. If it was correct, I was pleased and satisfied.

Once a take was successful for Mike and Robin, the day moved along better. Robin walked around making jokey comments as we changed seats or instruments. Mike's brisk, business-like studio manner relaxed back into easy friendship with all. In these circumstances we saw the best of their partnership. Undistracted by minor annoyances, the music flowed from both as they played for their future audiences and one another. Once a final take was mixed and agreed on as the best that could be done, I was very aware of the privilege of being in the studio with them. Unlike most, I had seen every day from the first attempts at a new song to the finished tapes. A tune I had heard Mike playing and replaying, adding to and elaborating, was now a set piece. Little pencil notes on scraps of paper were now the lyric to a song everyone was going to hear. I was pleased other people could now share it.

ISB at play

Sometimes Mike and Robin made outlandish demands on Joe's patience, which Licorice and I aided and abetted. We believed in their work, but this was also part of the game of being ISB. We often had tremendous fun trying to make a sound one of them had dreamed up. The four-track machines we started off with at Sound Techniques made it hard to reproduce the mosaic of music, so we resorted to bizarre improvisations.

For 'The Water Song' on *The Hangman's Beautiful Daughter* Mike or Robin decided that they wanted the sound of a babbling brook. The rhythmic movement of water was absolutely essential to the imagined musical landscape. The nearest approximation was water sloshing around a tin bucket. The cleaner's plastic mop-bucket wouldn't do, because the mop-squeezer got in the way. We needed a metal one for the sharper sound of water slapping against hard surfaces.

There was no convenient ironmonger in the middle of the King's Road. After some running about, a bucket was found in the household basement of Peter Jones on the corner of Sloane Square. We all laughed a lot, getting very wet as the bucket was constant refilled from the hand basin in the toilet. We scooped gravel from a nearby gutter and tried that, to get the variation of pitch that water running over stones makes, but the shaking and tipping of the bucket put us in imminent danger of electrocution, blowing up all the circuits at Sound Techniques. Cables had to be fished out of the water running over the floor.

For 'Koeeoaddi There' Robin wanted the sound of skates cutting through ice. Eventually they discovered that a knife run along the fine flexible tongue of a Jew's Harp produced a fair imitation of the effect. If he was feeling particularly playful in concert he sometimes vocalised the sound, but the original was better.

Easier solutions included banging together random wood, metal or instruments, sliding one surface against another for a slithering sound, mistreating an instrument to produce its cry of pain, changing tunings or exploring the limited technical possibilities of the recording machines. But the band was interested in the physical, sensual interaction with the real organic world and the people in it, on stage and in the studio, so manufactured imitations were a last resort.

The willingness to make do and improvise was part of ISB's charm for the kids who had grown up, like ourselves, with the limited resources of the 1950s, and not yet earned the money that enabled them to choose other ways. It didn't seem particularly unusual to us that we had gathered instruments from all corners of the globe. Relatives returning from fighting or working in far-flung enclaves of the Empire had hung such objects in the suburban hallways of our childhoods, as decorative souvenirs. We all broke many when we pretended to play them, but Robin really could make music out of anything he picked up. The tour manager, Huw Price, told us about the baffled looks and the "What the hell is that thing?" that he had to put up with as he laid out our stages.

We had endless entertainment recording 'Queen Juanita' early in 1970 for *I Looked Up*. Now we had the luxury of being able to order in strange instruments, which upset the roadies with their size and complexity, and Joe with their cost. But they weren't much better than our earlier home-made inventions. Mike wanted to see how a 1930s electronic Ondes Martenot worked, but he never really found out how to play it. Even the studio tech wizards couldn't make much of it, and we only got the odd squeak from it. The "sea machine" did sound like waves on the beach but was little better than the bucket we used on 'Water Song'. The vast length of its wooden trough of water and pebbles took up half the studio. It got in the way of cables and mics, threatening a deluge and soaking any roadie called on to tip or shake it around to vary the effect.

Studio trials

Sound Techniques was keen on Mike and Robin's musical exploration, I assumed, because it too wished to change recorded music for the better, to undermine the rigid dominance of the mammoth names of the business. Things were different at the Island Records studio in Notting Hill.

We turned up as instructed, and were chivvied into what seemed a vast room, full of empty space and microphones. For the next hour or so all we heard was the Jimi Hendrix Experience, shut off and invisible in the next-door studio, their volume overwhelming their sound insulation. Our timid music would never win this battle of the reverberation of the joint studio wall.

We sat and waited until it was all over, never even getting a glimpse in compensation as they left. Compared to the image I had of them, we were small, shabby and ineffectual.

In Chelsea, it was never impressed upon us that recording time cost money, although I guess Joe made attempts to hurry things along. In studios more corporate than Sound Techniques, the atmosphere was very different, particularly in the US where technicians often looked dubious or disdainful. Many were musicians themselves, amazed at our chaos, and at Lic's and my sheer inadequacy. They made it evident that they could do far better themselves, given the chance.

I tried to be honest in such situations, without betraying the band, destroying anyone's dreams or claiming to be a dizzy girl who knew no better. I was not a musician and made no pretence of being one. I loved playing what I was taught and delighted in acquiring new skills but this was the extent of my expertise.

The difficulty arose when I was assumed to have musical abilities that were far beyond me and could therefore play along spontaneously with any jam-session that might arise socially. I could not. Joe tells that Steve Winwood had visited Sound Techniques to ask if he could borrow me, and Joe had to say, "Oh no, she has another appointment that day." Not that my skills were usually requested by the stars, but the limitation was a recurring embarrassment. An obvious solution, intensive music lessons, was never suggested. I would have been pleased to learn more and we all knew I had the dedication.

But Licorice and I were ideal as we were for what Mike and Robin wanted at the time. We didn't challenge their creative ideas or their skills and never tried to upstage them. And we added something to the band's performances and image. Most of the time I could do just enough. Increased skills would have brought greater demands. It was easier for everyone, including Joe, to limit the number of importunate voices. Having our instruments tuned for us was one small but public demonstration of our dependent status, musically and financially, and we both accepted it contentedly.

As studio equipment became more sophisticated, so did the recording process, moving away from the apparent "front-room" casualness of the early days. But by then Licorice and I were old hands. Now we sat singing or playing along in our own little corners, with the other tracks on our earphones, no longer feeling uncertain or isolated by our separation from Mike and Robin. This demonstrated some independence in our music-making and we rose to the challenges.

Smiling Men

By the time Mike Heron recorded his solo album *Smiling Men* in late 1970, I was more competent musically and less impressed by the novelty of recording. I was also less attached to Mike and more critical of ISB. Joe returned from the USA to spend some time with us. We all revelled in the freedom to do something different, although the transition was uneasy, as the cover-photo shows. Robert Plant, a neighbour for a while in Wales after the ISB days, believed that the barrier to Mike's wished-for pop career was ISB's esotericism. Robert admired Mike's music and, some time later, when we talked about the past, said that Mike had very nearly made it, that it was just bad luck he was never a superstar when many lesser talents were.

Nevertheless *Smiling Men* was a playtime chance of escape, for those of us closely involved with Mike. The overt personal and internal band conflicts had diminished, to be replaced by Scientology's repressive influence. Mike seemed more free and joyful when left to his own devices in the studio. He made sure that recording proceeded more quickly and formally. Musicians had tighter schedules, and Joe the confidence that time wouldn't be wasted. Whether due to Mike's reputation or Joe's, or from simply curiosity, the cast-list was spectacular. The names on the album cover only tell part of the story.

Previous ISB albums had involved few outside musicians, and Mike and Robin rarely played on others' work. While they were perfectly friendly with most people we met, at that time there was little effort to widen the scope of their musical acquaintanceship. This creative isolation had increased as Joe moved his interest to the USA from earlier in 1970. Mike's solo venture seemed about to change this.

The session with some of The Who was a revelation of the reviving power of music. Booked to play drums, Keith Moon was not going to

"It's a bit cold in here": Mike draped in Rose's jacket at Sound Techniques

be allowed to miss the appointment. From my dark corner, I saw him staggering through the doorway, seemingly hardly able to walk. Pete Townshend and a roadie collected him, one at each elbow, and virtually carried and dragged him in the direction of the drum kit, already set up for him. He was dropped down on the drum stool, swaying slightly and looking bemused.

The drumsticks were put in his hand and the track was played through his headphones. It was like turning on a switch. He was totally there, instantly, playing with a mastery and energy that looked entirely normal. The track stopped, he slumped back into semi-consciousness, muscles slackened and eyes hazy again. He was hauled off as he had arrived, but Mike had the track and the prestige of it.

Whoever was in the studio formed a chorus when Mike wanted one. Linda Thompson led the singing when I was there, while Susie Watson-Taylor rounded up all-comers, even Joe, to join in just for the hell of it. Mike was delighted with his project and with its progress. The heaviness of recent ISB sessions lifted. Mike laughed and talked with other musicians, sparkling and vivid in a way we hadn't seen for a long time. We realised how much things had changed for all of us. The effects on his music had not been beneficial.

The communal living at Penwern, then the Glen, for the last two years had been driven by Robin's desire to move into multi-media productions. Mike was now committed to the communal life, but the permanent proximity to Robin and to a group of performers more in harmony with Robin's inclinations than his own affected Mike's own music. The tenuous narrative structures in the film (and, later, those of our disastrous Scientology-influenced musical U) constrained his originality. Mike had been allowed some latitude, but, uneasy with the form and forced into these straitjackets, he was stripped of his free flow. Then U was a financial disaster, and this too was dispiriting. Neither ISB nor Stone Monkey had the skills or the inclination to follow him towards rock music.

For me too, the solo LP was a great opportunity. Mike had written a beautiful and fairly complex bass line for his song 'Flowers of the Forest', which I played alongside Dave Mattacks once more. Dave was quiet and approachable. We had played together recording 'The Letter', and knew each other by sight. It was fortuitous that my ventures into playing a bass-line with a proper drummer were with him. I could relax, he was good-natured, his generous skill filled out my limitations, making the best of it for both of us. I was not counting every beat, watching the guitarist as I so often did. I could feel the interchange of rhythms running into my fingers from the drums.

Rose, at Sound Techniques

It was a huge pleasure to hear the track being played back, as my own efforts reflected the whole glory of Dave's technique. It was thrilling and for once I felt like a real musician. I assumed the subject of the song was a newer love, not me, but the bass line was mine and that was even better.

Whether or not they involved me at the time, the honesty of Mike's songs has threaded them through my subsequent life. When his father died, he went into Edinburgh until evening. He came home, went away into another room overnight and wrote 'No Turning Back'. After all the years and turmoils in between, this was the only song for me to play at my own father's funeral. Hearing it again in a public space, it bridged the years with its expression of love and loss.

The Rainbow Fades

1970-1971

I Looked Up is released in April 1970, the month we begin performing *U* as a show, which we take to the US with Stone Monkey, against Joe Boyd's advice. Facing disappointed audiences and financial disaster, Stone Monkey are sent home and we carry on touring as a band only. *U* the album is recorded at great speed during this tour, to be released in October.

The long, long road

I couldn't withdraw from the life around me as Licorice could, but I often wanted to. Before, my reservations about the other three's ideas, activities or friends had always been outweighed by my admiration and affection for them. As they now disappeared into the maw of Scientology, I could only hope that this too was a fad, to run its course and be left behind.

The adulation and respect gained by earlier work carried the band forward for a while. The same audiences came to concerts and talked the same talk as before, but now our responses were different, and the admiration was less well founded. It was sad to watch the destruction of people's dreams. After a gig, hippies wanted to talk the universal language of peace and love to their idols. But Mike and Robin were often indifferent, sometimes falling into Scientology-speak. Eager faces fell and people turned away, looking puzzled. Sometimes the shift from wonder to disappointment was visible.

Our enthusiasms had always been facile and superficial, moving through our lives as fast as we did. At first this had been exciting, opening up new worlds of thought and activity. But as the novelty wore off, I thought more about what our ideas had been and had become. I began to question the value of it all, at least for me.

Every new guru told me how to direct my life. Every political activist claimed higher moral ground than sybarites like us. To anyone close, the emotional and intellectual rift between me and the other three was obvious, though it took a radio interview to establish the full mutual break in confidence.

Amsterdam, 1970

The interview was in the US, probably in November 1969. The interviewer mentioned the campus protests taking place throughout the country, especially in Golden Gate Park, which we had visited recently. They were against the Vietnam War, but generally just anti-establishment as then understood. Unlike other bands, Mike and Robin usually refused to play such events or show any solidarity. We were asked for our opinions. I said that I understood and supported the students' point of view. Mike demanded the interview be stopped and the tape erased. We left in deep silence and returned to the hotel.

We already had separate rooms when we toured, so when I went out to a nearby bar to drown my sorrows with the roadies, it went unnoticed. But this was the culmination of many small disagreements making life uncomfortable. They were stronger in the US than back home, where we had worked out ways to live that obscured differences between us in our little row of cottages. After this I held my peace, preferring to take time to think out the implications of my position.

Not long before this interview, we had spent the afternoon with some earnest representatives of the counter-culture, probably also

Scientologists. We ended up in a macrobiotic restaurant. Robin was now with Janet, and there he could get the swordfish steak that was his current health-food, while Licorice could balance yin and yang to her heart's content. Mike had also found some new friends and was happy enough to join them in their meal.

The menu was bleak and I couldn't face it any more. I slipped out and walked down the street to a nearby supermarket. I bought a steak from the butchery counter and a can of lager to go with it. There was a bench on a patch of grass near the car park. I spread out the carrier bag as tablecloth and ate my impromptu meal in the free, fresh air.

I tore the meat apart with teeth and fingers, savouring the gobbets of raw and bloody flesh, their taste and their texture. Washed down with the beer it felt real and good. I felt healthier after that, and more settled. This was better than all the contrived simplicity, the solemnity, the brown rice and sludgy soup. I rejoined the crowd, happier, more able to appreciate their genuine interest with good feeling.

I was by now convinced that Scientology was nonsense and had no intention of following its theories and rules. I would carry on in my own way, even though this meant the withdrawal of the safety net that ISB offered.

Audiences loved it, critics hated it

On our return to the Glen, Robin's collaboration with Stone Monkey became focused on the production of a full-length show. Following Scientology ideas of the trajectory of the spiritual path, Robin decided on *U* as the title and now the show became the priority. Janet worked on the graphics and lurid colour-schemes that marked its final production and its posters. The project was a follow-on from the fable that Robin had insisted take central position in *Be Glad*. Joe was unimpressed and, except as record-producer, more distanced than ever. Once again, Mike was not enthusiastic, and I shared his unease. I liked Stone Monkey better as individuals now, but I had little confidence they could sustain a long performance work and disliked ISB being relegated to musical accompaniment.

Preparations continued as haphazardly as ever. Robin was now strongly abetted by Stone Monkey's Malcolm le Maistre and, more significantly, by Janet. Scientology demanded formality and propriety and it was not long before their mutual commitment to the sect brought about the marriages of Robin and Janet, Mike and Susie. Janet's Scientology credentials were well established and she was an efficient and active influence on all Robin's views and activities, largely replacing Licorice in the daily organisation of his personal life. Her own artistic and managerial ambitions would be advanced by undertaking an entire stage show. She could claim scenery, props, costume, publicity and ultimately the album cover as her own concept. With Robin's backing and Mike's compliance, her position as production designer was assured.

The dramatic form of the show was never seriously discussed. Robin's sketchy narrative was an erratic series of scenes, with characters that lacked coherence. Their relationship to each other, let alone to the title, was tenuous and unclear. "Everyone involved in *U* had his own idea about what things should look like," Mike later admitted.

Called upon to choreograph such a lengthy piece and with their creative input circumscribed by Robin, Stone Monkey's limitations once again came to the fore. Malcolm and Rakis were aware of their limitations and unhappy with the design and the costumes they would wear. They laughed about the "Las Vegas" effect of black and silver in deco designs and parodied other roles to each other, never clear themselves whether to take the show seriously or not. The lack of conviction in the group's leaders carried over to the others.

Nor was there a director. Rehearsals took place mainly in the Estate's village hall, with no plan for the finished performances. After a couple of hours of aimless hopping around and chatting, people usually gave up. "It'll be all right on the night" was the fall-back position. Everything was amateur, every unskilled performer left to their own choices and devices. Stone Monkey were also the occasional lovers, handymen or random companions of our lives, their homes and employment dependent on ISB which meant there was little room for criticism or artistic negotiation on either side.

Janet brought in a friend, Jane Mock, who worked night and day to sew the costumes Janet designed. Linus, a girl who had played with Dr Strangely Strange also came to stay, helping out with the sewing and contributing to musical and theatrical ideas. She made me an outfit worthy of Abba, in startling yellow silk with short top and wide flares cut with green inserts, all embroidered with trailing flowers. It was too incongruous ever to wear but the design faults were mine. She probably grumbled about it with her friend Mary, but domestic patience was a necessary virtue on the Row, as husbands, fathers and lovers went their own way and demanded their partners did the same.

Mike and I obediently dressed up in the costumes provided and he wrote music, very aware of the demands imposed on his personal inclinations. None of us believed in the plot by the time of the first performance in The Roundhouse in April 1970, or even understood it. Critics disliked the show, reinforcing Mike's distrust in Robin's judgement, and Joe's predictions of doom and bankruptcy if we took it to America. But London audiences loved it. My father, who would have given all he had for the chance to appear on a London stage, turned up unexpectedly at one performance. I knew the strange antics of band and dancers could only look bizarre to him. I hoped that full houses, enthralled faces and wild applause allowed him to assume it said something to the youth of the day, and that he wasn't embarrassed for his daughter.

Robin pointed to the rapturous audiences to justify his belief in the show and insisted that we tour it with Stone Monkey in the US. Lic argued that our doubts were simply the residue of previous lives. As far as doctrine went, this was a Scientology show. Audiences didn't know this.

Joe was right. In the US the four nights at the Fillmore East were a disaster, whether the critic's line was city cool or suburban conservatism.

Ed Ochs in *Billboard* (9th May 1970): "The two-part pop pantomime *U* overworked a cosmic parable of generally pleasant String Band tunes with the mime troupe's mock-oriental illustrations… The two failed to come together, lacking commitment to any new theatrics or story line."

Lisa Mehlman in *The Rockland County Journal* (also 9th May 1970): "The entire production was too long and often extremely confusing. The music alone stands up very well."

The Stone Monkey dancers were sent ignominiously back home. Joe called them in, told them we couldn't take the financial loss any longer and gave them air tickets for the next day. That wasn't pleasant for any of us. These were our friends and they were unhappy and humiliated. After this, it was not a happy tour, the programme reduced to a miserable re-hash of *U* songs, without drama or dancing. Robin was perpetually irritated, Licorice withdrawn and Mike sullen. It wasn't easy to turn on the ISB magic.

We recorded the *U* album in a hurry on that tour, in a studio in San Mateo, just outside San Franciso. Joe Boyd had managed to get a 48-hour weekend deal and, he told us, that was all the time he could book. There would be no opportunities for creative angst or group dissensions. When we arrived at the studio we knew nobody, there was no feeling of sympathy for the music or sense of personal interaction. Technicians seemed to resent the demands made upon them, and no wonder. There was no joy in the work. The large, tidy, efficient-looking studio was bare and desolate, and we huddled in the middle of it, resigned to the process but without pleasurable anticipation.

Evening wore into early morning with Licorice still trying to master a simple rhythm on a basic drum kit, refusing to give up or move on, looking totally bizarre in a fairy dress with a flowered hair band in a bleak night-time studio. Everyone else was desperate, even Robin, who offered to play the part for her. Engineers wanted to go home and we were frantic at the waste of time. She refused any help. Joe even walked out for a while but thought better of it and came back.

It seemed hours later when she finally stopped. We were all hungry, tired and maddened by the repetition. Joe pointed out that we'd just spent any profits the rest of the tour could possibly make on studio time. We might as well have stayed in Scotland.

Fillmore West

If I was getting disillusioned, those who came to see us perform and who knew the music were not. They were willing to be bewitched from the moment they walked in to see our stage set-up, so unlike anyone else's, to the moment they left, singing one of the choruses. The Fillmore West had always been a good venue for us and even if the audience knew about U and felt they were getting second-best, we thought it would turn out alright.

On some tours we arrived in San Francisco direct from London, with a couple of days to recover and plenty of time for a leisurely run through of our plans at the hotel. This time we arrived late afternoon after a long drive in the blazing sun, too hot and too crowded together.

We were dragged in through the stage-door at the same time as all the gear and into a sound-check, then a snack in the dressing-room before the performance. This was California just after the Summer of Love, and someone had thought of us. So there was a bowl of fruit and lots of water, but still no time. We had all been unwell in minor ways in recent days, and, dosed to the eyebrows with prescription painkillers, we were tired and cross.

The two cockney roadies had laid out all our gear, plugged in and disappeared. They never really understood what all this poetry and wailing was about, but they knew what they had to do. Drugs, sex and rock n'roll were what they were after. They probably found it, but they kept out of our way and we never noticed. The resident crew with their hippie talk and quiet drawly accents were looking after us now, and I needed it. I don't suppose the others felt too good either but there was no point in talking about it.

The energy to get through the evening required more than natural adrenaline, which was anyway exhausted somewhere along the road. "I can't make this, I'm worn out," I said to the nearest person. Where from I wasn't sure, but coke appeared as if by magic. Exactly what I'd been thinking of. Maybe Mike, Robin and Licorice all also had their secret stash. But Scientology took a strong line against habits from which they could derive no profit.

In the Fillmore West, the air is always heavy with incense and hazy with cannabis fumes. It's not a theatre but a ballroom, the Carousel Ballroom, with the sprung floor for tangos of yesteryear and ornate plasterwork on pillars, ceilings and cornices that made dancers feel like Hollywood stars. The stage was made for the Big Bands who played for the dancers under glitter balls. By the time we get out there, the room is always packed. People sit on the floor, leaving small gangways around the sides and up the middle. To get out you have to climb over one another. As the hours go by, all the spaces fill up. People relax, edging nearer the stage, leaning against each other as emotions overflow or moving to the side to sway along with the music, if there's any bare floor left by then.

It's not much fun doing the *U* songs out of context. Mike's heart wasn't in it when he wrote them, so they were never my favourites. The songs he cares about and plays with enthusiasm are heading for his solo album. I'm playing bass on many of them, and I stand sideways to the audience and gaze at the amps, which saves on smiles. I always enjoy the bass lines, feeling more free of the others when I'm playing them.

Many of the *U* songs are so obviously Scientology anthems that I can't hear them as a writer's personal outpouring. The songs written for pantomime dance, like 'Hirem Pawnitof', don't work too well without that background, or so it feels to me. But we flog through them and, if not enthralled, the audience is appreciative. The others all drink strong black coffee during the interval, desperate to keep awake. It was only a few days since our 48-hour shift in the recording studio. I have coffee, but I feel like a vibrating string, with all my nerves from top to toe firing on all cylinders.

The second half is more demanding for me. I have a solo to sing and a fiddle line from way back to remember, and I can't hide away. I'm not happy singing 'Walking Along with You'. It works as a kind of parody, with Rakis and John doing their gigolo act in the background, but my voice isn't up to it. I'm fine joining in with Licorice, but I have none of her distinctive quality and can't carry the burden of a song with any power. It sounds all right, and everyone claps. We move on to Mike's very powerful 'This Moment', which raises the mood on-and off-stage. Here is the Mike of earlier times, with a song that's tuneful, thoughtful and simple, and has a lively significance for hippie idealists cherishing every second of the timeless life, enjoying it and not living in fear.

We end the set with 'Log Cabin Home in the Sky'. This proves that Robin and Licorice have given up on the tour. It's an old song, something upbeat to end on, but we play it on automatic pilot. It has no great significance for any of us now. We hope the audience will go out satisfied. Another gig over and we can each get away. I am starting to tremble slightly, from near-total exhaustion, caffeine and cocaine, my shaky hands making it impossible to just carry on and go to a restaurant, as normal. There seems to be no hope of calming down in the company of an after-gig meal.

On a previous trip to San Francisco, as an escape after a gig from the hippie hordes and the Scientologists, I had made friends with a drug-dealer. I thought of this as I stood outside waiting to be collected with the others. I left them and caught a cab. When I told the taxi-driver where I wanted to go he suggested that this was not suitable for a young lady, perhaps assuming from my accent that I was a tourist who needed looking after. I should think twice about visiting the sort of people who lived in that area, he told me. He insisted on waiting in the cab until I was through the front door.

The people that lived behind the door had seemed perfectly reasonable to me in the dressing room last time we were in San Francisco. The dark curly-headed boy was an art student at UCLA and his looks guaranteed a welcome. His friend was the sort of older hippie we picked up as supplementary crew in the US, who had often left respectable family and career to indulge in irresponsibility and freedom.

They had not been invited to the gig and were surprised to see me. I explained that I wasn't proud of the tour and didn't want to share it. I complained about the shaking exhaustion. Black, sticky opium might do the trick, the older one said, and it helped. Now I was losing the tension, relaxing in the company of friends. Drug-dealer friends. The local grass led to a lively conversation continuing late into the night. I fell asleep happily and woke in the new California morning quite normally. Just another day.

When I sat down in the kitchen with a cup of tea I suddenly blacked out, fell off the chair onto my nose, smashing a front tooth. Instinctively I picked myself up and jumped back onto the chair. As I sat there poking my bent tooth, I realised that while I was quite conscious, I was entirely sightless. At the time this was curiously unterrifying, and I was almost calm. There was very little fuss from my hosts either. We did all the right things, I had more tea and a warm bath, and mentally put a time-limit on my unaided recovery before a trip to the hospital was needed. I was lucky, again. The black mist cleared, sight came back, and I didn't feel ill.

We called into a clinic on the way back to the safety of the group hotel, but I didn't bother with the offered brain scan. As long as it was working enough that I could see and talk that was fine. I just needed quiet time alone to relax and watch the TV, and make sure I could

think again. I was too scared to go to sleep in case the awakening was disastrous once more.

As I walked back to my room, the other three were coming along the hotel corridor towards me, going out to lunch I guessed. From their faces, surprised, amused, disapproving, I concluded I didn't look well. But there was a whole afternoon left to recover in. I suffered no after-effects from the escapade. In my extra-mural activities in the US, I wanted to meet people and see what was happening beyond the band and the attractions. When Joe was away, nobody knew the localities to show us around, so I took my chances, and sometimes came across a strange and diverse world.

Sun, Sea and Surf:
California Dreaming

September 1969-1971

As well as musical meetings, Scientology group activities now sometimes spread into days. Increasingly I try to escape into spaces without agendas, itineraries or schedules. The great open spaces, bright suns and inky nights of California give us much-needed opportunities to get away from one another. We tour the US again in late 1970, ending at the Fillmore West in December. I can't wish for a better venue to end a tour. As we leave the stage that night, to the usual happy applause, I don't know it's for the last time. The full *Be Glad* soundtrack is issued in March 1971.

Lightning strikes and setting suns

A few months earlier, flying into the US on a cold night, we had crossed paths with Crosby, Stills and Nash in some airport as we waited for yet another connecting flight. We had been tired after a long journey, dispirited at leaving home and cross with each other. They had looked an image of cheerful good fellowship and I had mourned the vigour of times past, when we too walked around arm in arm and laughed together. They had brought the California sun into that grey airport hall and I envied their bright, successful lives. I imagined them as very different from our dreary, Scientology-directed routines.

To date, my closest encounters with the private life of stars had been brief meetings in theatres, airports and shops, or performing on the same big bill, as at Woodstock. We had never wanted a glitzy life but now it looked better to me than reading Scientology pamphlets in a hotel room, with a cardboard cup of tea from the lobby and the others droning on in the background.

Then one day in New York, out of the blue, there came a phone call, "Hi, it's Elliott, you know, the manager of Crosby, Stills and Nash". After being shut up with ISB for weeks, meeting him in the coffee shop at the end of the street was a tear in the dullness, a window opening on a sparkling landscape. Invitations to outings and parties followed but Mike and the others rarely came along. I got to know him and the band as my own friends.

By now Mike was so thoroughly entangled in Scientology that he was impatient of anything that interfered with his path to perfection, as he saw it. In his daily conversations he was harder and more tense, smiling less cheerfully. In dealing with necessary business he now had a speed and efficiency which suggested that his days as an accountant were not as alien to his present self as he had us believe.

Once back in London again, I went straight down the King's Road to a chic boutique, buying a leather coat to celebrate new liberty and new pleasures, just as I bought Indian skirts in the early ISB days. Friendship with a Supergroup meant I needed new clothes.

The coat was a remarkable garment, a fashion statement that captured all the keen delight of the moment. A clinging sheath of soft silver leather slithered from its high collared neck to my toes, with a single long zip down the front. It stretched and flexed silkily with the body living within. Once wrapped in its embrace you were caught, with no need to worry what was underneath, when you shed its skin you were renewed. Purple and green patches reinforced seams and elbows like the joints of a spacesuit: it was the gear for strange journeys.

But the whole point of it was the appliquéd leather motif on the back. Streaking down the centre, from neck to toe, was a shaft of orange-edged green lightning, splitting the large scarlet heart at the waistline in two. This made the wearer's feelings unmistakeably clear and public. There was never another like it. I needed this coat, to establish for myself the difference between the areas of my present life and to reclaim a core Rose which was slipping away as I clung onto ISB despite misgivings. Every day was an attempt to reconcile home with away.

There could still be happy ISB days. Susie Watson-Taylor, Mike's new girlfriend and manager, was buoyant and vivacious, ready to laugh like a "best friend" from schooldays. She could bring Mike's sun from behind the clouds. In Scotland she and I went on long walks over the hills while Mike stayed back down on the Row. Mike matched her high spirits when she was around, and then all was well. We enjoyed the work together still, sharing an unspoken conspiracy, which had nothing to do with Scientology. We were a family with fundamental disagreements, who nonetheless remained together via shared interests and the memories of closer times.

I was vaguely aware that I should be looking out for other ways of living my life but could envisage no permanent role for myself among the possibilities that presented themselves. I spent a day on a California ranch, courtesy of Elliott, and felt as if I was on a film set. The horse was a real enough challenge though. I soon found it was a lot less scary on horseback with clear sparkly cocaine to help me along and give at least the illusion of strength and ability. It did occur to me that this was probably not the best way to learn to ride in a hurry, but the saddles were wide with pommels to hold onto and if I could stay on the animal's back and persuade it not to gallop that was enough.

The next day Joe collected me to drive up the coast road to the next gig. He and I had stayed an extra day or two, while the others went ahead. I suppose he was pursuing his latest conquest, and I was enjoying mine. I must have looked worse than exhausted when he picked me up because he asked if I felt OK. Such concern was unusual, as he was rarely one to comment on our lives. I didn't feel too bad, nor did I feel the need to explain myself. Joe guessed straight away why I was pale and shaky and chatted to me about the evils of cocaine as we drove along.

I listened with total respect as I always did to Joe and took notice of his advice. He knew all these lives much better than I and I trusted him absolutely. Our brief affair had been a matter of snatched nights in a hotel room on tour or at the Glen, less significant for both of us I think than the months and years of my admiration at a distance as I watched him at work and play.

It was impossible to match his energy as he seized the morning, racing out to play tennis with friends before I was really awake. Once the business of the day had begun he was perpetually on the move and totally involved. He paid little attention to anything he considered irrelevant to the current project. As he walked home over Westminster Bridge at three o'clock in the morning after a night in the studio, he was still looking for new ideas and new challenges. On one of those early-morning walks, he told me, he stopped for a coffee at the all-night burger van and got the idea for the film *Scandal*. He always had the American fascination with British aristocracy, as well as the contacts to turn curiosity into a good film. He tells a different story about it now, or so I heard.

His glossy outside layer seemed to repel all encumbrances without effort and I never saw him angry, although he must often have been irritated beyond forbearance as he tried to keep together the disorderly lives of so many musicians and their attachments. He had a way of looking smiley and bland while making a cutting remark. It was difficult to retort without seeming petty. This kept us at a distance, and when that was not enough, he got on a plane and went away. Life alongside Joe was either skin contact or arm's length, with no comfortable familiarity in between.

But the Crosby, Stills and Nash connection had changed my life, and I felt more of an equal as we drove through the California sun that afternoon.

Euphoria

It was after a day at Big Sur that Joe and I went one evening with Dave Crosby, Joni Mitchell and the rest up the coast to the hot springs at Esalen. As we meandered down the steps to the pools, my whole world was in that happy group and, in the delight of the moment, I couldn't see beyond the warm bodies, the voices and the sheer brilliance of those around me.

The sun was dipping below the horizon. Seemingly suspended over the surf below, the stone basin of the pool seemed to have grown out of the cliff itself. The evening was quiet. Small waves gently licked the shore and the smell of sea-salt rose on the soft breeze, soothing after a hot day and drive. All around was an ancient wilderness of moor and pine, and the rustles of the land joined the whisper of the sea. This was the archetypal landscape of a New World and it felt as though we were the first settlers, alone in the perfect peace. It was a blissful, rhapsodic vision of heaven on earth, amplified by a dreamy, dopey softness, and we melted into one great closeness.

Sitting round the pool, leaning back against its warm stones and each other, tanned California skin against my Northern paleness, we paddled our feet like children playing in the bath. The games got wilder then along with Joni Mitchell, Crosby, Stills, Nash and Young began to sing the old folk songs I knew from ISB and from home. As their voices soaring in the silence I could even join in, very quietly. They harmonised and laughed, playing with the tunes in the sheer joy of the surroundings and the evening. A shared bathing became a simple, ecstatic, coming-together of young people on a summer evening.

As we drifted into night the closeness continued and it seemed natural and inevitable to stay with them. Waking with Dave Crosby's curly head on the pillow beside me was good, but the evening before had been perfect.

The next encounter with them all followed some weeks later, as soon as ISB had a few days free of all commitments. It was a thrill to fly on my own from London into LA, to hear my name over the plane's PA system as the plane landed and be told that a car would be waiting for me on the tarmac. This sort of thing didn't happen with ISB. I looked down from the plane window and felt more Orphan Annie than LA chic. I imagined what the other travellers would think, seeing my small person in second-hand finery from Antiquarius on the King's Road being ushered to the limo.

The driver had a proper uniform with cap and all, just like in the movies. I felt like a film star as I was driven to Laurel Canyon past the big LA houses. It was still hot and dusty, but the road was almost

Rose in California, 1970

countryside, with little traffic and trees everywhere, real trees with thick old branches covered in moss and green leaves like back home, not the frond-mopped lollipop palm trees of the city.

The houses were laid back and relaxing after a day in town, with shrubberies melting into the woods, cats lying in the sun and dogs running around. I was met at Joni Mitchell's door, though I didn't realise this immediately. I also guessed that there must be a system limiting access, but it was not obvious. It seemed as open as Mary Stewart's Temple Cottage, with people just arriving and picking up their lives without formal introduction or routine.

The ways of the house were harder to guess than Mary's. I recognised faces and knew names, but I didn't know how their home lives ran or what I should do with myself as they carried on with the business of their days. After the first greeting they seemed to think I would just fit in. They knew as little of my quiet home life as I did of theirs.

I wandered outdoors and looked around at a house with complicated terraces, its paths perhaps leading somewhere private. I was curious about the lives inside. It was odd to be precipitated into that close familiarity and have nothing to do there. Everyone knew each other so well and me hardly at all, yet I was still included: "Hi, I'm going into town, d'you want to come along?" But what would I do, dropped off in LA for an indefinite time and knowing nobody?

As guitars were picked up and played for a moment to explain, entertain or just have fun, I was thoroughly relieved that I had never pretended to any great musical skills. I felt vividly at times like this the

227

anomaly of playing with a band without being a proper musician. No one else seemed to think of it. I was just another girlfriend who may or may not turn up again, so I settled into the role and made the best of it.

This looked like a good life, a super-sized, super-beautiful, super-everything Glen Row. But there I had a place. Here I was simply waiting around in someone else's house as other people lived out their day. I was soon bored. I'd done enough of this already in Scottish cottages. By now I knew I wanted to be living my own life not attending on someone else's. But in a day or two it was back to London and the life I knew. Returning to ISB and its Scientological gossip was a big come-down, all very small and insignificant, low-key and low-volume. Yet the time I spent with them was far richer and more amazing than any life that would otherwise have come my way. I loved all three on some level and appreciated everything we had together. I could sit at the side of the stage and still watch them play with the wonderment of any fan.

When Crosby, Stills, Nash and Young played the Royal Albert Hall in January 1970, I was on the guest list. Once more I was star-struck. Songs heard on record and stage became personal, photographs and films took on breathing warmth. Like all their fans I saw their performances as near-perfect. And I wasn't around long enough to become blasé.

But eventually, as with ISB, the music stopped, the stage packed up and meals needed to be eaten. Nights passed, morning came again, a dreary normality returned. We all spent our lives on the move, someone always had to be leaving to fly to the next city and then the joy faded. Being left behind wasn't very different, whether in the quiet luxury of a Knightsbridge Mews or a utilitarian flat off Oxford Street. I felt bereft and found it hard to pass the time. I wanted someone who would stay with me, a life to share. How uncool that sounded to me now.

I no longer felt part of ISB's present incarnation and I belonged nowhere else.

But there was no need to think too hard about it, as gig followed gig and the group life took me along with it. I drifted through the weeks with the stimuli of new faces and places to distract me.

Frisco nights

San Francisco had always been a more sympathetic venue for all of ISB, and it was easier to pass my free California days there. The atmosphere was very different from LA's hyper-glitz. We could walk down the streets, visit markets, look around Chinatown, although the butchered ducks hanging up outside restaurants haunted me, and I looked the other way the whole time.

Pagoda in Chinatown, San Francisco, 1969

Haight Ashbury was already was a tourist attraction, with coach tours full of Mid-West Americans come to see the hippies from the safety of the bus. We visited too, but this wasn't the totality of the San Francisco experience to me. As an iconic destination for artists and the alternative culture it must be more than hilly streets and sun. I needed someone who knew the town to show me around, and to bring me home safely.

None of the roadies fitted this bill at that time. The two who travelled with us everywhere were English and while I could probably rely on them in a tight spot I didn't necessarily want to spend time in their company. We had met a man on a business trip in the lobby of the Chelsea in New York. His long blond hair and frontiersman leather clothes suggested the business was not corporate, as did the fact that he recognised us. Yet he didn't seem to be a drug dealer either. He conveniently appeared again in San Francisco just when I was looking out for an escort.

Here and in England, an entire breed of hippies came from wealthier homes, with indulgent parents who had sown their own wild oats and saw such rebellion as a rite of passage. These scions of the establishment bought land in backwoods places, for a life free from all the modern conveniences that had made their life so easy. They knew there was always a home and a job to return to, if that ever looked appealing again.

They read *Mother Earth News* and *Whole Earth Catalog*. In a bucolic idyll they chopped trees and ploughed, looked after livestock, spun and wove and raised children. It wasn't all self-indulgence: they also

229

cared about conservation and campaigned against the exploitation of natural resources.

The present representative of this class was exactly what I was hoping for, as he arrived in our dressing room. Perhaps he had once been the hero of the basketball team or a college football quarterback, but now his tall and powerful frame was exercised in agricultural work, hacking a living out of virgin soil like the first settlers. This kind and independent spirit, with the confidence that comes from a secure family background, helped me feel safe in my night-time outings around the town.

Self-sufficient in Arkansas or Vermont, men like him came to town with the same escapist motives as me. They wanted to get away from the settled moral and ethical life of the homestead and the organic tepees, where their patient companions were stirring the pot and guarding the children. Women wouldn't want to be worried by the unpleasantness of lawyers or deals, they said. Such important business needn't concern them. But what they really intended was to enjoy all the benefits of the civilisation they had rejected and have some fun before they returned to the backwoods.

The blond and I had good nights in the less polite bars of New York and San Francisco. He introduced me to a different and a wilder society, a relief from the clean-living adherents of Scientology, who seemed so narrow-minded and bitter. In North Beach San Francisco we met friends of Lenny Bruce who took me on a tour of his favourite bars. Once he had fallen out of a window after a heavy evening, thinking it was the door he was opening, and I stayed most of the night in that same room.

Waking up before anyone else, I headed back to respectability and breakfast on foot. I was a good walker and wasn't worried, heading through the long streets at that early hour. There were few taxis around at that time, as the nightlife slept it off, and I had no phone-number to call them anyway.

I blended into the life of the streets and it was fine. This was the experience I had been looking for. Walking along as the sun rose over the blue bay, and the day warmed up after the night chills, I never came to harm or even felt threatened. It gave me time to settle back into ISB Rose of the daytime.

Changing horses again

These escapes made it possible to stay longer with the band, spending time with people the others didn't know dissipating all the frustrations and unsaid words with people who could play as hard as they worked. None of the band were really aware what we each did once we'd retreated behind our private doors into our separate lives. This was not so much indifference as a determination to claim and to acknowledge the freedom to walk separate paths.

This freedom was overruled by Scientology, with its corporate ethic and its demands for conformity and regulation. And in the end I could not accept the control of a belief-system I had no respect for. In the final months I was telling roadies when I needed collecting or dropping off for some personal escapade, which meant letting them into my secrets. But they were on my side, so we were conspirators. And my righteous indignation towards Scientology was offset by a lurking sense of betrayal. The demand for ideological unity was repressive, but I recognised that all these deceits and silences were also a denial of ISB's original nature.

Personal strains affected us in different ways. Robin and Janet were working out a permanent life together, as Licorice lived alone next door. Mike pursued a fluctuating relationship with Susie and I wondered what would happen next. Yet on-stage we maintained, and largely felt, the joys and wonders of the first days, and this carried us through photo sessions and other public encounters. We still depended on one another and trusted each other musically on-stage and off.

The autumn tours of the UK and the US followed one another and Mike and I still kept company in free hours. We went to a Tom Rush concert and, according to an observer, "loved it". We knew each other's ways. It was comfortable and supportive to be together. Janet was often with Robin. Licorice followed her own path as usual. We met in dressing rooms and theatres and in those places reverted to type: "If you haven't seen them in person then it may be hard to understand the radiant innocence they have, the completely unpretentious character they show that never fails to warm an entire audience," enthused *The Tech* magazine: "The two guys along with their girlfriends/accompanists have such a happy time up there on the stage that you can't help smile along with them. Their whole presence brings to mind such words as delightful, heartwarming, charming which sound overly dramatic but are accurate descriptions of the responses they inspire. That is why it doesn't matter that their voices sound strained or that they hit occasional bad notes…their shows are a real joy in every sense."

But mentions of "strain" and dissonance appeared more often in reviews now, as in the *Trinity Tripod*: "Robin Williamson tried now and then to keep things going… but his thick brogue and the poor acoustics made his jokes inaudible… Mike Heron actually stopped playing… [and] seemed to get somewhat tense about the balance of the sound. He seems to be the serious force behind this group, as opposed to Williamson who gets too silly at times."

Others, like *The Spectrum*, were still enthusiastic and saw the band as it wished to be seen: "The music holds a beauty that sweeps you away to the greatest heights of pleasure and contentment... Their ladies Licorice and Rose are as different as night and day. Rose appears like a cute, fun-loving tomboy, dancing around the stage and really working on her instruments. Licorice on the other hand gives the appearance of a beautiful, soft, fragile flower, gently flowing with the music."

After a performance of the *U* show at the Roundhouse in London I had met a journalist recently returned from California, who now worked for a pacifist newspaper in London. We stayed together between tours for a few months, and a shared future seemed possible.

Mike, Robin and Licorice were now fully devoted to Scientology and making it clear that I must join them in their commitment. We had all been so bound together ideologically and physically for so long that my compromises, my distances and my apostasy was impossible for all of us. I felt cornered and desperate. We returned to Scotland together for Christmas after the US tour, but I couldn't start another New Year as part of the band. I walked out on all of it, on my home at the Glen, on my future with ISB and on my friendships of the moment.

There were no discussions, no notifications of intent. I decided to make a new life with the journalist before New Year's Eve launched us all into another year. The decision emerged from the depths of my mind, with no need for thought or consideration. For a second time I left everything behind me that had been the scenery of my life. The silver leather coat still hung on the peg in the hallway, my shoes lay in the bedroom, jewellery in odd boxes around the house. I took some instruments with me, as I would have taken a pet, but the cottage I left just as it was, ready for any new tenant. One day I was a member of a successful band, the next just an anonymous face in the bedsit world of London's suburbs.

My going was treated as that of any other of the Glen's inhabitants. We never talked. The customary silence reigned. But it was different, because a sudden gap in the band now had to be filled.

◆ ◆ ◆

I don't know what happened next, I wasn't there. I was mildly surprised to learn that concerts were cancelled and that new people were brought in, with greater and lesser degrees of success. It confirmed my sense that the four of us had been a special grouping, working together in ways not easily definable, but somehow creating for some years the environment in which Mike and Robin could write and perform happily. Licorice and I had been part of their creative lives, not simply decorative additions to their stage-performances.

The new beginning that 1971 brought with it was, as usual, unexpected but nevertheless welcomed wholeheartedly. My daughter was born in October of that year.

I had no contact with any of ISB for some time after my sudden departure from Scotland. There was nothing to be said that could make it better for any of us. One final occasion put a seal on the ISB time for me. Eighteen months after I left Glen Row, I felt I needed to face the past and the present together, to seek some reconciliation between the different lives.

With my young baby in my arms I went alone on the train to Fairfield Halls in Croydon to see ISB in a new line-up with new songs. Now I was simply one of those asking the roadies to see the band after the gig. My baby girl's warm little hands clutched my hair as I held her tight. She was my teddy bear, a refuge and consolation for the pain of a loss that I wouldn't admit to myself or anyone else. She was my talisman against all the temptations and evils of the past and my hope for the future.

Epilogue

31ˢᵗ January 1971

I leave officially, moving out of Glen Row some days before. The upcoming booked tour is cancelled and rescheduled for March 1971, with Malcolm le Maistre. My daughter is born in October 1971.

◆

After my sudden departure, the insistent problem on waking every day and in all hours after that was how to define "real life" for myself and get on with it. I still clung to the idea that "real life" had been my original relationship with Mike and our early time together as The Incredible String Band.

We had been truthful and genuine, sharing ideals and acting them out, without repressing or constricting one another. While we did not always identify with every detail of the other's ideas, the general direction was the same. The loosening of our romantic and sexual bonds hadn't led to anger or despair. Cottage doors were left open long after we ceased to be exclusively together.

Now I was free of the band, with hardly any money, nowhere to live and nothing to do, the situation was clear and simple. Real life was defined by an income and a home. The great advantage of doing early-morning cleaning at Global Tours on Tottenham Court Road – my first job since leaving ISB – was that it swept away all leftover illusions of fame from my life with the band. My baby I left sleeping beside her father in the bedsit we rented near Regent's Park. The cycle ride through early-morning London, with everyone rushing to work like me, got me back on a more even keel, as did the empty offices with no critical eyes and the simple physical work of cleaning.

Very many years later, Robin asked a new audience "How has it been up to now?" This was one of those unsuccessful Mike and Robin reunion occasions, where all the conflicts of the past remain while everyone tries to ignore them. Robin spoke in the same tones, and with the same expression and stance as I remembered from being on-stage with him. Like his other fans, I felt his acknowledgement of all the time that had passed, and all the ways our lives had diverged from what we were imagining in 1968.

I had landed in the orbit of ISB from a completely different world, and afterwards I spun off into another life. I knew that however close I was to the three of them, the music of the band did not depend on my presence. Mike and Robin would always make music, whoever was beside them.

Together we waved our banners of truth and beauty, believing they were worth more than anything else. On-stage we were the best people we could be, living almost instinctively for that little while, carried beyond the worries and concerns of daily life to a purer state of being. We responded to others from that better self as long as it lasted. Then the show ended, and all the confusions of living in a material world took over once more.

Each of us four saw the same events through different eyes and now we all wander through the labyrinths of a mind which has imposed its own order on the past. None of us can claim to represent the others, or tell what it was like for them. They travelled the same paths as me for a while, but with very different aims and intentions. We never assumed there was only one truth to be told.

First group photo session, Queensway Flats, Spring 1968

The Incredible String Band: Key releases and dates

Albums before Rose joined

The Incredible String Band   Elektra, 1966
The 5000 Spirits or the Layers of the Onion   Elektra, 1967

Albums Rose played on

The Hangman's Beautiful Daughter   Elektra, March 1968
Wee Tam and the Big Huge   Elektra, November 1968
Changing Horses   Elektra, November 1969
I Looked Up   Elektra, April 1970
U   Elektra, October 1970
Be Glad For the Song Has No Ending   Island, March 1971
(film soundtrack)
Smiling Men with Bad Reputations   Island, April 1971
(Mike Heron's solo LP)

Compilations Rose plays on

Relics of The Incredible String Band   Elektra, 1971
Seasons They Change   Island, 1976
Across The Airwaves: BBC Radio   Hux Records, 2007
Recordings 1969-74
Tricks of the Senses: Rare and   Hux Records, 2008
Unreleased Recordings 1966-1972

Key ISB live performances 1968-70

The list is only what can be derived from sources mentioned so other performance dates are now lost or uncertain.

Many thanks for the careful archival work of Wolfgang Rostek. Shane Pope also helped.

From Rose

In early 1968 I was sitting on-stage or at the edge of it on most English dates. I was left at home during the American tour that Spring. From 29th June 1968 until 14th December 1970 I was on-stage as a performer.

1968

February

3rd BBC Television – *Once more with Felix*
13th Leicester University w/ The Scaffold, Ron Geesin
17th Ansom Room, Bristol (w. Ewan McColl, Peggy Seeger, Young Tradition) (*IT* – ad)

March
Release of *The Hangman's Beautiful Daughter*

1st Glasgow Concert Hall
2nd Manchester Free Trade Hall
4th Recording session for John Peel's *Nightride* ('Bid You Goodnight'/ 'Won't You Come See'/ 'You Get Brighter'/ 'All Too Much for Me')
8th Brighton Dome with Pentangle
9th Philharmonic Hall, Liverpool – *A Mystical Pantomime*
16th Birmingham Town Hall – *A Mystical Pantomime*
        March: Albert Hall, London (with Donovan, Tyrannosaurus Rex) (Felix, newspaper)
30th Royal Festival Hall, London – *A Mystical Pantomime* (supported by Tim Buckley)

June

23rd Warwick University Arts Festival
29th Royal Albert Hall, London – *On a Summer Evening* (This was Rose's first gig on-stage)

July

5th Queen's Hall, Barnstaple
19th Central Hall, Westminster, *Folkfestival* with David Campbell, Dorris Henderson, Stephen Delft

August

11th   *8th National Jazz Blues & Pop Festival*, Sunbury, with
       Herd, Jethro Tull, Fairport Convention, Traffic and others
24th   Magical Mystery Tour (Middle Earth Club, London)
       (part of a 48 hour "freak out")
       and/or
25th   Magical Mystery Tour (Middle Earth Club, London)
       (part of a 48 hour "freak out")
30th   ABC Regal, Edinburgh

September

30th   Sheep Meadow, Central Park NY, with Jefferson
       Airplane, Ten Years After, Country Joe and the Fish

October

9th   Sheffield City Hall
13th   Glasgow Concert Hall – *A Mystical Pantomime*
18th   Manchester Free Trade Hall
25th   Birmingham Town Hall
26th   Liverpool Philharmonic Hall
27th   Newcastle City Hall
30th   Albert Hall, Nottingham

November

Release of *Wee Tam and the Big Huge*

1st   Brighton Dome
2nd   Royal Albert Hall, London
9th   Manchester Free Trade Hall (supported by Pentangle)
26th   Live broadcast from WBAI studios in New York
27th   Fillmore East, New York.
29th   Lincoln Center's Philharmonic Hall, New York.

December

7th   Jordan Hall, Boston, Boston Tea Party (which is a festival)

1969

February

5th   Recording of BBC Session *Nightride*
      ('All Writ Down', 'Dust Be Diamonds', 'Theta', 'Fine
      Fingered Hand', Studio S1, Broadcasting House)
15th BBC Television, *Once More with Felix*
19th Belfast

March

1st   Colston Hall, Bristol
2nd   Fairfield Hall, Croydon
5th   Lanchester Polytechnic, Coventry
8th   Leeds Town Hall
9th   Rex Theatre, Cambridge
16th Newcastle City Hall
23rd De Montfort Hall, Leicester

April

27th Fillmore East, New York

May

2nd   New England Life Hall, Boston (presented by the Boston
      Tea Party and WBCN Radio)
3rd   Alexander Hall, Princeton, New Jersey
4th   Academy of Music, Philadelphia
6th   Memorial Chapel at Wesleyan University, Middletown
11th Fillmore East, New York
16th Ford Auditorium, Detroit
24th Fillmore West, San Francisco
26th Aquarius Theatre, Los Angeles

June

8th-11th   Cambridge *Midsummer Pop Festival*

July

2nd Royal Albert Hall – *Pop Proms* with Family, Fairport Convention, John Peel
12th York University
19th Newport Folk Festival

August

5th Recording of Peel Session, Maida Vale 4 ('Letter', 'This Moment', 'Gather Round', 'Waiting for You', 'BJD'), transmission date 24th August
13th Carnegie Hall, New York
16th *Woodstock Festival of Peace and Love*
16th *Singer Bowl Folk Festival*, Flushing Meadow Park, New York, with Ian & Sylvia, Sea Train, Odetta, Tim Harding, Tom Paxton
21st Merryweather Post Pavilion, Columbia
23rd-24th *Philadelphia Folk Festival*
27th Electric Factory, Philadelphia
31st *Texas International Pop Festival*, Dallas

September

3rd The Electric Factory, Philadelphia
4th Fillmore East, New York
5th New England Life Hall, Boston
7th Music Hall, Houston
8th Aquarius Theatre, LA
10th Fillmore West, San Francisco
13th *6th Annual Big Sur Festival*
14th Fillmore East, New York

October

17th Regal Cinema, Cambridge
18th Concertgebouw Amsterdam (supported by Fairport Convention)
19th Sheffield City Hall,
24th Birmingham Town Hall
25th Philharmonic, Liverpool
26th Newcastle City Hall
31st Manchester Free Trade Hall

November
Release of *Changing Horses*

1st	Usher Hall, Edinburgh

1st   Usher Hall, Edinburgh
2nd   New City Hall, Glasgow
7th   Fairfield Hall, Croydon
8th   Dome, Brighton
11th   Royal Festival Hall, London
22nd   University of Maryland, Baltimore
23rd   Boston Tea Party
25th   Place des Arts, Montreal
28th-29th   Ludlow Garage, Cincinnati
30th   Guthrie Theatre, Minneapolis

December

4th   University of Wisconsin, Milwaukee
5th   Powell Symphony Hall, St. Louis, with Sun
7th   Jordan Hall, Boston Tea Party
10th   Fillmore West, San Francisco
12th   Public Hall, Cleveland, with Crosby, Stills, Nash & Young
14th   Fillmore East, New York
31st   Berkeley Community Theatre, San Francisco

1970

February

20th   Exhibition Hall, Newcastle
25th   Sophia Gardens, Cardiff
26th   De Montfort Hall, Leicester
28th   University of Bradford, attending a seminar on 'Pop-culture and deviance'

April
Release of *I Looked Up*

8th-11th,   The Roundhouse, London (performing *U* two shows each
13th-18th   night on 10th, 11th, 17th & 18th April)
23rd-26th   Fillmore East, New York, performing *U*, with Stone Monkey

May

1st	Bronx Campus, New York University, performing *U*
2nd	Syracuse University, NY, performing *U*
3rd-4th	Boston Tea Party, with Stone Monkey, performing *U*
5th	SUNY, New York, performing *U*
8th-9th	Ludlow Garage, Cincinnati, performing *U*
11th, 13th	Fillmore West, San Francisco
17th	Berkeley Community Theatre

July

17th	Usher Hall, Edinburgh.
18th	Manchester Free Trade Hall
19th	Hull City Hall
23rd	Fairfield Hall, Croydon
24th	Birmingham Town Hall
25th	*Reading Festival*
26th	London Palladium, with Fairport Convention

August

9th	*10th National Jazz and Blues Festival*, Plumpton
12th	Plymouth Guildhall
19th	Farx, Potters Bar

September

4th-5th, 11th-12th	Empire Theatre, Edinburgh
18th	Van Dyke, Plymouth
19th	Farx, Potters Bar
20th	Mothers, Birmingham
24th	Recordings for NCRV-TV, Hilversum (NL)
26th	Albert Hall, London, with Pentangle
30th	Newcastle City Hall

October
Release of *U*

1st	Apeldoorn, NL
2nd	NL-TV broadcast (NCRV)

2nd   DeDoelen, Rotterdam, NL
3rd   Concertgebouw, Amsterdam, NL
4th   Stadsschouwburg, Enschede, NL
7th   Sheffield City Hall
8th   Keynes College, Canterbury
10th   Brighton Dome
11th   Fairfield Hall, Croydon
18th   Usher Hall, Edinburgh
20th   Royal Albert Hall, London
21st   Albert Hall, Nottingham
23rd   Lancaster University
24th   Manchester Free Trade Hall, with Trees
24th   German TV broadcast: Beatclub (recorded September 1970)
25th   Birmingham Town Hall
26th   Bristol Colston Hall
28th   Liverpool Philharmonic
29th   Leeds Town Hall
30th   Newcastle City Hall
31st   Birmingham Town Hall

November

1st   Victoria Hall, Hanley
13th-14th Pepperland, San Francisco, with Doug Kershaw, Joy of Cooking
15th   Freeborn Hall, University of California LA (produced
           by KZAP Radio)
20th-21st Armadillo World Headquarters, Austin
29th   Fillmore East, New York (two shows)

December

3rd   Scott Hall, Northwestern University, Evanston IL
4th-6th Boston Tea Party, Jordan Hall, with Doc Watson, Mimi Fariña
8th   SUNY at Buffalo, Fillmore Room (supported by Joe Mama)
11th   Vassar College, Poughkeepsie, NY
13th   Ludlow Garage, Cincinnati
14th   Fillmore West, San Francisco

Reviews

Extended extracts from reviews and press write-ups quoted in the main text, 1968-70:

August 1968, Sunbury Festival

"Sunday afternoon was sublime with the Incredible String Band in the Marquee. The Incredibles were, as usual off the wall, charming, weird, wonderful and unique. Mike Heron and Robin Williamson played a multitude of instruments, Rose was a good 10 years before her time as a real novelty item on bass – wow a chick playing bass man – I remember some idiot remarking – but she proved she was more than up to the job and Licorice provided sweet backup vocals. A Very Cellular Song was a highlight, but this was their heyday, their whole set was stellar, unique, gems of songs just seemed to spring forth effortlessly from their pens in those days – stuff like 'Waltz of the New Moon', 'October Song', 'Swift as the Wind', 'Chinese White' – were all part of the set list at that time in 1968."

— anonymous online comment

28th November 1968

"There was the aura of a trance ritual at the Fillmore East last night as the Incredible String Band from England gave its first major concert here. The trance was engendered by the haunting and evanescent music of the group… The Incredible String Band is both avant-garde and avant-pop. In vocal adventuresomeness and lyrical audacity the group is quite without parallel… But the gifted musicianship, the fertile imaginations and the boundless stylistic fusions are important. They cast their spell even on ears tired by gimmickry and shock-novelty."

— Robert Shelton, *New York Times*

December 1968, New York

"Neither avant-garde nor deviant garde, and denying an exact name or origin, the company's music represents an exact slice of history, both yesterday's and tomorrow's. Though gentle in nature, their tunes are weird, defying empathy and a communicable warmth. But whether not of this earth – or moon music like the lonely whinings of two cats on a fence – the virtuosity of the Incredible String Band is something else."

— Ed Ochs, *Billboard*

20th March 1969, Yonkers, New York

"In worn velvets and beads, amid puffs of incense, the group camps on the stage in a cluster of guitars, lute, mandolin, oud, sitar, dulcimer, harmonicas and organ. In soft burrs they sing of archery and swans, amoebae and love."

— *Herald Statesman*

20th April 1969

"I saw the Incredible String Band use the Fillmore Stage for a picnic and turn the Lower East Side into a woodland glade & do a very far out thing & then return on a backwards trip to the fields of childhood innocence... How beautiful to find that England shimmering on New York air and I fell in love with the Incredible String Band... When they move on stage they are private but close together like new lovers and lit with a clean fire that talks of peace and apple-cheek country weather. What can I say but child innocence? It sings across their music and dances at the corner of their eyes... Somewhere in Wales near the wet sands and the magic stones live the Incredible String Band. No electronics, perms, peroxide. The girls' hair sticks out, newly washed in rainwater, faces newly scrubbed."

Robin on writing: "Writing was a necessity. Acid opened my eyes... You name it I've tried it. Like the mysterious ancient things. Tarot, magic, astrology"

Robin on Scientology: "A year ago I would have said I was in touch with the Spirit which wrote all the songs. I would have said I wasn't responsible for their existence it was the music but now I'm starting to take responsibility for actually creating them."

Licorice on Scientology: "It has removed past pain in me so that now I am able to play instruments on stage which frightened me before."

On Rose: "Rose has a smile which goes on and on and on. Go down the tunnel of Rose's smile and find Mike at the end with his silver sitar. Been together since the beginning of time and before as Licorice and Robin have… Now Rose plays to spread her insistent happiness like butter on a brown bread stage."

Rose on herself: "I wanted to show more people how happy I was and started playing on gigs and just get happier all the time… What's holding you back from loving everyone? Everyone is basically good, so if you try to understand why people are acting in weird ways, being abrupt, being ridiculously angry then you get to know how the mind works, you get through that and really love them."

— text and all quotes from *Oz* No.20, April 1969

5th May 1969

"Barefoot, wearing shoulder-length hair, dressed in embroidered vests and peasant dresses, they look simultaneously like a 14th century minstrel band and a 21st century family. During the evening the four played guitars, piano, organ, sitar, violins, electric bass, washboard, gongs, flute, gimbri, mandolin, harmonica and a variety of percussion instruments; not only did they play all these superbly, they created beautiful, coherent arrangements from such diverse materials… The Incredible String Band offers a unique musical experience, a celebration of music, myth, poetry and love an invitation to be joyously and completely stoned on the beauties of existence."

— Andrew Wilson, *The Princetonian*

14th May 1969

"When a boo-bird whistles, the team turn on/Bring home all the kicks Saturday night's concert at the Fillmore East was capped by a surging ecstasy of applause equalled seldom. They are Robin Williamson, Mike Heron and two nameless and unnameable girl/children. Their sound defies description being a conglomerate of influences ranging from the Highland Fling through Debussy to the Ming Dynasty... The element of surprise is a constant factor in the ISB sound but it never degenerates into novelty. There is a zen-ish awareness of the freshness and constancy of change here. Three hours of ISB seemed hardly enough to fill anyone's appetite. An all-day concert would be more like it!... Because it takes five minutes or more to set up the instruments in between selections, what could have turned into very ugly hand-clapping and whistling developed but Williamson let them know where it was at by just telling them, in effect, to clam up. This was done so gently that suddenly there was a strange quiet. American audiences are not used to such stage-cool... When a brawl broke out in the first row over someone with a camera in 'Creation', Williamson vaporised it in an instant by stopping the music in midstream. That was more of a shock to the combatants than any blow with a fist would have been: "How can I sing about Creation while you're... " This was all said so naturally that no person could have failed to respond. In a way that incident says more about the Incredible String Band and their music than anything else does. They are organic musicians above everything else and when they sing of the clear light within you leading you all the way home there is no sermonising, no teaching, no exemplifying, only truth. Though the Fillmore was filled, it seemed, three-quarters with obnoxious 11-year-olds from Scarsdale, there is no doubt that this message got through. The ISB is more than a musical group, it is a vision of music that can be made and shared throughout the Aquarian Age. The ISB is loved wherever they go."

— Joe Melz, *The Other*

16th May 1969

"Although most of the vast Ford Auditorium on May 16 was empty, the stage was filled before Mike Heron, Robin Williamson, Rose, and Licorice came on. An organ, piano, two amplifiers, bass, gongs, sitar and an array of unusual Eastern instruments graced the large stage with the tremendous and gaudy gold curtain... They were in person, as their songs and stories are: gentle, peaceful, full of love, concerned about living and understanding life and all that is around them. Most of all, they came to Detroit with a message:... learn, create, try all types of music, not 'scholarly' to 'broaden your knowledge' but to feel and know more; more music, sounds, human experience."

— Mike Kerman, *Fifth Estate*

19th June 1969

"Do not confuse the Incredible String Band with any of the feather-clad, golden slipper crowd that marches on Broad Street in Philadelphia every year in the Mummers Parade... 'Underground is a term used by people who like to think they are in it,' Heron said in an interview, 'We're just a group that perform what some people like.'"

— *The Stars and Stripes*

18th November 1969

"The ISB is one of England's most popular recording acts. At times they have been compared to the Beatles as an innovative music force... Mike Heron states, 'The music is a force that permeates our existence and though people can't fully comprehend our songs they can share our experience... We set no limitations. Our songs are not preconceived, they just flow.'"

— Bob Godd, *The Retriever*

26th November 1969

"Together, they looked like a band of gypsies – dressed in robes of many colours, their hair long enough to blow in the wind... What makes the String Band so appealing is its combination of things we know and things we don't. All the way through their songs you can pick out influences or licks and harmonies you've heard somewhere before but they've never been put together like that before. Their words to their songs are in the language we know and phrases and sentences, even moods are familiar. But in sum, the lyrics are a mystery and therein lies their fascination... Listening to the String Band is an adventure into something ancient and modern and weird everyday, strange and known. And last night it all came across far more clearly than their records even hint at."

— Dane Lanken, *Montreal Gazette*

26th November 1969

"They are entirely pleasant people full of hope and love and beauty and things like that and they sing basically of their experience with the wonders of this and any other world... In a word, it was sloppy. Self indulgent. The evidently feel a lot of feelings but they betrayed them, in my view, by countless amateurisms. Simply, the singing was pretty awful, whiney, uncontrolled, bereft of any sense of drama, timing and pace... They state the obvious, which is fine in its way, but they do not make it worthwhile hearing because they drown these simple everyday revelations with a posture which dictates, 'Look here, this is the inner light,' or to quote a particularly gushy line, 'I swear you have the power as the angels do'... The Incredible String Band pluck and strain away taking themselves and their thoughts far too seriously to be believed... I don't think it was sporting of them to subject their audience to about seven minutes of tuning up and moving about between practically every song."

— Juan Rodriguez, *Montreal Star*

4th December 1969

"At the Place des Arts, the four singers came out with a series of hellos then settled down, longhaired and comfortable, booted and velvet dressed, to sing a programme of medieval stories wedded to Eurasian instrumental tunes... Each of the four individuals played an inestimable number of instruments and a sort of low-English drawing-room comedy was bantered about among the members as they tuned and retuned their instruments... I guess you'd call them the new romanticism. Pastoral tales of love, life, death, rebirth and the countryside... The songs are filled with European mysticism and seemed to be relics of the time the world was young and chivalrous... it was part of the band's mysticism that the under-15-year-olds, who had bought half-price tickets and the dyed blonde girls who stood up to take Kodak starflash pictures, believed them... During the last song, a meditation about a girl and an octopus called Anita [Juanita] I saw people around me lost in contemplation of the band's story. In the song, after hearty choruses of foghorns, the beautiful maiden is rescued by the virtuous fisherman and GOOD as always triumphs. The song ended with a joyous smile and the band walked offstage... The audience demanded more of the depression-dispelling music, the ballads that made you forget your problems and enter their life."

— *The Georgian*

5th December 1969

"'subtlety and gentleness rather than the surge of rock rhythms' – It was a concert that was filled with fragile and sometimes esoteric beauty... The ineptness of the girls, however, in no way affected the quality of the final product. In fact it helped provide a simple, almost rustic touch... This reviewer kept having visions of shepherds and their flocks."

— Keith Spore, *Evening Times Wisconsin*

April 1970: "The Incredible String Band Comes to Town"

"The Incredible String Band is a special taste, and they usually come to the Fillmore East for two performances, Sunday evenings, a week apart, and the house is sold out (as usual) and the audiences are pretty distinctly ISB audiences... ISB people are arty, poetic,... You won't like this music, Dick, there's nobody going wham-wham-wham all the time... Rhythm it has, but not the kind of driving, pounding wham-wham... more the droning, hypnotic kind of rhythm... and it has melodies, but a kind of long-line, non-pop sort that you might almost expect from Benjamin Britten not those rock and roll bands... Leaving the theatre at 10.40 pm we pass 100 people lying on the Sixth Street sidewalk waiting for the box office to open tomorrow so they can buy tickets to Crosby Stills Nash Young. They will not be puzzled as we have been."

"Mike and Rose decided to come with Jim and me to the Bitter End to see Tom Rush (they loved him). They seem to easily bridge the dichotomy between their (reality) and the city. Both know how to fluidly draw people into themselves. They seek and deal with people on their own levels, with the seeming ease and 'knowingness' that is so evident in the music of the Incredible String Band."

— Dick Lupoff, *Crawdaddy* vol.4 no.6

11th November 1970

"The String Band is by far one of the best groups, if not the best group, in music today. Their music is a general uplifting in times of depression and an inspiration during periods of difficulty… The music holds a beauty that sweeps you away to the greatest heights of pleasure and contentment… Their ladies Licorice and Rose are as different as night and day. Rose appears like a cute, fun-loving tomboy, dancing around the stage and really working on her instruments. Licorice on the other hand gives the appearance of a beautiful, soft, fragile flower, gently flowing with the music and adding her high sweet voice to the songs. The four of them switched flawlessly from one instrument to the next, thus proving the merit of the name The Incredible String Band and by the last song they had everyone up and dancing."

— Wendy Gruber, *The Spectrum*

1st December 1970

"One group continues to move forward, constantly producing, constantly progressing… Their songs contain complex images and beautiful fantasies. Their ballads are unmatched. Recently they have taken to rock and roll type songs which are largely parodies… If you haven't seen them in person then it may be hard to understand the radiant innocence they have, the completely unpretentious character they show that never fails to warm an entire audience. The two guys along with their girlfriends/ accompanists have such a happy time up there on the stage that you can't help smile along with them. Their whole presence brings to mind such words as delightful, heartwarming, charming which sound overly dramatic but are accurate descriptions of the responses they inspire. That is why it doesn't matter that their voices sound strained or that they hit occasional bad notes… their shows are a real joy in every sense."

— Jay Pollack, *The Tech*

7th December 1970

"The String Band plays perhaps the most gentle satisfying music in the entire universe… A lot of their material deals with love and religion. Their tunes generate a lot of spiritual good feeling and you find yourself turning on their records at times of crisis… Williamson's songs are very deep and he has a unique way of cramming three or four melodies into a cohesive unit."

— *The Spectrum*

12th December 1970

"These Elektra Records artists actually comprise the smallest distinct ethnic group in the world."

— Nancy Ehrlich, *Billboard*

15th December 1970

"Concert at Vassar – Mike Heron and Robin Williamson are two of the most unique contemporary songwriters. Their excellent musicianship and vocalising is unquestionable. Together with their friends Licorice and Rose they make up the Incredible String Band and they produce some of the freshest music today…no matter how intricate the style may become, no matter how symbolic the lyrics may get, the predominating mood on each of their eight albums has been happiness. They are a joyful celebrating band… A disappointing feature of the concert was the amount of time which passed silently as the group tuned and retuned instruments. Robin Williamson tried now and then to keep things going by telling stories but his thick brogue and the poor acoustics made his jokes inaudible… Mike Heron actually stopped playing a song he had started.

He had to get the tone adjusted on his mic... Heron seemed to get somewhat tense about the balance of the sound. He seems to be the serious force behind this group, as opposed to Williamson who gets too silly at times... The spirit they give off, the excitement they obviously feel (Licorice dancing fairy-like, Williamson jumping as he fiddles, Rose and Heron smiling at each other) is contagious. The last song had people clapping and dancing in the aisles... It was refreshing not to hear any pseudo-political speech between numbers. It was refreshing not to have to put my fingers in my ears for fear of going deaf. And it was refreshing to see four superb musicians in love with what they were doing, turning on an audience with the joy that comes from real and honest music."

— John Speziale, *Trinity Tripod*

Strange Attractor Press 2020